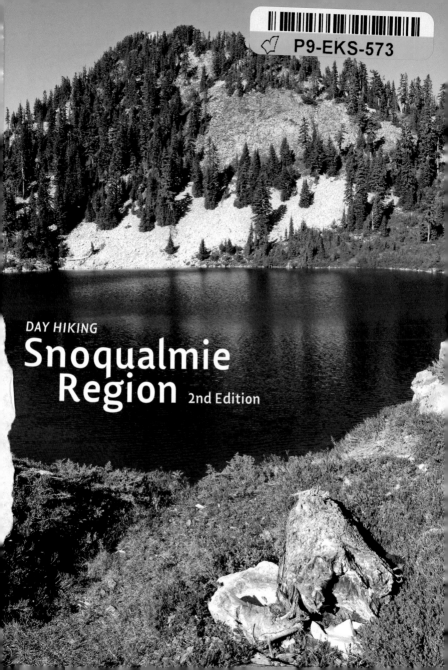

DAY HIKING
Snoqualmie
Region 2nd Edition

Old weathered log surrounded by huckleberry shrubs near Lake George

Previous page: Autumn day at Gem Lake with Wright Mountain rising to the north

Left: Massive old-growth Douglas fir along the Asahel Curtis Nature Trail

Franklin Falls along the South Fork Snoqualmie River

Views toward Mount Stuart from the summit of Iron Peak

Spectacular golden alpine larch trees in autumn with views of Mount Stuart from the trail leading to Lake Ingalls

Below, left: Red columbine flowering along the Cooper River
Below, right: Huckleberries make for stunning fall color along the hike up Granite Mountain.

Open views of the Stuart Range looking across the Ingalls Creek valley from near Navaho Pass

A hiker enjoys the lonely last stretch to the lookout at the summit of Kelly Butte.

The upper trails at Tolt MacDonald Park pass through lush, mossy forests.

DAY HIKING

Snoqualmie Region 2nd edition

cascade foothills · I-90 corridor · alpine lakes

Dan A. Nelson
photography by
Alan L. Bauer

MOUNTAINEERS
BOOKS

Mountaineers Books is the nonprofit publishing division of The Mountaineers, an organization founded in 1906 and dedicated to the exploration, preservation, and enjoyment of outdoor and wilderness areas.

MOUNTAINEERS BOOKS

1001 SW Klickitat Way, Suite 201 • Seattle, WA 98134
800.553.4453 • www.mountaineersbooks.org

Copyright © 2014 by Dan A. Nelson and Alan L. Bauer

All rights reserved. No part of this book may be reproduced or utilized in any form, or by any electronic, mechanical, or other means, without the prior written permission of the publisher.

Printed in the United States of America
First edition, 2007. Second edition, 2014

Copy Editor: Kerrie Maynes
Design: Mountaineers Books
Layout: Emily Ford
Cartographers: Moore Creative Designs and Marge Mueller, Gray Mouse Graphics
Photographer: Alan L. Bauer

Cover photograph: *Mount Stuart towers over the golden autumn alpine larch trees in Headlight Basin along the trail to Lake Ingalls.*
Frontispiece: *An ant appreciates the beauty of a big-headed clover blooming on Whiskey Dick Mountain.*

Library of Congress Cataloging-in-Publication Data
Nelson, Dan A.
  Day hiking Snoqualmie region : Cascade Foothills, I-90 Corridor, Alpine lakes / Dan A. Nelson, Alan L. Bauer. — Second edition.
    p. cm.
  Includes index.
  ISBN 978-1-59485-768-3 (pbk) — ISBN 978-1-59485-769-0 (ebook) 1. Hiking—Washington (State)—Snoqualmie Pass (King County and Kittitas County)—Guidebooks. 2. Snoqualmie Pass (King County and Kittitas County, Wash.)—Guidebooks. I. Title.
  GV199.42.W22S567 2014
  796.5109797—dc23
                          2013039161

Maps shown in this book were produced using *National Geographic's* TOPO! software.

♻ Printed on recycled paper
ISBN (paperback): 978-1-59485-768-3
ISBN (ebook): 978-1-59485-769-0

Table of Contents

Snoqualmie Pass Area

Snoqualmie Pass Corridor: East

Teanaway and Blewett Country

LEGEND

Symbol	Description	Symbol	Description
84	Interstate Highway	℗	Parking
197	US Highway	▲	Campground/Campsite
14	State Route	■	Building/Landmark
—	Secondary Road	▲	Summit
=======	Unpaved Road	) (	Pass
== 24 ==	Forest Road	~	River/Stream
....	Hiking Route	~	Falls
....	Other Trail		Lake
—·—·—	Wilderness Boundary	)(	Bridge/Trestle
❶	Hike Number	←	Gate
❶	Trailhead		Lookout
Ⓣ	Alternate Trailhead		

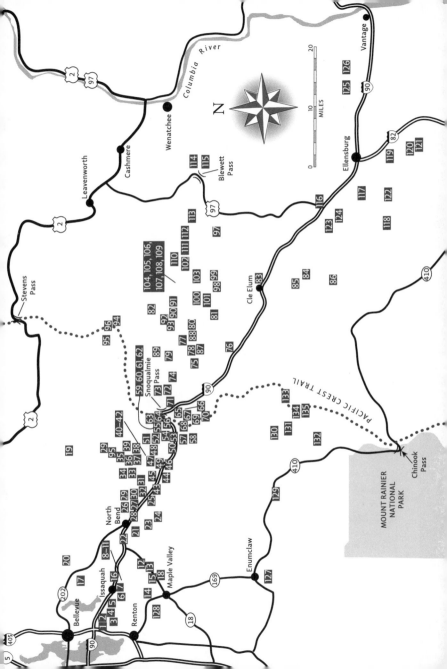

Hikes at a Glance

HIKE	DISTANCE (ROUND-TRIP)	DIFFICULTY	HIKABLE EARLY SEASON	KID-FRIENDLY	DOG-FRIENDLY
ISSAQUAH ALPS					
1. Wildside Trail–De Leo Wall	4 miles	2	•	•	•
2. Red Town Meadow	1.5 miles	1	•	•	•
3. Coal Creek Falls	2.5 miles	2	•	•	•
4. Anti-Aircraft Peak	6 miles	2	•	•	•
5. Wilderness Peak	4 miles	3	•	•	•
6. Poo Poo Point–High School Trail	7.4 miles	3	•		•
7. Pilots Trail to Poo Poo Point Launch	4 miles	3	•	•	•
8. West Tiger Railroad Grade	10 miles	4	•		•
9. West Tiger 3	5 miles	4	•		•
10. Tradition Lake Loop	4 miles	2	•	•	•
11. Tiger Mountain Trail: North	5 miles	3	•		•
12. Northwest Timber Trail	5 miles	2	•	•	•
13. Middle Tiger Loop	8.6 miles	4	•		•
14. Tiger Mountain Trail: South	4 miles	2	•	•	•
15. Tiger Mountain Trail	16 miles	5	•		•
16. Grand Ridge Trail	9 miles	3	•	•	•
17. Soaring Eagle Park	7.5 miles	2	•	•	•
18. Taylor Mountain–Holder Knob Loop	6 miles	2	•	•	•
NORTH BEND					
19. Bare Mountain	8 miles	5			•
20. Tolt MacDonald Park	2.5 miles	1	•	•	•
21. Rattlesnake Ledge	4 miles	3	•	•	•
22. Rattlesnake Mountain	4.5 miles	3	•	•	•
23. Cedar Butte	5 miles	3	•	•	•
24. Iron Horse Trail–Change Creek	12 miles	2	•	•	•
25. Twin Falls	3 miles	2	•	•	•
26. Little Si	5 miles	4	•	•	•
27. Mount Si	8 miles	5	•		•
28. Old Si–Boulder Garden Loop	2.4 miles	2	•	•	
29. Mount Teneriffe	14 miles	5	•		•
30. Kamakazi (Teneriffe) Falls	6.5 miles	3	•	•	•
31. Granite Lakes	12 miles	4	•		
32. Mailbox Peak	6 miles	5	•		

WILD-FLOWERS	OLD GROWTH	FISHING	BIRD-WATCHING	WILDERNESS	HISTORICAL	WHEEL-CHAIR-ACCESS	BIKES OK	CAR CAMP NEAR	BACK-PACKING
					•				
					•				
•					•				
			•		•				
			•		•				
			•						
			•						
			•						
	•		•				•		
			•						
					•				
•			•				•		
			•				•		
				•	•				
		•							
					•		•		
		•							
		•	•						

HIKE	DISTANCE (ROUND-TRIP)	DIFFICULTY	HIKABLE EARLY SEASON	KID-FRIENDLY	DOG-FRIENDLY
33. CCC Road: Blowout Creek	7 miles	2	•	•	•
34. Bessemer Mountain	12 miles	4			•
35. CCC Road: Upper Trailhead	4 miles	2	•	•	•
36. CCC Road: Campground	6 miles	2	•	•	•
37. Middle Fork Snoqualmie: Downstream to Pratt	7 miles	3	•	•	
38. Middle Fork Snoqualmie: Upstream	6 miles	2	•	•	•
39. Big Creek Falls	10 miles	3	•	•	•
40. Rock Creek Falls	11 miles	3			•
41. Dingford Creek–Hester Lake	12 miles	4			
42. Upper Middle Fork Snoqualmie Meadows	12 miles	4			
SNOQUALMIE PASS CORRIDOR: WEST					
43. Mount Washington	8 miles	5			•
44. Deception Crags	1 mile	1	•	•	•
45. Dirty Harry	5 miles	3		•	•
46. McClellan Butte	9 miles	5			
47. Ira Spring Trail	6 miles	4		•	•
48. Mount Defiance	11 miles	5			•
49. Little Bandera Mountain	7 miles	4			•
50. Talapus and Olallie Lakes	4 miles	2	•	•	
51. Island and Rainbow Lakes	10 miles	4			•
52. Pratt Lake Basin	8 miles	4			•
53. Granite Mountain	8 miles	5			
54. Denny Creek	4 miles	2		•	•
55. Melakwa Lake	9 miles	4			•
56. Franklin Falls	2 miles	1		•	
57. Asahel Curtis Nature Trail	0.5 mile	1		•	•
58. Annette Lake	7.5 miles	3		•	•
SNOQUALMIE PASS AREA					
59. Commonwealth Basin	10 miles	4		•	
60. Kendall Katwalk	11 miles	4			
61. Snow Lake	6 miles	3		•	
62. Gem Lake	10 miles	4			
63. Source Lake	4 miles	3		•	•
64. Lodge Lake	3 miles	2		•	•
65. Iron Horse Trail Tunnel	6 miles	3	•	•	
66. Silver Peak	8.5 miles	3			•

WILD-FLOWERS	OLD GROWTH	FISHING	BIRD-WATCH-ING	WILDERNESS	HISTORICAL	WHEEL-CHAIR-ACCESS	BIKES OK	CAR CAMP NEAR	BACK-PACKING
					•				
					•				
					•				
			•		•		•		
							•		
		•					•		
							•		
							•		
	•	•	•	•			•		
•			•	•			•		
•									
			•						
					•				
					•				
		•		•	•				
			•	•					
•				•					
			•	•					
			•	•					
			•	•					
•				•	•				
							•		
		•		•			•		
					•		•		
	•				•				
		•					•		
•			•	•			•		
•			•	•	•		•	•	•
•		•		•			•	•	
•			•	•	•		•	•	•
			•				•		
		•							
					•				
•			•						

HIKE	DISTANCE (ROUND-TRIP)	DIFFICULTY	HIKABLE EARLY SEASON	KID-FRIENDLY	DOG-FRIENDLY
67. Twin Lakes–Tinkham Loop	8 miles	3			•
68. Mount Catherine	3 miles	3			
69. Mirror Lake	3 miles	2			•
70. Stirrup Lake	4 miles	3		•	•
71. Gold Creek Pond Loop	1 mile	1	•	•	
72. Margaret Lake	6 miles	3		•	•
73. Twin Lakes and Lake Lillian	9 miles	4			•
SNOQUALMIE PASS CORRIDOR: EAST					
74. Rachel Lake	8 miles	4		•	•
75. Kachess Ridge	6 miles	4			•
76. Easton Ridge	6 miles	4			•
77. Thorp Lake	7 miles	4			•
78. Knox Creek–Thorp Mountain	4.4 miles	3			•
79. No Name Ridge–Thorp Mountain	9 miles	3			•
80. Howson Creek	5 miles	4			•
81. Hex Mountain	6 miles	4			
82. Boulder Creek–Gallagher Head Lake	9 miles	4			
83. Coal Mines Trail	6.5 miles	1	•	•	•
84. North Fork Taneum Creek	8 miles	2	•	•	•
85. Taneum Ridge–Fishhook Flats Loop	14 miles	3			•
86. Lost and Manastash Lakes	7 miles	3		•	•
87. French Cabin Creek	7 miles	3			•
88. French Cabin Mountain	10 miles	5			•
89. Pete Lake	9 miles	3		•	•
90. Cooper River	6 miles	2	•	•	•
91. Polallie Ridge	8 miles	5			
92. Davis Peak	11 miles	5			
93. Jolly Mountain	12 miles	5			
94. Paddy-Go-Easy Pass	7 miles	4			•
95. Cathedral Rock	9 miles	4		•	•
96. Hyas Lake	4 miles	1		•	•
TEANAWAY AND BLEWETT COUNTRY					
97. Redtop Lookout and Agate Beds	3 miles	2		•	•
98. Middle Fork Teanaway	7 miles	2	•	•	•
99. Elbow Peak	10 miles	4			•
100. Koppen Mountain	7 miles	4			•
101. De Roux Creek–Gallagher Head Lake	8 miles	3	•	•	•

WILD-FLOWERS	OLD GROWTH	FISHING	BIRD-WATCH-ING	WILDERNESS	HISTORICAL	WHEEL-CHAIR-ACCESS	BIKES OK	CAR CAMP NEAR	BACK-PACKING
•			•						
•			•						
		•							
•			•						
•						•	•	•	
•		•		•					
•		•	•	•					
				•			•	•	•
•					•		•		
•			•				•		
•		•					•		
•					•		•		
•					•				
•								•	
•			•				•		
•		•	•				•	•	•
					•	•			
•	•		•			•	•		
			•				•		
•	•	•						•	•
•			•						
•									
•	•	•		•			•	•	•
		•	•				•	•	
•			•		•		•	•	
•			•				•	•	
•			•					•	
•			•	•			•	•	•
•					•		•	•	•
		•		•			•	•	•
•					•				
•		•	•				•	•	•
•			•				•	•	
•			•		•		•		
•		•							

HIKE	DISTANCE (ROUND-TRIP)	DIFFICULTY	HIKABLE EARLY SEASON	KID-FRIENDLY	DOG-FRIENDLY
102. Johnson Creek–Medra Pass	8 miles	3			•
103. Way Creek Trail–Middle Fork Teanaway	4.4 miles	2	•		•
104. Bear Creek	3.5 miles	1	•	•	•
105. Standup Creek to Stafford Creek Overlook	7 miles	4			•
106. Esmeralda Basin	7 miles	3			•
107. Lake Ingalls	9 miles	5			
108. Longs Pass	5 miles	4			
109. Bean Creek Basin	5 miles	3			•
110. Beverly Creek–Fourth of July Creek Overlook	7 miles	3			
111. Navaho Pass	11 miles	3			•
112. Miller Peak	8 miles	3			•
113. Teanaway Ridge	6 miles	3			•
114. Tronsen Ridge	8 miles	2		•	•
115. Mount Lillian	3 miles	2		•	•
ELLENSBURG BASIN					
116. John Wayne Trail	6+ miles	1	•	•	•
117. Westburg Trail	4 miles	2	•	•	•
118. Observation Road–Manastash Ridge	10 miles	2	•	•	•
119. Rattlesnake Dance Ridge Trail	2.2 miles	2	•	•	
120. Umtanum Creek Canyon	6+ miles	1	•	•	•
121. Umtanum Ridge	4+ miles	2	•		•
122. Umtanum Creek Falls	6+ miles	2	•		•
123. Joe Watt Canyon	6+ miles	3	•	•	
124. Robinson Canyon	10+ miles	3	•		
125. Whiskey Dick Mountain: Wind Farms	5 miles	3	•	•	
126. Whiskey Dick Mountain: Rocky Coulee	8+ miles	3	•	•	•
ENUMCLAW PLATEAU					
127. Pinnacle Peak	2 miles	2	•	•	•
128. Echo Mountain	3.2–4 miles	2	•	•	•
129. Federation Forest	2–12 miles	2	•	•	
130. Kelly Butte	3.6 miles	2		•	•
131. Colquhoun Peak	1.1–2.6 miles	2		•	•
132. Lake George–Noble Knob's Backdoor	3.5 miles	2		•	•
133. Blowout Mountain	6.8 miles	2		•	•
134. Pyramid Peak	6.5 miles	2		•	•
135. Greenwater–Echo Lake	14 miles	3	•	•	

WILD-FLOWERS	OLD GROWTH	FISHING	BIRD-WATCH-ING	WILDERNESS	HISTORICAL	WHEEL-CHAIR-ACCESS	BIKES OK	CAR CAMP NEAR	BACK-PACKING
•								•	
•							•		
•		•	•						
•			•						
•			•				•	•	•
•			•	•			•	•	
•			•						
•			•					•	•
•			•					•	•
•			•				•	•	•
							•		
•			•				•		
•			•				•		
•							•		
					•	•			
•			•		•				
•			•						
•			•						
•			•		•		•	•	•
•			•					•	
•									
•			•		•		•		
•			•		•		•		
•			•		•				
•			•		•				
					•				
	•		•				•		
•					•				
					•				
•		•	•						
•									
	•				•				
	•	•		•			•	•	•

Acknowledgments

This book and series would not have been possible without the support of our families. Throughout the years of frequent trips away from home and odd hours we spent in our home offices while we researched, photographed, and wrote about these routes, our immediate families have kept us grounded, focused, and happy. This book is dedicated to them.

A meadow of bear grass on Granite Mountain

Introduction

The more advanced we become with labor-saving technology, the less time we have to ourselves. All those time-saving tools merely open the door for other time-eating traps at work and home. Americans are working more hours each year, with less vacation time taken, than they have at any time since World War II.

This helps explain why more and more hikers are foregoing multiday backpacking trips in favor of day-long outings. With fewer free hours—and more hobbies competing for that free time—hikers seem to favor trail excursions that can be done in a day.

This Day Hiking series steps in to help modern hikers get their wilderness fix, offering up the best routes in a region that can be enjoyed as day trips. Of course, the length of day will vary, depending on where you start—drive times to, say, the Teanaway Valley are considerably longer for hikers starting from Olympia than those coming from Issaquah.

Day Hiking: Snoqualmie Region focuses on hikes in the southern portion of the central Cascades—that is, the trails found off I-90, State Route 18, the west end of State Route 410, and US Highway 97 from Blewett Pass south. These routes explore some of the Cascades' most varied terrain, delving into deep forested valleys, cresting high craggy peaks, and exploring dry pine basins, broad alpine meadows, and high desert steppes. You'll find some of the richest ecosystems and some of the most abundant and varied wildlife available in the country.

A bear grass–filled meadow and views of Mount Rainier from near the summit of Kelly Butte

The trails cross the habitat of black-tailed deer as well as their larger cousins, mule deer. There are Rocky Mountain elk (wapiti) and their chief predator, mountain lions (aka cougars or pumas). There are snowy white mountain goats and dun-colored bighorn sheep. Scan the skies and you might see eagles (bald and golden) as well as an array of other raptors, big and small. You might hear the screech of an owl, the *thump-thump-thump* of grouse, and the trilling calls of a multitude of songbirds.

This region is home to ancient cedar and hemlock forests, as well as stands of tall Douglas fir. Massive ponderosa pines fill the eastern slopes, which are also dotted with beautiful larches that change from soft emerald green to radiant golden hues each year. From forest to meadow to alpine

A male blue grouse puts on a show in the open pine forest regions on the eastern slopes of the Cascades.

slopes, you'll also enjoy glorious bursts of color thanks to a plethora of wildflowers—from the beautiful (though unfortunately named) skunk cabbage to aptly named carpet pinks (aka spreading phlox). You'll find forest floors covered in the tall stalks of bear grass with their bulbous blooms, and hillsides covered in the ubiquitous lupine.

Best of all for those who love to hike, the trails of the central Cascades are just as varied as the environs they cross, and plentiful, too. I hope this book will help you find your own special moments in this wonderful wild country.

USING THIS BOOK

Day Hiking: Snoqualmie Region strikes a fine balance. It was developed to be as easy to use as possible while still providing enough detail to help you explore a region. As a result, it includes all of the information you need to

find and enjoy the hikes, but leave enough room for you to make your own discoveries as you venture into areas new to you.

What the Ratings Mean

Every trail described in this book features a detailed "trail facts" section. Not all of the details here are facts, however.

Each hike starts with two subjective ratings: each hike has a **rating** of 1 to 5 stars for its overall appeal, and each route's **difficulty** is rated on a scale of 1 to 5. This is subjective, based on the author's impressions of each route, but the ratings do follow a formula of sorts. The overall rating is based on scenic beauty, natural wonder, and other unique qualities, such as solitude potential and wildlife-viewing opportunities.

The difficulty rating is based on trail length, the steepness of the trail, and how difficult it is to hike. Generally, trails that are rated more difficult (4 or 5) are longer and steeper than average. But it's not a simple equation. A short, steep trail over talus slopes may be rated 5, while a long, smooth trail with little elevation gain may be rated 2.

To help explain those difficulty ratings, you'll also find the **roundtrip mileage** (unless otherwise noted as one-way), total **elevation gain,** and **high point** for each hike. The distances are not always exact mileages—trails weren't measured with calibrated instruments—but the mileages are those used by cartographers and land managers (who have measured many of the trails). The elevation gains report the cumulative difference between the high and low point on the route. It's worth noting that not all high points are at the end of the trail—a route may run over a high ridge before dropping to a lake basin, for instance.

Another subjective tool you'll find is the hikable **season.** Many trails can be enjoyed from the time they lose their winter snowpack right up until they are buried in fresh snow the following fall. But snowpacks vary from year to year, so a trail that is open in May one year may be snow-covered until mid-July the next. The hiking season for each trail is an estimate, so before you venture out it's worth contacting the land manager to get current conditions.

To help with trip planning, each hike also lists which **maps** you'll want to have on your hike, as well as what agency to **contact** to get current trail conditions (for complete contact information, see Appendix A). Hikes in this guidebook use Green Trails maps, which are based on the standard 7.5-minute USGS topographical maps. Green Trails maps are available at most outdoor retailers in the state, as well as at many US Forest Service visitors centers.

Given that we now live in a digital world, **GPS coordinates** (in degrees and decimal minutes) for each trailhead are provided—use them both to get to the trail and to help you get back to your car if you get caught out in a storm or wander off-trail.

You will also note small **icons** throughout the book. Trails that we found to be dog-friendly, kid-friendly, good for bird-watching, or of historical interest, for example, are marked by these icons. The icons are meant to be merely helpful suggestions, however, and should not be a limiting factor for your hiking. If you and the kids want to hike a trail that does not have a "kid" icon, go for it! Same holds true for dogs, though you might want to check with the land manager before venturing out with your dog, since canines are restricted in some areas, especially on trails outside the National Forest Service lands.

 Kid-friendly

 Dog-friendly

 Exceptional wildflowers in season

Exceptional waterfalls

Fishing options

Exceptional old growth

Bird-watching

Historical relevance

The route descriptions themselves provide a basic overview of what you might find on your hike, directions to get you to the trailhead, and in some cases additional highlights beyond the actual trails you'll be exploring.

Of course, you'll need some information long before you ever leave home. So, as you plan your trips, consider the following several issues.

PERMITS AND REGULATIONS

You can't set foot out your door these days without first making sure you're not breaking the rules. In an effort to keep our wilderness areas wild and our trails safe and well maintained, the land managers—especially the National Park Service and the US Forest Service—have implemented a sometimes-complex set of rules and regulations governing the use of public lands.

Virtually all trails in national forests in Washington (and Oregon) fall under the Region 6 forest pass program. Simply stated, in order to park legally at these designated national forest trailheads, you must display a **Northwest Forest Pass** or an **America the Beautiful Interagency Annual Pass,** which is good nationwide for all US Forest Service, National Park Service, Bureau of Land

ALL LIT UP

The following are suggestions for reducing the dangers of lightning should thunderstorms be forecast or develop while you are in the mountains:

- Use a NOAA weather radio (a radio tuned in to one of the national weather forecast frequencies) to keep abreast of the latest weather information.
- Avoid traveling on mountain tops and ridge crests.
- Stay well away from bodies of water.
- If your hair stands on end, or you feel static shocks, move immediately—the static electricity you feel could very well be a precursor to a lightning strike.
- If there is a shelter or building nearby, get into it. Don't take shelter under trees, however, especially in open areas.
- If there is no shelter available, and lightning is flashing, remove your pack (the metal stays or frame are natural electrical conduits) and crouch down, balancing on the balls of your feet until the lightning clears the area.

Of course, thunderstorms aren't the only weather hazard hikers face. A sudden rain-squall can push temperatures down 15 or 20 degrees Fahrenheit in a matter of minutes. Even if you're dressed for hot summer hiking, you should be prepared for such temperature drops and the accompanying soaking rain if you want to avoid hypothermia.

If the temperature drop is great enough, you can miss the rain and get hit instead by snow. Snowstorms have blown through the Cascades every month of the year, with as much as a foot falling on some routes in late August.

Besides fresh-fallen snow, summer hikers also need to be aware of snowfields left over from the previous winter's snowpack. Depending on the severity of the past winter and the weather conditions of the spring and early summer, some trails may melt out in June, while others will remain snow-covered well into August or beyond—some years, some sections never melt out. In addition to making for treacherous footing and difficulties in routefinding, these lingering snowfields can be prone to avalanches or slides.

Hikers roaming the ridge below the summit of Noble Knob

Management (BLM), and National Wildlife Refuge lands. The Northwest Forest Pass sells for $5 per day or $30 for an annual pass good throughout Washington and Oregon (which constitute Region 6). The Northwest Forest Pass is also required at most trailheads within the North Cascades National Park complex. The America the Beautiful Pass sells for $80 and works nationwide. Learn more at www.fs.usda.gov/detail/r6/passes-permits/recreation/?cid=fsbdev2_027020.

If recreating on state lands, you'll need a **Washington Discover Pass,** which covers day use on lands managed by Washington State Parks, the Washington State Department of Natural Resources (DNR), and the Washington Department of Fish and Wildlife (WDFW). The Washington Discover Pass costs $10 per day or $30 annually. Learn more at www.discoverpass.wa.gov/.

In addition to getting a parking pass, when you hike in wilderness areas you must also pick up and fill out a wilderness permit at the trailhead registration box (sometimes located at the wilderness boundary if the trail doesn't immediately enter a designated wilderness). These are free and unlimited (though that may change).

WEATHER

Mountain weather in general is famously unpredictable, but the Cascade Range stretches that unpredictability to sometimes-absurd lengths. The high, jagged nature of the mountains, coupled with their proximity to the Pacific Ocean, makes them magnets for every bit of moisture in the atmosphere.

As moist air comes rushing in off the Pacific, it hits the western front of the Cascades. The air is pushed up the slopes of the mountains, often forming clouds and eventually rain, feeding the wet rain forests that dominate the western slopes. By the time the airstream crests the Cascades and starts down the east slopes, the clouds have lost their moisture loads, leaving the east-side forests dry and filled with open stands of drought-resistant pine.

Where east meets west, the wet clouds hit the dry heat, often creating thunderstorms. Hikers on the trail must be aware

Looking down at Rachel Lake from the trail that extends beyond the lake and heads up to the Rampart Lakes region

of this potential, because such storms can brew up any month of the year. Thunderstorms can also develop quickly, with little warning, and a hiker stuck on a high pass becomes a good target for a lightning bolt (see "All Lit Up" for how to avoid this).

ROAD AND TRAIL CONDITIONS

Trails in general change little year to year. Though they truly are man-made structures in rugged wilderness settings, trails are quite durable. But change can and does occur, and sometimes it occurs very quickly. One brutal storm can alter a river's course, washing out sections of trail in moments. Wind can drop trees across trails by the hundreds, making the paths difficult if not impossible to travel. And snow can obliterate trails well into the heart of summer.

Access roads face similar threats and are in fact more susceptible to washouts and closures than the trails themselves. With this in mind, each hike in this book lists the appropriate land manager to contact so you can call or email prior to your trip to ensure that your chosen road and trail are open and safe to travel. (See Appendix A for contact information.)

On the topic of trail conditions, it is vital that we thank the countless volunteers who donate tens of thousands of hours to trail maintenance each year. The Washington Trails Association (WTA) alone coordinates upward of one hundred thousand hours of volunteer trail maintenance each year.

As massive as the volunteer effort has become, there is always a need for more. Our wilderness trail system faces increasing threats, including (but by no means limited to) ever-shrinking trail funding, inappropriate trail uses, and conflicting land-management policies and practices.

Broad views from the Pacific Crest Trail north of Snoqualmie Pass look on Snoqualmie Mountain and Red Mountain.

With this in mind, this guide includes several trails that are threatened and in danger of becoming unhikable. These endangered trails are found throughout the region. Sometimes, we listed trails as "Endangered" even though land managers may consider them fine—this is especially true when destructive uses are allowed, such as motorcycle use of trails on steep terrain or in sensitive meadow or wetland areas. These trails are marked with the following icon in this book:

 Endangered trail (threatened with loss or closure)

On the other side of the coin, we've also been blessed with some great trail successes in recent years, thanks in large part to that massive volunteer movement spearheaded by the WTA. As you enjoy these saved trails, stop to consider the contributions made by your fellow hikers that helped protect our trail resources. These saved trails are marked with this icon:

 Saved trail (rescued from permanent loss)

WILDERNESS ETHICS

As wonderful as volunteer trail maintenance programs are, they aren't the only way to help save our trails. Indeed, these on-the-ground efforts provide quality trails today, but to ensure the long-term survival of our trails—and the wildlands they cross—we all must embrace and practice sound wilderness ethics.

Strong, positive wilderness ethics include making sure you leave the wilderness as pure or purer than it was when you found it. As the adage says, "Take only pictures, leave only footprints." But sound wilderness ethics go deeper than that, beyond simply picking up after ourselves when we go for a hike. Wilderness ethics must carry over into our daily lives. We need to ensure that our elected officials and public land managers recognize and respond to our wilderness needs and desires. If we hike the trails on the weekend but let the wilderness go neglected—or worse, allow it to be abused—on the weekdays, we'll soon find our weekend haunts diminished or destroyed.

TRAIL GIANTS

I want to add a personal note here. As I began my career as a guidebook author, I was blessed with the opportunity to learn from the men

Wonder pooch getting ready to hike the Northwest Timber Trail on Tiger Mountain

and women who helped launch the guidebook genre for Mountaineers Books. Throughout the 1990s I enjoyed many conversations with Ira Spring—we would talk for hours about our favorite trails and how we needed to diligently fight for those trails. I exchanged frequent correspondence with Harvey Manning, debating the best means of saving wildlands. I was advised and mentored by Louise Marshall. I worked alongside Greg Ball—founder of the WTA's volunteer trail maintenance program—for more than a decade.

In short, I served my apprenticeship with masters of the trail trade. From them, and from my own experiences exploring the wonderful wildlands of Washington, I discovered the pressing need for individual activism. When hikers get complacent, trails suffer. We must, in the words of the legendary Ira Spring, "get people onto trails. They need to bond with the wilderness." This green bonding, as Ira called it, is essential in building public support for trails and trail funding.

As you get out and hike the trails described here, consider that many of these trails would have long ago ceased to exist without the phenomenal efforts of people such as Ira Spring, Harvey Manning, Louise Marshall, and Greg Ball, not to mention the scores of unnamed hikers who joined them in their push for wildland protection, trail funding, and strong environmental stewardship programs.

When you get home, bear in mind these people's actions and then sit down and write a letter to your congressperson asking for better trail funding. Call your local Forest Service office to say that you've enjoyed the trails in their jurisdiction and that you want these routes to remain wild and accessible for use by you and your children.

Endless views extend into the Columbia Basin from the high ridge of Whiskey Dick Mountain near Wild Horse Wind Farm.

And if you're not already a member, consider joining an organization devoted to wilderness, backcountry trails, or other wild-country issues. Organizations such as The Mountaineers, the Washington Trails Association, Volunteers for Outdoor Washington, the Cascade chapter of the Sierra Club, Conservation Northwest, the Cascade Land Conservancy, and countless others leverage individual contributions and efforts to help ensure the future of our trails and the wonderful wilderness legacy we've inherited.

TRAIL ETIQUETTE

Anyone who enjoys backcountry trails should recognize their responsibility to those trails and to other trail users. We each must work to preserve the tranquility of the wildlands by being sensitive not only to the environment but to other trail users as well.

The trails in this book are open to an array of uses. Some are open to hikers only, but others also allow horseback riders, mountain bikers, hikers with dogs, and—on occasion—motorcycles.

When you encounter other trail users—whether they are hikers, climbers, runners, bicyclists, or horseback riders—the only hard-and-fast rule is to follow common sense and exercise simple courtesy. It's hard to overstate just how vital these two things—common sense and courtesy—are to maintaining an enjoyable, safe, and friendly situation when different types of trail users meet. See "The Golden Rules of Trail Etiquette" for what you can do during trail encounters to make everyone's trip more enjoyable.

THE GOLDEN RULES OF TRAIL ETIQUETTE

- **Right-of-way.** When meeting other hikers, the uphill group has the right-of-way. There are two general reasons for this. First, on steep ascents hikers may be watching the trail and not notice the approach of descending hikers until they are face-to-face. More importantly, it is easier for descending hikers to break their stride and step off the trail than it is for those who have gotten into a good climbing rhythm. But by all means if you are the uphill trekker and you wish to grant passage to oncoming hikers, go right ahead with this act of trail kindness.
- **Moving off-trail.** When meeting other user groups (like bicyclists or horseback riders), hikers should move off the trail. This is because hikers are more mobile and flexible than other users, making it easier for them to step off the trail.
- **Encountering horses.** When meeting horseback riders, hikers should step off the downhill side of the trail unless the terrain makes this difficult or dangerous. In that case, move to the uphill side of the trail, but crouch down a bit so you don't tower over the horses' heads. Also, make yourself visible so as not to spook the big beastie, and talk in a normal voice to the riders. This calms the horses. If hiking with a dog, keep your buddy under control.
- **Stay on trails,** and practice minimum impact. Don't cut switchbacks, take shortcuts, or make new trails. If your destination is off-trail, stick to snow and rock when possible so as not to damage fragile alpine meadows. Spread out when traveling off-trail; don't hike in a line if you are in a group, as this greatly increases the chance of compacting thin soils and crushing delicate plant environments.
- **Obey the rules** specific to the trail you are visiting. Many trails are closed to certain types of use, including hiking with dogs or riding horses.
- **Hiking with dogs.** Hikers who take their dogs on the trails should have them on a leash or under very strict voice command at all times.
- **Avoid disturbing wildlife,** especially in winter and in calving areas. Observe from a distance, resisting the urge to move closer to wildlife (use your telephoto lens). This not only keeps you safer, but it also prevents the animal from having to exert itself unnecessarily to flee from you.
- **Take only photographs.** Leave all natural things, features, and historic artifacts as you found them for others to enjoy.
- **Never roll rocks off trails or cliffs.** You risk endangering the lives of people below you.

These are just a few of the things you can do to maintain a safe and harmonious trail environment. And while not every situation is addressed by these rules, you can avoid problems by always remembering that common sense and courtesy are in order.

Also part of trail etiquette is to pack out everything you packed in, even biodegradable things such as apple cores.

Another important Leave No Trace principle focuses on the business of taking care of personal business. The first rule of backcountry bathroom etiquette says that if an outhouse exists, use it. This seems obvious, but all too often folks find that backcountry toilets are dark, dank affairs, and they choose to use the woods rather than the rickety wooden structure provided. It may be easier on your nose to head off into the woods, but this disperses human waste around popular areas. Privies, on the other hand, concentrate the waste and thus minimize contamination of area waters. The outhouses get even higher environmental marks if they feature removable holding tanks that can be airlifted out. These johns and their accompanying stacks of tanks aren't exactly aesthetically pleasing, but having an ugly outhouse tucked into a corner of the woods is better than finding toilet paper strewn about.

When privies aren't provided, the key factor to consider is location. You'll want to choose a site at least 200 feet from water, campsites, and trails. A location well out of sight of trails and viewpoints will give you privacy and reduce the odds of other hikers stumbling onto the site after you leave. Other factors to consider are ecological: surrounding vegetation and some direct sunlight will aid decomposition.

A pika stands alert and on guard on a talus rock, very aware of human presence.

Once you pick your place, start digging. The idea is to make like a cat and bury your waste. You need to dig down through the organic duff into the mineral soil below—a hole six to eight inches deep is usually adequate. When you've taken care of business, refill the hole and camouflage it with rocks and sticks—this helps prevent other humans, or animals, from digging in the same location before decomposition has done its job.

WATER

You'll want to treat your drinking water in the backcountry. Wherever humans have gone, germs have gone with them—and humans have gone just about everywhere. That means that even the most pristine mountain stream may harbor microscopic nasties such as *Giardia* cysts, *Cryptosporidium*, or *E. coli*.

Treating water can be as simple as boiling it, chemically purifying it (adding tiny iodine tablets), or pumping it through one of the new-generation water filters or purifiers (Note: Pump units labeled as filters generally remove everything but viruses, which are too small to be filtered out. Pumps labeled as purifiers use a chemical element—usually iodine—to render viruses inactive after all of the other bugs are filtered out.) Never drink untreated water, or your intestines will never forgive you.

CLEANUP

When washing your hands, rinse off as much dust and dirt as you can in just plain water first. If you still feel the need for a soapy wash, collect a pot of water from a lake or stream and move at least 200 feet away. Apply a tiny bit of biodegradable soap to your hands, dribble on a little water, and lather up. Use a bandanna or towel to wipe away most of the soap, and then rinse with the water in the pot.

When camping, practice Leave No Trace principles when possible. Specifically, consider using a stove even where wood fires are permitted. If you do make a fire, keep it small and build only in existing fire rings and only where safe and legally permitted. Use only dead and downed wood from outside the camp area. Leave flowers, rocks, and other natural features undisturbed. Visualize potential impacts when selecting campsites. Hang food out of reach of animals: four feet from tree trunks and ten feet off the ground, or use a bear-proof box.

WILDLIFE
Bears

There are an estimated thirty to thirty-five thousand black bears in Washington, and the big bruins can be found in every corner of the state. The central and southern Cascades are especially attractive to the solitude-seeking bears. Watching the bears graze through a rich huckleberry field or seeing them flip dead logs in search of grubs can be an exciting and rewarding experience—provided, of course, that you aren't in the same berry patch.

Bears tend to prefer solitude to human company and will generally flee long before you have a chance to get too close. There are times, however, when bears either don't hear hikers approaching, or they are more interested in defending their food source—or their young—than they are in avoiding a confrontation. These instances are rare, and there are things you can do to minimize the odds of an encounter with an aggressive bear (see "Bear in Mind" in this section).

Cougars

Very few hikers ever see a cougar in the wild. Not only are these big cats some of the

A small Northern Pacific rattlesnake on the trail

BEAR IN MIND

Here are some suggestions for helping to avoid running into an aggressive bear:

- **Hike in a group** and hike only during daylight hours.
- **Talk or sing as you hike.** If a bear hears you coming, it will usually avoid you. When surprised, however, a bear may feel threatened. So make noises that will identify you as a human—talk, sing, rattle pebbles in a tin can—especially when hiking near a river or stream (which can mask more subtle sounds that might normally alert a bear to your presence).
- **Be aware** of the environment around you, and know how to identify bear signs. Overturned rocks and torn-up deadwood logs often are the result of a bear searching for grubs. Berry bushes stripped of berries—with leaves, branches, and berries littering the ground under the bushes—show where a bear has fed. Bears will often leave claw marks on trees, and, since they use trees as scratching posts, fur in the rough bark of a tree is a sign that says "A bear was here!" Tracks and scat are the most common signs of a bear's recent presence.
- **Stay away from abundant food sources and dead animals.** Black bears are opportunistic and will scavenge food. A bear that finds a dead deer will hang around until the meat is gone, and it will defend that food against any perceived threat.
- **Keep dogs leashed and under control.** Many bear encounters have resulted from unleashed dogs chasing a bear: The bear gets angry and turns on the dog. The dog gets scared and runs for help (back to its owner). And the bear follows right back into the dog owner's lap.
- **Leave scented items at home**—perfume, hair spray, cologne, and scented soaps. Using scented sprays and body lotions makes you smell like a big, tasty treat.
- **Never clean fish within 100 feet** of camp.

most solitary, shy animals in the woods, but there are just twenty-five hundred to three thousand of them roaming the entire state of Washington. Still, cougars and hikers do sometimes encounter each other. In these cases hikers should, in my opinion, count their blessings—they will likely never see a more majestic animal than a wild cougar.

To make sure that the encounter is a positive one, hikers must understand the cats. Cougars are shy but very curious. They will follow hikers simply to see what kind of beasts we are, but they very rarely (as in, almost never) attack adult humans. See "Cool Cats" in this section for how to make the most of your luck.

GEAR

No hiker should venture far up a trail without being properly equipped, starting with the feet. A good pair of boots can make the difference between a wonderful hike and a horrible death march. Keep your feet happy and you'll be happy.

But you can't talk boots without talking socks. Only one rule here: wear whatever is most comfortable unless it's cotton. Corollary to that rule: never wear cotton.

COOL CATS

If you encounter a cougar, remember that these animals rely on prey that can't, or won't, fight back. So, as soon as you see the cat:

- **Do not run!** Running may trigger a cougar's attack instinct.
- **Stand up and face it.** Virtually every recorded cougar attack on humans has been a predator-prey attack. If you appear as another aggressive predator rather than as prey, the cougar will back down.
- **Try to appear large.** Wave your arms or a jacket over your head.
- **Pick up children and small dogs.**
- **Maintain eye contact** with the animal. The cougar will interpret this as a show of dominance on your part.
- **Back away slowly** if you can safely do so.

Cotton is a wonderful fabric when your life isn't on the line—it's soft, light, and airy. But get it wet and it stays wet. That means blisters on your feet. Wet cotton also lacks any insulation value. In fact, get it wet and it sucks away your body heat, leaving you susceptible to hypothermia. So leave your cotton socks, cotton underwear, and even the cotton T-shirts at home. The only cotton I carry on the trail is my trusty pink bandanna (pink because nobody else I know carries pink, so I always know which is mine).

While the "to pack" list varies from hiker to hiker, there are a few things each and every one of us should have in our packs. For instance, every hiker who ventures more than a few hundred yards away from the road should be prepared to spend the night under the stars (or under the clouds, as may be more likely). Mountain storms can whip up in a hurry, catching sunny-day hikers by surprise. What was an easy-to-follow trail during a calm, clear day can disappear into a confusing world of fog and rain—or even snow—in a windy tempest. Therefore, every member of the party should pack the Ten Essentials and a few other items that aren't necessarily essential but would be good to have on hand in an emergency.

The Ten Essentials

1. **Navigation (map and compass):** Carry a topographic map of the area you plan to be in and knowledge of how to read it. Likewise a compass—again, make sure you know how to use it.
2. **Sun protection (sunglasses and sunscreen):** In addition to sunglasses and sunscreen (SPF 15 or better), take along physical sun barriers such as a wide-brimmed hat, long-sleeve shirt, and long pants.
3. **Insulation (extra clothing):** This means more clothing than you would wear during the worst weather of the planned outing. If you get injured or lost, you won't be moving around generating heat, so you'll need to be able to bundle up.
4. **Illumination (flashlight/headlamp):** If caught after dark, you'll need a headlamp or flashlight to be able to follow the trail. If forced to spend the night, you'll need it to set up an emergency camp, gather wood, and so on. Carry extra batteries and a bulb, too.
5. **First-aid supplies:** Nothing elaborate needed—especially if you're unfamiliar

with how to use less familiar items. Make sure you have plastic bandages, gauze bandages, some aspirin, and so on. At minimum a Red Cross first-aid training course is recommended. Better still, sign up for a Mountaineering Oriented First-Aid course (MOFA) if you'll be spending a lot of time in the woods.

6. **Fire (firestarter and matches):** An emergency campfire provides warmth, but it also has a calming effect on most people. Without one the night can be cold, dark, and intimidating. With one the night is held at arm's length. A candle or tube of firestarting ribbon is essential for starting a fire with wet wood. And of course matches are an important part of this essential. You can't start a fire without them. Pack them in a waterproof container and/or buy the waterproof/windproof variety. Book matches are useless in wind or wet weather, and most disposable lighters are unreliable.

7. **Repair kit and tools (including a knife):** A knife is helpful; a multitool is better. You never know when you might need a small pair of pliers or scissors, both of which are commonly found on compact multitools. A basic repair kit includes such things as a twenty-foot length of nylon cord, a small roll of duct tape, some one-inch webbing and extra webbing buckles (to fix broken pack straps), and a small tube of superglue.

8. **Nutrition (extra food):** Pack enough so that you'll have leftovers after an uneventful trip—those leftovers will keep you fed and fueled during an emergency.

9. **Hydration (extra water):** Figure what you'll drink between water sources, and then add an extra liter. If you plan on

DAY HIKER'S CHECKLIST
In addition to the Ten Essentials, consider the following:

THE BASICS
- Day pack (just big enough to carry all your gear)

CLOTHING
- Polyester or nylon shorts/pants
- Short-sleeve shirt
- Long-sleeve shirt
- Warm pants (fleece or microfleece)
- Fleece jacket or wool sweater
- Wicking long underwear
- Noncotton underwear
- Bandanna

OUTERWEAR
- Raingear
- Wide-brimmed hat (for sun/rain)
- Fleece/stocking hat (for warmth)
- Gloves (fleece/wool and shell)

FOOTWEAR
- Hiking boots
- Hiking socks (not cotton!). Carry one extra pair. When your feet are soaked with sweat, change into the clean pair, and rinse out the dirty pair and hang them on the back of your pack to dry. Repeat as often as necessary during the hike.
- Liner socks
- Extra laces
- Gaiters
- Moleskin (for prevention of blisters) and Second Skin (for treatment of blisters). Carry both in your first-aid kit.

relying on wilderness water sources, be sure to include some method of purification, whether a chemical additive, such as iodine, or a filtration device.

10. **Emergency shelter:** This can be as simple as a few extra-large garbage bags, or something more efficient such as a reflective space blanket or tube tent.

TRAILHEAD CONCERNS

Sadly, the topic of trailhead and trail crime must be addressed. As urban areas contin-uously encroach upon our green spaces, societal ills follow.

But by and large our hiking trails are safe places—far safer than most city streets. Common sense and vigilance, however, are still in order. This is true for all hikers, but particularly so for solo hikers. Be aware of your surroundings at all times. Leave your itinerary with someone back home. If something doesn't feel right, it probably isn't; take action by leaving the place or situation immediately. But remember, most hikers are friendly, decent people. Some

may be a little introverted, but that's no cause for worry.

By far your biggest concern should be with trailhead theft. Car break-ins are a far too common occurrence at some of our trailheads. Do not—absolutely under any circumstances—leave anything of value in your vehicle while out hiking. Take your wallet, cell phone, and listening devices with you, or better yet, don't bring them along in the first place. Don't leave anything in your car that may appear valuable. A duffle bag on the back seat may contain dirty T-shirts, but a thief may think there's a laptop in it. If you do leave a duffle of clothes in the car, unzip it so prowlers can see that it does indeed just have clothes inside. Save yourself the hassle of returning to a busted window by not giving criminals a reason to clout your car.

If you arrive at a trailhead and someone looks suspicious, don't discount your intuition. Take notes on the person and his or her vehicle. Record the license plate number and report the behavior to the authorities. Don't confront the person. Leave and go to another trail.

While most car break-ins are crimes of opportunity, organized bands intent on steal-ing IDs have also been known to target parked cars at trailheads. While some trailheads are regularly targeted and others rarely if at all, there's no sure way of preventing this from happening to you other than being dropped off at the trailhead or taking the bus (either of which is rarely an option). But you can make your car less of a target by not leaving anything of value in it.

ENJOY THE TRAILS

Above all else, I hope that you safely enjoy the trails in this book. These trails exist for our enjoyment and for the enjoyment of future generations. We can use them and protect them at the same time if we are careful with our actions and forthright with our demands on Congress to continue and to further the protection of our country's wildlands.

Throughout the twentieth century, wilderness lovers helped secure protection for the lands we enjoy today. Now we must see to it that those protections continue and that the last bits of wildlands are also preserved for the enjoyment of future generations.

Please, if you enjoy these trails, get involved. Something as simple as writing a letter to Congress can make a big difference.

Opposite: A large adult black bear stands up to get a better view of the photographer.

A NOTE ABOUT SAFETY

Safety is an important concern in all outdoor activities. No guidebook can alert you to every hazard or anticipate the limitations of every reader. Therefore, the descriptions of roads, trails, routes, and natural features in this book are not representations that a particular place or excursion will be safe for your party. When you follow any of the routes described in this book, you assume responsibility for your own safety. Under normal conditions, such excursions require the usual attention to traffic, road and trail conditions, weather, terrain, the capabilities of your party, and other factors. Keeping informed on current conditions and exercising common sense are the keys to a safe, enjoyable outing.

—*Mountaineers Books*

Opposite: Moss-covered maple trees line the trail through Soaring Eagle Regional Park.

issaquah alps

Western Washington boasts many wonderful and unique features, but one thing truly sets the Seattle-area megalopolis apart from all other urban areas: the Issaquah Alps. These peaks comprise the section of the Cascade foothills straddling the I-90 corridor, from the North Bend area to Bellevue. In the mid-1970s, Mountaineers Books author Harvey Manning gave these low but spectacular peaks the moniker "Alps" as a way to help promote, and thus preserve, the beautiful wildlands before developers marred them. Recreation became the focus for the public lands within the Alps, and the land-management agencies—from King County Parks and Recreation to the Washington State Department of Natural Resources—helped make this a trail user's mecca in a state already rich in hiking opportunities.

The Issaquah Alps offer residents of the Puget Sound basin wonderful year-round hiking. The trails in this region range from short, scenic strolls along rivers and streams to long hikes into rich forest ecosystems to even a few view-rich mountain summits. Best of all, these wildland trails are mere minutes from downtown Seattle, so even the busiest corporate type can get off work at 5:00 p.m. and, with Superman-like speed, convert into a hiker type and be on a pristine trail by 6:00 p.m. for an evening hike.

Map: Green Trails Cougar Mountain No. 203S; **Contact:** King County Parks and Recreation; **GPS:** N 47 32.090, W 122 07.728

Humans have been trekking through this Cougar Mountain forest for ages. Native Americans wandered the slopes for as long as seven thousand years, and after the new Americans moved west, trappers, prospectors, loggers, and traders pushed goods through the wagon traces along the slopes above Coal Creek basin. Today, hikers and horse riders can enjoy the cool forests and gentle trails year-round, even November through May, when the high-country Cascades are locked in snow.

GETTING THERE

From I-90 take exit 13 onto Lakemont Boulevard Southeast. Drive south on Lakemont Boulevard Southeast. After crossing "The Pass" and starting down, cross Coal Creek and find the trailhead on the east side of the road at a sharp bend in Newcastle Golf Club Road.

ON THE TRAIL

Red Town. Coal Creek Town. Rainbow Town. There's a lot of American history here, going back nearly 150 years. Of course, Native American history goes back much further. Local tribes hunted these woods, gathered foodstuffs in the meadows, and harvested cedar for various uses.

As you hike the Wildside Trail (W1), you'll cross the clear waters of Coal Creek in a deep gorge, striding past an old homesite (the Wash House). Stay right at the junction with the Rainbow Town Trail to continue a scenic woodland walk to a high old mine site, where you'll find a massive concrete piling. Once, a massive cable nearly a half mile long

1 Wildside Trail–De Leo Wall

RATING/ DIFFICULTY	ROUNDTRIP	ELEV GAIN/ HIGH POINT	SEASON
***/2	4 miles	350 feet/ 950 feet	Year-round

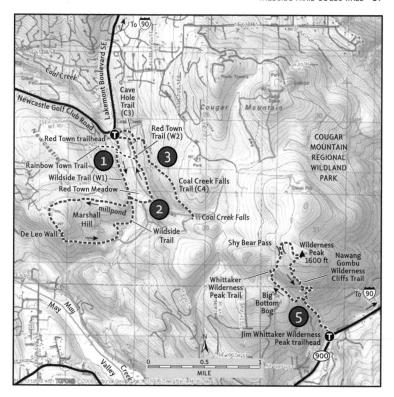

was used to haul ore-laden containers up the steep slope below—this section of trail, dubbed the Steam Hoist Trail, is named for the massive coal-fired engines that powered that ore-hauling cable system.

The trail continues past this bit of Americana to Curious Valley—a U-shaped gorge carved by glaciers at the tail end of the last ice age—before it loops around the upper flank of Marshall Hill. An old millpond still sits, cool and dark, in the woods on Marshall Hill. Its waters once rushed down an old, closed flume system to power lumber mills in Coal Creek valley.

Past the pond, the trail leads across the spine of De Leo Wall. Here you'll find views from the open madrona forest atop the wall. Leave the spine of De Leo Wall by descending gradually toward Newcastle Hills to rejoin the Wildside Trail in the Coal Creek valley near Red Town Meadow.

EXTENDING YOUR TRIP

Several linkages exist to make this, and other area hikes, longer. A secondary trail links Curious Valley on the southwestern end of this route to the trails leading to Red Town Meadow (Hike 2) and Coal Creek Falls (Hike 3).

The view south from De Leo Wall shows a lenticular cloud hovering near Mount Rainier.

2 Red Town Meadow

RATING/ DIFFICULTY	LOOP	ELEV GAIN/ HIGH POINT	SEASON
***/1	1.5 miles	150 feet/ 800 feet	Year-round

Map: Green Trails Cougar Mountain No. 203S; **Contact:** King County Parks and Recreation; **GPS:** N 47 32.090, W 122 07.728

Sometimes we humans do get it right, and this area proves it. The old mining community of Red Town built a ball field in a previously spectacular meadowland, and when King County Parks and Recreation reclaimed Cougar Mountain, a few advocates—most notably the venerable guidebook author and wildlands protector Harvey Manning and his daughter and fellow advocate, Penny Manning—fought to restore the meadow to its natural state. Hundreds of volunteers helped plant native grasses, trees, and shrubs, clearing out invasive species such as Scotch broom and blackberry vines. They toted tons of topsoil and cleared human relics. As the native plants took root and flourished, native birds and beasts moved in and prospered. Today, this area offers a stunning experience of a native foothills forest meadow—complete with mosquitoes, so come fall through spring to avoid these summer pests.

GETTING THERE
From I-90 take exit 13 onto Lakemont Boulevard Southeast. Drive south on Lakemont Boulevard Southeast. After crossing "The Pass" and starting down, cross Coal Creek and find the trailhead on the east side of the road at a sharp bend in Newcastle Golf Club Road.

ON THE TRAIL
Leave the parking lot and follow the Wildside Trail (W1). Stay right at the first three junctions, then go left at about 0.25 mile from the trailhead, and in mere yards go right to stay on the Wildside Trail (this short jog to the left was on the Rainbow Town Trail).

The Wildside Trail reaches a junction with the Red Town Trail (W2) on the left at just

Coal Creek flows along the trail that returns from Red Town Meadow.

0.7 mile. The Red Town Meadow awaits you. Stop and enjoy the fragrant meadows—many of the wildflowers bloom April through May—but please don't tromp through the fragile field. Benches invite those who want to spend some quality time contemplating this native restoration.

Once you've had your fill, continue on the Red Town Trail as it sweeps left around the upper Coal Creek basin before turning north and rolling back down toward the trailhead.

3 Coal Creek Falls

RATING/ DIFFICULTY	ROUNDTRIP	ELEV GAIN/ HIGH POINT	SEASON
***/2	2.5 miles	350 feet/ 1000 feet	Year-round

Map: Green Trails Cougar Mountain No. 203S; **Contact:** King County Parks and Recreation; **GPS:** N 47 32.090, W 122 07.728

Water, water everywhere, and quite a drop it takes! Cougar Mountain's Coal Creek Falls is the primary attraction here, but it's the water underfoot that really makes the area special. Such abundance helps keep the forest green and fragrant, with wildflowers in season—and abundant summer mosquitoes. Come in November through May, when the nights are too cold for these pesky biters and the falls is full of runoff. In the spring you'll find skunk cabbage, and through early summer you'll enjoy plump, juicy salmonberries. And at the end, you'll enjoy the cool cascade of Coal Creek Falls.

GETTING THERE
From I-90 take exit 13 onto Lakemont Boulevard Southeast. Drive south on Lakemont Boulevard Southeast. After crossing "The Pass" and starting down, cross Coal Creek and find the trailhead on the east side of the road at a sharp bend in Newcastle Golf Club Road.

ON THE TRAIL
From the trailhead, head up toward Red Town on the Red Town Trail (W2), where you'll find the Cave Hole Trail (C3) veering off to the left. Take the Cave Hole Trail. Once upon a time, mules pulled wagonloads of coal down this trace, and later, as the

Coal Creek Falls

coal veins played out, folks used it as an access route to another easily accessible fuel source: firewood. Today's trail uses that same old track.

As you climb away from the old Red Town site, you'll notice areas where the ground seems to have slumped in on itself—these are the cave holes that give the trail its name. The holes formed when miners pushed their underground extractions too close to the surface, leaving a void that eventually caved in, creating a "cave hole" in the ground above.

Less than a quarter mile after leaving the trailhead, you'll find the Coal Creek Falls Trail (C4) leading off to the right. The path meanders around the upper slopes of Curious Valley before slanting down into a small gulch carved by the tumbling waters of Coal Creek. Here, about 1.25 miles out, you'll find the falls.

Coal Creek Falls can be spectacular during the rainy season of January through March as it thunders down the rocky chute. Venture out during a particularly cold spell and you'll find marvelous ice sculptures formed by the splashing and spray from the falls. By midsummer, the falls usually shrinks to nothing more than a small splattering of dribbling streams between the rocks.

4 Anti-Aircraft Peak

RATING/ DIFFICULTY	ROUNDTRIP	ELEV GAIN/ HIGH POINT	SEASON
****/2	6 miles	625 feet/ 1525 feet	Year-round

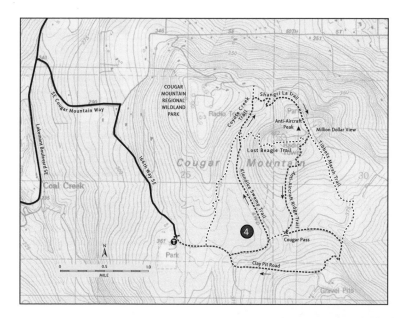

Map: Green Trails Cougar Mountain No. 203S; **Contact:** King County Parks and Recreation; **GPS:** N 47 32.465, W 122 05.762

🚶 🐾 🏠 ↩ *If you want views from Cougar Mountain, this is the trail to take—best from November through May, to avoid the summer clouds of mosquitoes. The route climbs to one of the highest points in the western Issaquah Alps, and along the way you'll find plenty of open viewpoints to take in the scenery of the central Puget Sound basin. The military recognized the value of these high peaks early on and built a missile launch and missile-command radar station atop Anti-Aircraft Peak.*

GETTING THERE

From I-90 take exit 13 onto Lakemont Boulevard Southeast. Drive south on Lakemont Boulevard Southeast. After crossing "The Pass," turn left (east) onto Southeast Cougar Mountain Way. Continue about a half mile before turning right (south) onto 166th Way Southeast. Drive about 0.75 mile to a gate and park, being sure not to block the gate.

ON THE TRAIL

The route starts by rounding the gate and heading up the road toward the Newcastle Brick Works clay pit. At about 0.75 mile, you'll leave the road by veering hard left onto the Klondike Swamp Trail. This swampy basin was once a shallow impoundment behind a long dam across these headwaters of Coal Creek. The lake behind the dam filled with sediment (largely the result of runoff from area logging), creating the current boggy swamp. Birds of all varieties thrive in this accidental ecosystem—even wood ducks!

Views toward Mount Pilchuck and Three Fingers Mountain from near Anti-Aircraft Peak

Almost a mile up the Klondike Trail through this rich environment, stay on the Klondike, passing the Lost Beage Trail on the right. Soon after, take a right at the next junction onto Coyote Creek Trail. This trail climbs slightly for half a mile to a junction with the Shangri La Trail. Turn right and follow this new trail through the wild woods to a reminder of this area's military might—a high fence around Radar Park. Continue along the trail as it skirts the park perimeter and, shortly after crossing the access road leading into the park compound, stop and enjoy the best views of

the day at a small knob locals have dubbed Million Dollar View. The panoramic splendor includes Mount Baker in the North Cascades (on especially clear days) as well as the Seattle skyline and the Olympic Mountains beyond.

After soaking in the scenery at the top, descend along the Shangri La Trail a short 0.1 mile before going right and then right again at the very next junction. This puts you on Anti-Aircraft Ridge Trail. Shortly, you'll encounter yet another fork in the trail. (Warning: There are myriad trails here, and if signposts get knocked down it's easy to take a wrong turn—a great reason to carry a map.) To the right is Lost Beagle Trail, leading straight back to your starting point. Go left instead to descend along Anti-Aircraft Ridge.

You'll soon find yourself at Cougar Pass (elev. 1250 feet)—about 1.25 miles from Million Dollar View. This pass separates the drainages of Coal Creek and West Tibbetts Creek. Go right to cut your hike short (this leads straight down to the Klondike Swamp Trail), or stay left for the longer loop. This path skirts another swamp before merging into Tibbetts Marsh Trail. Stay right and climb a long 0.25 mile to the blue-sky views above the open cuts of the clay pits (elev. 1375 feet). Hop on Clay Pit Road here and follow it west and then north to 166th Way Southeast and your waiting vehicle.

5 Wilderness Peak

RATING/ DIFFICULTY	LOOP	ELEV GAIN/ HIGH POINT	SEASON
***/3	4 miles	1200 feet/ 1600 feet	Year-round

Map: Green Trails Cougar Mountain No. 203S; **Contact:** King County Parks and Recreation; **GPS:** N 47 32.465, W 122 05.233

If your definition of wilderness includes remote wildlands untouched by the hands of man, this is a misnamed peak. But if you can accept that wilderness includes lands returned to a state of wildness, you'll love this simple little Cougar Mountain hike in a natural wonderland that's just minutes from an urban jungle. Though the trail is usually hikable year-round (snowfall is scarce at this elevation), the route is best enjoyed fall through spring because mosquitoes buzz here in great numbers during the summer.

GETTING THERE

From I-90 take exit 15 onto Newcastle Way (State Route 900). Drive south about 2.5 miles to the Wilderness Creek trailhead and a small parking area on the right (west) side of SR 900.

ON THE TRAIL

The Wilderness Creek Trail, now called the Whittaker Wilderness Peak Trail in honor of Jim Whittaker, crosses a sturdy, picturesque bridge over the pretty creek before climbing immediately up a series of switchbacks to lead you up and out of the creek canyon. The creek itself can be seen frequently from the trail as it tumbles down the steep draw, rushing over rocks and dropping over small falls. At around a half mile you'll reach a trail fork.

To the right is the path you'll return on. For now, go left and you'll soon recross the creek and continue up the creek valley. Here, the forest boasts stands of maple, cottonwood, alder, and fir. This mixed forest allows great light penetration to the forest floor, which makes the moisture-rich creek valley an emerald basin of mosses and ferns that seem to cover every surface. From huge

Weathered signpost near the snowy winter summit of Wilderness Peak

A happy dog shares the views from Poo Poo Point.

boulders to old, rotting logs, greenery grows everywhere. This rich world of green can be a wonderful place to escape the heat of summer. But for our purposes it's simply a grand landscape to enjoy while hiking on to greater adventures.

Continue up the trail as it veers up the lower slopes of nearby Ring Road Peak (not-so-creatively named for the old road that circled the peak to its top). At the next trail junction stay right to recross the creek again, and then move onto a long section of boardwalk trail that keeps you above the murk on Big Bottom Bog. The forest here is largely very old second growth and even some native deciduous stands.

After crossing the boggy bottomlands at the upper end of the creek valley, the trail starts up the flank of Wilderness Peak. You'll find yourself among majestic old Douglas-firs in a forest largely untouched by man—only a few old stumps reveal the hand of hard-working independent loggers (*gypos*) who harvested single trees. Look closely and you'll see the notches cut for the sawyers' springboards—long planks stuck into the ax-hewn notches so the loggers could stand and saw through the tree trunk above the wide spread at root level.

After hiking just 1.3 miles, you'll cross Shy Bear Pass at 1320 feet, and in another 0.25 mile find yourself at the junction with the Far Country Lookout Trail—the lookout itself is several miles out and not worth the effort it would take to get there from here. At the junction here, go right to ascend to the summit of forest-crowned Wilderness Peak. You'll find scant views other than of the forest around you. Continue on down the far side of the peak on the newly named Nawang Gombu Wilderness Cliffs Trail on the southern slope before reaching that original trail split at the top of the first set of switchbacks you encountered on your trek out.

6 Poo Poo Point–High School Trail

RATING/ DIFFICULTY	ROUNDTRIP	ELEV GAIN/ HIGH POINT	SEASON
***/3	7.4 miles	1650 feet/ 1850 feet	Mar–Nov

Map: Green Trails Tiger Mountain No. 204S; **Contact:** Department of Natural Resources, South Puget Sound Region; **GPS:** N 47 31.425, W 122 1.571

It's time to go back to high school. Or maybe flight school. This Tiger Mountain path starts at Issaquah High School and ends at Poo Poo Point, where many paraglider pilots learn to fly their featherweight crafts. In between, you'll find wonderful old forests to explore and a grand path to follow.

GETTING THERE

From I-90 take exit 17 (Front Street) and turn right (south). After 0.6 mile turn left (east) onto East Sunset Way, and in two blocks turn right onto 2nd Avenue Southeast. In about a half mile, park near the high school. The trail begins just south of the school on the switchback of the old railroad grade. The trail is on the left (east) side of

the road about 200 yards south of the actual high school. There is adequate parking for about six cars.

ON THE TRAIL

Hike up the old railway-turned-trail about a quarter mile before veering right onto the service road known as Old State Road. Walk around the gate on this road and continue about 1 mile. Just after crossing an old clear-cut, climb under some high-tension powerlines and continue up the rocky slope. Stay right at the next trail junction (to the left is the Section Line Trail) to hop onto the Poo Poo Point Trail. Limited views southwest reveal Squak Mountain.

Like so many Issaquah Alps trails, the Poo Poo Point Trail was born from an old road. The path is still wide enough for two hikers to trek side-by-side much of the time. More often, however, thick wildflowers and bushes (some laden with delicious salmonberries) line the route and crowd it down to a single-track trail.

At about 2 miles, you'll cross a broad plateau (elev. 1150 feet) before starting up into Many Creeks Valley. Some of the creeks giving the valley its name are seasonal, running only in spring, while others—notably Gap Creek—runs year-round. The well-built Gap Creek bridge is at 2.5 miles, from which you can view the creek's stair-step falls and the remains of an old road bridge.

Past the creek, the trail continues to weave upward through the forest. You'll find some wonderful ancient trees, and plenty of reminders of the region's logging history (hint: look for old stumps with springboard notches). At 3.2 miles, stay right at the intersection with the West Tiger Railroad Grade (Hike 8).

In just another 0.5 mile, you'll come out into a small parking area, complete with

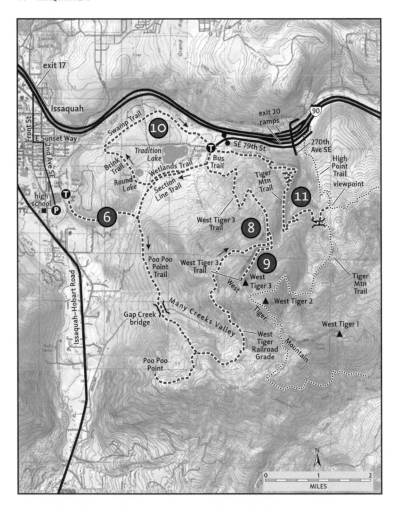

high-tech composting toilet. Follow the trail around to the right side of the parking area to burst out into the bright sunshine on the grass bench that is Poo Poo Point. Hang gliders and paragliders launch off this grassy swale most afternoons spring through early autumn. Nonpilots can rest on the grassy hillside above the launch area, enjoying views of Issaquah Valley, Lake Sammamish, and the Bellevue skyline beyond. On clear days, Mount Baker can even be seen in the distance.

7 Pilots Trail to Poo Poo Point Launch

RATING/ DIFFICULTY	ROUNDTRIP	ELEV GAIN/ HIGH POINT	SEASON
***/3	4 miles	1650 feet/ 1850 feet	Feb–Nov

Map: Green Trails Tiger Mountain No. 204S;
Contact: Department of Natural Resources, South Puget Sound Region; **GPS:** N 47 31.425, W 122 1.571

While hikers usually opt for the longer and less steep trail starting near the Issaquah High School, paraglider pilots and hikers seeking a more strenuous workout climb this trail from the small King County Park off Issaquah-Hobart Road to the two launch points atop Poo Poo Point. The south-facing launch looks out over the Enumclaw Plateau to Mount Rainier, while the north launch offers views to the north and west to the Bellevue area.

GETTING THERE

From I-90 take exit 17 (Front Street) and turn right (south). Continue southeast along Front Street as it leaves town, and about 2.8 miles from the I-90 interchange turn left into a gravel parking lot alongside a long grassy field. The trail starts in the middle of the field, opposite the parking lot. Note: Due to the nature of air currents, most paraglider pilots fly mid- to late afternoon from May through October. During those months the parking is full to overflowing by noon, lasting into the evening every weekend day (except when it is raining). Hit this trail early to avoid the full lot and crowded trail.

ON THE TRAIL

Before leaving the parking lot, check the sky to the north and south to make sure there

The Pilots Trail passes through upper open meadows near the south launch area.

are no aircraft (hang gliders or paragliders) trying to set down in the field. These glides lack motors, so once they commit to landing, they will land. If there are pilots approaching the ground, wait for them to land before crossing the field. The trail enters the forest opposite the parking lot and soon turns south and starts to climb the steep flank of Tiger Mountain.

The Washington Trails Association has rebuilt this previously rough-hewn trail, installing rock steps and curbs to make the climb safer and easier. You'll climb steadily for the next mile, switching back periodically as the path ascends through a thick second-growth forest.

At about 1 mile, the climb moderates and the trail drops onto an old logging road track briefly. The "road" is more a wide trail these days, and in less than a tenth of a mile,

you'll leave it and start climbing once more. From here the trail is more open, with more chance to see the varied growth along this southern flank of the Poo Poo ridge.

At about 1.7 miles, a switchback to the left skirts a patch of sunshine at the base of a long, steep open slope. This is the bottom of the clear-cut slope that serves as the southern launch for hang gliders and paragliders. Step out onto the small side trail at the apex of the switchback and look skyward. If the winds are blowing out of the south, you might see gliders launching above you.

Continuing up the trail, you'll switchback several times, and might occasionally miss the main trail since the next quarter mile features heavily braided trail—trail runners seeking the most direct route down have cut several "shortcuts" through the trees. Your best bet, however, at any intersection is to stay on the

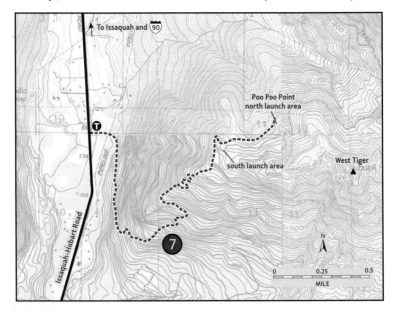

trail that climbs the most gradually.

At about 1.9 miles, the trail bursts into a grassy clearing. This is the top of the south launch. Pause here to enjoy the views to the south. On clear days, Mount Rainier looms large far beyond the expanse of the Enumclaw/Black Diamond Plateau.

The trail crosses the grassy clearing and reenters the forest just north of a small road spur. A short tenth of a mile brings you through a somewhat marshy stand of forest to the north launch. Hang gliders and paragliders launch off this sloping lawn most afternoons spring through early autumn. Nonpilots can rest on the grassy hillside above the launch area, enjoying views of Issaquah Valley, Lake Sammamish, and the Bellevue skyline beyond. The large panels of AstroTurf were installed by the paragliders to help them keep their lines weed-free during the launch cycles. Note that the AstroTurf was recycled and repurposed from the football field of the old Kingdome stadium in Seattle.

8 West Tiger Railroad Grade

RATING/ DIFFICULTY	ROUNDTRIP	ELEV GAIN/ HIGH POINT	SEASON
****/4	10 miles	1600 feet/ 2000 feet	Feb–Nov

Map: Green Trails Tiger Mountain No. 204S; **Contact:** Department of Natural Resources, South Puget Sound Region; **GPS:** N 47 31.779, W 121 59.742

Follow Tiger Mountain's finest old rail line while exploring some of the wildest and most remote stands of forest remaining on the mountain. You'll even find some outstanding views during this long, gentle hike. If you want to keep from swatting mosquitoes with every step, visit fall through spring.

GETTING THERE

From I-90 take exit 20 and then turn right onto Southeast 79th Street, which parallels the interstate. In just under a half mile the road ends at a gate. The gate opens daily, though it is closed and locked at 7:00 p.m. Park outside the gate if you'll be returning late in the day. Otherwise, continue another 0.4 mile to the Tradition Plateau trailhead.

ON THE TRAIL

Tiger Mountain's rich stands of timber and its close proximity to the booming city of Seattle proved too enticing for lumber barons to ignore. Trucking in the early 1900s wasn't efficient—to haul big loads you needed steam, and that meant railroads. As a result,

Skunk cabbage lines the wet areas along the West Tiger Railroad Grade Trail.

short-line railroads were laid all over the mountain. Most wound through long series of switchbacks—the log trains would run forward up the first leg and out onto a long spur at the corner of the switchback turn. A lineman would switch the track so the train could back off the spur and continue backward up the next leg onto another corner spur—and so on until the log trains were at the top of the mountain. They'd then reverse the process to descend. Today, hikers enjoy those same switchbacks, though the rails are long gone and the remaining forest is mixed second and third growth, with a few remnant stands of old growth.

From the trailhead, head south on the Bus Trail as it swings around the east side of Tradition Lake. The trail pierces the second-growth forests of the lower flank of West Tiger. You'll cross under the high-tension powerlines and turn left onto the Section Line Trail, following the lines for more than a half mile.

At 1.5 miles out, turn left onto the Poo Poo Point Trail, climbing steeply up the rocky slopes before climbing through the middle of Many Creeks Valley. At 4 miles out (elev. 1200 feet), cross Gap Creek on a stout bridge. Enjoy the views of the creek as it tumbles over a series of steps.

Beyond Gap Creek, the trail ascends steeply through a rare stand of old-growth Douglas-fir before crossing the West Tiger Railroad Grade at 4.6 miles. Turn left onto this trail to continue the loop (the right fork leads to Poo Poo Point, Hike 6). Stay on West Tiger Railroad Grade as it sweeps around the head of Many Creeks Valley, crossing as many as eight seasonal streams (and a couple of year-round creeks). Stick to the main trail at all intersections and trail forks—there are many side trails leading away on both sides of the West Tiger Railroad Grade.

At about 6 miles, you'll cross the route's high point (2000 feet) on the ridge below West Tiger's summit. From here the trail descends gently for the next mile, before turning left onto the West Tiger 3 Trail to drop steeply for the last 2 miles as it follows a series of switchbacks, crosses Tradition Creek, and runs straight down to the trailhead.

9 West Tiger 3

RATING/ DIFFICULTY	ROUNDTRIP	ELEV GAIN/ HIGH POINT	SEASON
****/4	5 miles	2100 feet/ 2525 feet	Mar–Nov

Map: Green Trails Tiger Mountain No. 204S; **Contact:** Department of Natural Resources, South Puget Sound Region; **GPS:** N 47 31.779, W 121 59.742

Don't expect solitude here— this is perhaps the most heavily used trail on Tiger Mountain, and for good reason. Fortunately, there is plenty of room to share. This close-to-the-city wildland trail provides stunning views, great forestlands, and ample opportunities to see birds and critters. West Tiger—one of the sprawling mountain's four primary peaks (West, Middle, South, and East)—is itself a tri-crowned peak. Numbered 1 through 3, the third of the West Tiger peaks offers the best views, despite being the shortest of the triplets.

GETTING THERE

From I-90 take exit 20 and then turn right onto Southeast 79th Street, which parallels the interstate. In just under a half mile the road ends at a gate. The gate opens daily, though it is closed and locked

A spot just below the summit of West Tiger 3 overlooks a fog-filled Snoqualmie Valley.

at 7:00 p.m. Park outside the gate if you'll be returning late in the day. Otherwise, continue another 0.4 mile to the Tradition Plateau trailhead.

ON THE TRAIL

Start up the Bus Trail, and after just 0.25 mile, veer left onto the West Tiger 3 Trail. Stay to the right just after that trail fork (the second left leads to the seemingly endless Tiger Mountain Trail, or TMT). Sticking to West Tiger 3 Trail can be problematic if trail signs are missing or hard to find, since multiple trails slant away left and right over the next 2 miles. Stick to the primary path as it ascends a long series of steep switchbacks.

At 2 miles out, the trail crosses the West Tiger Railroad Grade (elev. 1960 feet). Continue upward, heading into a tight series of switchbacks. The trail gets steeper, it seems, the closer you get to the top. But finally, you burst out onto the summit of West Tiger 3 (elev. 2525 feet), just 2.5 miles from the trailhead.

The open views you'll find here sweep in Squak Mountain, the sprawling town of Issaquah, the blue waters of Lake Sammamish, the skyscrapers of Bellevue, and even the snowy crown of Mount Baker far to the north. On hot summer days you might see hang gliders and paragliders launching off Poo Poo Point (just to your south), riding the thermal lift that spins out of Many Creeks Valley and off the summit.

10 Tradition Lake Loop

RATING/ DIFFICULTY	LOOP	ELEV GAIN/ HIGH POINT	SEASON
****/2	4 miles	400 feet/ 800 feet	Year-round

Map: Green Trails Tiger Mountain No. 204S;
Contact: Department of Natural Resources, South Puget Sound Region; **GPS:** N 47 31.779, W 121 59.742

When the pressures of the office get to be too much, this Tiger Mountain trail is just close enough to hike after business hours, and just wild enough to make you forget those urban cares for a while. The plethora of trails around the Tradition Lake plateau make for an array of loop options, this one being the longest of the short loops possible. You'll find yourself wandering deep green woods. You'll smell the rich foliage bursting from the damp earth of woodland swamps. You'll hear the song of countless birds. And you'll see a spectrum of native flora and fauna, all within a few moments' walk of the busy interstate corridor.

GETTING THERE

From I-90 take exit 20 and then turn right onto Southeast 79th Street, which parallels the interstate. In just under a half mile the road ends at a gate. The gate opens daily, though it is closed and locked at 7:00 p.m.

Park outside the gate if you'll be returning late in the day. Otherwise, continue another 0.4 mile to the Tradition Plateau trailhead.

ON THE TRAIL

This route makes use of several trails. Start on the Bus Trail as it climbs south before sweeping west along the long slope of West Tiger Mountain. At 0.4 mile, you can take a short spur on the right to see Tradition Lake. The Bus Trail crosses several small creeks (some running year-round, some seasonal freshets) before reaching the Bonneville powerlines at 0.8 mile. Cross under them and slant west onto the Wetlands Trail.

In another 0.1 mile, you'll find a small spur path that drops a short hop down to the small basin of Round Lake. Look for songbirds around this pond any time of year,

Tradition Lake

and in the winter you might see migratory waterfowl resting here.

Continue along the trail as it runs northwest, descending slightly before reaching a junction at 1.8 miles. Go right (to the second trail on the right—the first is Big Tree Trail) to follow Brink Trail as it swings around at about the 400-foot-elevation level for another short mile to yet another junction.

Stay left to continue along the Swamp Trail as it stays near the same elevation for another mile. This path pierces some thick foliage, utilizing raised boardwalks for a good portion of the route. Volunteers from the Issaquah Alps Trail Club chopped this route out of the swamp vegetation below Tradition Lake—so it can be hot and buggy during the midday heat of summer. But come evening, it can be a cool escape from the hot urban jungle.

The trail ends at the powerline access road just west of the trailhead. Hike the last few hundred yards back to the trailhead on this road.

11 Tiger Mountain Trail: North

RATING/ DIFFICULTY	ROUNDTRIP	ELEV GAIN/ HIGH POINT	SEASON
***/3	5 miles	1100 feet/ 1500 feet	Mar–Nov

Map: Green Trails Tiger Mountain No. 204S; **Contact:** Department of Natural Resources, South Puget Sound Region; **GPS:** N 47 31.779, W 121 59.742

The crown jewel of the Tiger Mountain trail network turned thirty years old in 2009: the Tiger Mountain Trail (TMT) officially opened on October 13, 1979. This long trail meanders across the three main Tiger peaks, running some 16 miles from the southeast side of the big mountain all the way across to the northwest corner of the Tiger Mountain State Forest. This hike—the northern end of the TMT—is one of the more scenic stretches you'll find, with grand views and plenty of natural habitat to explore.

GETTING THERE

From I-90 take exit 20 and then turn right onto Southeast 79th Street, which parallels the interstate. In just under a half mile the road ends at a gate. The gate opens daily, though it is closed and locked at 7:00 p.m. Park outside the gate if you'll be returning late in the day. Otherwise, continue another 0.4 mile to the Tradition Plateau trailhead.

A hiker approaches a small footbridge along the northern portion of the Tiger Mountain Trail.

Low Oregon grape surrounding a large tree along the Northwest Timber Trail

ON THE TRAIL

With the maze of trails leading away from the trailhead, make sure you are heading south on the path signed "TMT." The trail leads out from the parking lot on the Bus Trail. In just a few paces, turn left onto the West Tiger 3 Trail, then make a quick left again onto the TMT.

The TMT leads east along Tradition Plateau, running under the broken canopy of a mixed-age forest. In less than 1 mile the route turns south and climbs a steep series of switchbacks, ascending the northern

spine of West Tiger Mountain. This steep climb can be a scorcher in midsummer, since the forest around the trail is mostly young alder and maple. This area was logged repeatedly in the first half of the twentieth century.

At around 1 mile (elev. 1350 feet) the trail sweeps southeast around the nose of the ridge and then climbs more gradually as it traverses into the headwaters of West Fork High Point Creek. During this traverse of the ridge nose you'll encounter increasingly older and mature forest as past logging operations fall behind you. You'll find massive Douglas-firs and hemlocks—even a few cedars. A high, wide bridge spans the deep cut of the creek.

A final 0.75 mile leads around another ridge nose into the main branch of High Point Creek. Just past the creek crossing you'll intersect the High Point Trail at a viewpoint. Turn back here and enjoy a relaxing hike back down the forested path.

12 Northwest Timber Trail

RATING/ DIFFICULTY	ROUNDTRIP	ELEV GAIN/ HIGH POINT	SEASON
***/2	5 miles	200 feet/ 1500 feet	Year-round

Map: Green Trails Tiger Mountain No. 204S; **Contact:** Department of Natural Resources, South Puget Sound Region; **GPS:** N 47 28.015, W 121 55.997

With little elevation change and a modest distance, this is a great Tiger Mountain trail for after work, especially on hot summer days. The cool forest tempers the worst summer heat wave

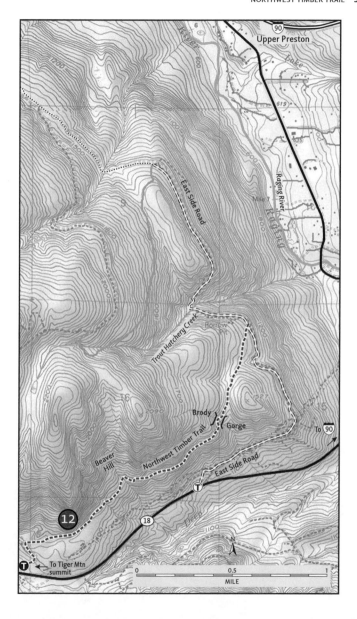

while the lush forests provide all the relaxation you could want. As you trek along this multiuse trail (open to horses and mountain bikes as well as hikers), keep silent and you're likely to hear the raucous calls of ravens, the screams of hawks, the chirps of juncos, and the rat-a-tat-tats of woodpeckers.

GETTING THERE

From I-90 take exit 25 and drive south on State Route 18 to the Tiger Mountain summit. At the summit, turn right (west) into the large parking lot.

ON THE TRAIL

Head for the gated road farthest to the right as you start walking out of the parking area. You'll walk a scant quarter mile on this road before turning right onto the well-signed path. The forest, lush second growth that resulted after the harvest of the original forest by northwest timber companies in the early 1900s, is a mix of old maples and alders—many draped beautifully with long beards of moss and lichen—as well as hemlocks and firs.

The trail contours northeast along the base of Beaver Hill for 2 miles, crossing a few creek basins along the way. One of these features a high bridge over the deep creek gorge. Below the bridge, waters cascade over a rocky ledge, creating a pretty waterfall to entertain hikers. The trail continues on, slowly descending toward Trout Hatchery Creek. The trail ends at a junction with East Side Road.

EXTENDING YOUR TRIP

For more mileage, hike north on the East Side Road and hook up with the Preston Railroad Grade in 2.6 miles.

13 Middle Tiger Loop

RATING/ DIFFICULTY	ROUNDTRIP	ELEV GAIN/ HIGH POINT	SEASON
****/4	8.6 miles	2200 feet/ 2607 feet	Feb–Nov

Map: Green Trails Tiger Mountain No. 204S; **Contact:** Department of Natural Resources, South Puget Sound Region; **GPS:** N 47 27.152, W 121 57.222

Two hikers passing a large blowdown along the Tiger Mountain Trail below Middle Tiger

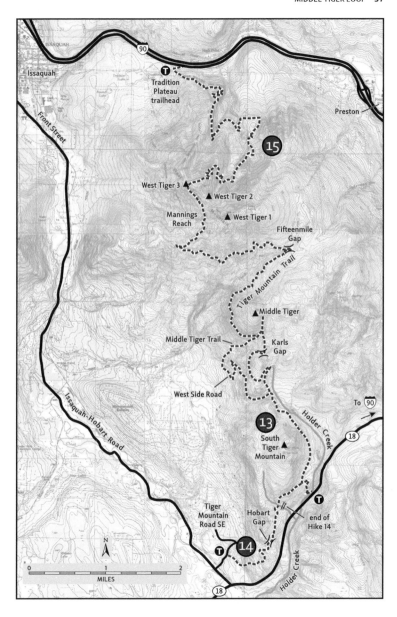

Issaquah

90

Tradition Plateau trailhead

Preston

Front Street

15

West Tiger 3

▲ West Tiger 2

Mannings Reach

▲ West Tiger 1

Fifteenmile Gap

Tiger Mountain Trail

▲ Middle Tiger

Middle Tiger Trail

Karls Gap

West Side Road

Issaquah-Hobart Road

To 90

Holder Creek

13

18

South Tiger Mountain ▲

Tiger Mountain Road SE

Hobart Gap

end of Hike 14

14

Holder Creek

N

0   1   2
MILES

18

When you want to simply stretch your legs and enjoy the woods, this is the trail to explore. The summit of Middle Tiger is wooded, so you won't find grand views. In fact, the entire route is wooded. But that's okay. This area is rich with wildlife, from the winged variety (woodpeckers, flickers, red-tailed hawks, and Steller's jays) to the four-legged kind (deer, bobcats, black bears, cougars, martens, coyotes, raccoons, and beavers). There are also the usual suspects when it comes to forest flora—with a variety of trees, bushes, wildflowers, ferns, and mosses—and the usual suspects in summer when it comes to mosquitoes, so visit in fall through spring for swat-free hiking.

GETTING THERE

From I-90 take exit 25 and drive south on State Route 18 to the Tiger Mountain summit. Continue over the summit about 2 miles to a parking area on your right. There is parking for only a few vehicles. The trail starts here mid-parking lot.

ON THE TRAIL

Head up the trail as it climbs through old second-growth forest on a road to reach the Tiger Mountain Trail in 0.3 mile at the powerline clearing. Go right, under the powerlines, and at about 0.5 mile, you'll pass through a brushy clearing with high-tension powerlines overhead and then slide back under the forest canopy. The forest is frequently alive with bird calls, with a variety of avian species, including woodpeckers and thrushes, residing here. Listen for their drumming even if you can't see them.

At 1.8 miles, the trail forks; stay right and soon reach West Side Road #1000.

Straight ahead will be your return route. Go left and hike West Side Road for 1.4 miles, losing 300 feet in elevation as the road winds past streams and wildflowers. At 3.2 miles, go right on the Middle Tiger and Hobart Railroad Grade trails, next to a lovely creek.

About 100 feet up the trail, veer right onto Middle Tiger Trail. Climb a steep mile, and about 4.2 miles from the trailhead, you'll encounter another trail junction. The right-hand path is the one you'll descend to close the summit loop. For now, stay left and keep climbing. A half mile farther on—climbing nearly 500 feet—you'll reach the Middle Tiger summit at 2607 feet.

After relaxing atop Middle Tiger, drop back to that trail junction a half mile below the summit and go left. You'll soon encounter a relatively small but fresh clear-cut, then more second growth before entering an older clear-cut at Karls Gap 5.5 miles into the hike, with views of the surrounding valleys and peaks. Another 1.3 miles of forest with frequent open views gets you to the end of the loop section of this route. Proceed straight across West Side Road to close out the route with the final 1.8 miles back to the trailhead.

14 Tiger Mountain Trail: South

RATING/ DIFFICULTY	ROUNDTRIP	ELEV GAIN/ HIGH POINT	SEASON
***/2	4 miles	600 feet/ 1100 feet	Year-round

Map: Green Trails Tiger Mountain No. 204S;
Contact: Department of Natural Resources, South Puget Sound Region; **GPS:** N 47 26.553, W 121 58.656

A happy border collie pauses along the Tiger Mountain Trail's southern section near Hobart Gap.

The Tiger Mountain Trail (TMT) is to Tiger Mountain what the Pacific Crest Trail is to the Cascades—a long, winding trail that crosses many summits and offers a long through hike or short section hikes. This is the shortest, but possibly most scenic, of the main TMT sections. It's an outstanding introduction to Tiger Mountain and its wonderful wildland trails.

GETTING THERE

From Issaquah head south on Front Street (which becomes Issaquah–Hobart Road after it leaves town). About 6 miles past the city limits, turn left onto Tiger Mountain Road Southeast. Continue for about 0.1 mile before parking on the left shoulder at a wide pullout. The trail is on the right.

ON THE TRAIL

As you set off up the wide trail, look for the old historical marker that reads "Route of Woods–Iverson Railroad Grade." The trail climbs gently but steadily for the next 1.5 miles through very old mixed-species forest. There are hemlocks, alders, and firs, as well as maples and even a few madronas.

At 1.5 miles, the climb turns into a traverse as the trail slants along the slope, heading for Hobart Gap (elev. 1100 feet). About 0.4 mile past the gap, you'll find a picture-perfect little waterfall on the trailside creek at 2 miles out. Stop here for photos and a snack before turning back.

15 Tiger Mountain Trail

RATING/ DIFFICULTY	ROUNDTRIP	ELEV GAIN/ HIGH POINT	SEASON
*****/5	16 miles	2200 feet/ 2607 feet	Mar–Nov

Map: Green Trails Tiger Mountain No. 204S;
Contact: Department of Natural Resources, South Puget Sound Region; **GPS:** N 47 26.553, W 121 58.656

Hiking the crown jewel of Tiger Mountain State Forest is a rite of passage for serious Issaquah Alps explorers. The trip isn't to be taken lightly, however. It requires a long day and good conditioning. It also requires some planning, as you'll need to arrange for a car at the trail's end. The 16-mile route weaves around or over most of the primary peaks on Tiger, and since it crosses scores of other trails and not all of the intersections are well marked, good routefinding skills are essential.

GETTING THERE

From Issaquah head south on Front Street (which becomes Issaquah–Hobart Road after it leaves town). About 6 miles past the city limits, turn left onto Tiger Mountain Road Southeast. Continue for about 0.1 mile before parking on the left shoulder at a wide pullout. The trail is on the right.

ON THE TRAIL

The Tiger Mountain Trail (TMT) was first conceived of in 1972, with construction getting underway in 1977. The first official hike on the new trail was opened in 1979. The route can be hiked north to south, but most Tiger Mountain aficionados agree it is best traveled south to north, as described here.

The trail begins climbing steadily right from the start, heading north onto the wooded slopes of South Tiger Mountain. At 1.6 miles, after passing under a band of cliffs, the trail pops out on an old railroad grade-turned-road at Hobart Gap, the first trail junction you'll encounter. Stay right on the railroad grade—occasionally, you'll see railroad ties still embedded in the trail tread.

At 2.6 miles, the TMT rolls under the high-tension powerlines. The long clearing under the powerlines reveals views of the East Tiger summit. Head straight across this clearing, keeping a sharp eye out for trail signs, to find the trail heading off into the woods on the far side.

Old signs on trees still dot the Tiger Mountain Trail.

The path continues to make use of the old railroad grade to a junction with Road 1400 at 3.1 miles. Follow this road about a half mile to Holder Creek and West Side Road. The TMT continues straight across West Side Road from this junction. Continue on the TMT as it rolls north on the old Holder Creek Railroad Grade. At 5 miles out, you'll cross Karls Gap. An optional 0.5-mile side trail leads to the (treed) summit of Middle Tiger (elev. 2607 feet). Continue on the main trail and you'll enjoy broken views of Mount Rainier and the country between you and that big peak.

Around the halfway point, the trail runs through the woods alongside Fifteenmile Creek. An interesting bit of human history can be found here—a massive steel cable lies across the trail. This two-inch braided bit of steel was suspended overhead and used to drag huge logs out of the forest to a landing where they could be loaded on railcars.

The TMT crosses Fifteenmile Gap at 9.3 miles, and 1 mile later the trail bursts out onto the sun-drenched viewpoint of Ricks Rock (elev. 2250 feet). Outstanding views are found here and continue on as you hike north to West Tiger 2. At 10.5 miles, you'll stride through Mannings Reach—named for guidebook author and legendary wildland protector Harvey Manning—which marks the high point of the TMT (elev. 2607 feet).

From Mannings Reach, you'll descend past junctions with the West Tiger Railroad Grade, the West Tiger 3 Trail, and the West Tiger 2 Trail. Grand views can be found at West Tiger 2.

The rest of the TMT is a rolling descent to the Tradition Plateau trailhead.

A boardwalk bridge built by volunteer WTA crews passing through wetlands in the far northern portions of the Grand Ridge Trail

16 Grand Ridge Trail

RATING/ DIFFICULTY	ROUNDTRIP	ELEV GAIN/ HIGH POINT	SEASON
***/3	9 miles	600 feet/ 1050 feet	Year-round

Map: King County Parks and Recreation, Grand Ridge Map; **Contact:** King County Parks and Recreation; **GPS:** N 47 31.916, W 121 58.845

 *Though perhaps best known for its sprawling housing developments, Grand Ridge also claims one of the finest pieces of wildlands in the Issaquah area. That was by design—planners required this park to be set aside as part of the mitigation for development, and the Washington Trails Association worked with King County Parks and Recreation to develop a wonderful recreational trail that explores the 1200 acres of rich second-growth forest on the 1100-foot ridge in the Cascade foothills. Plan to share the trail with mountain bikers on nice weekends.*

GETTING THERE

From Seattle, drive east on I-90 to exit 20. Turn left after exiting, passing under I-90, to find a broad gravel parking lot on the west side of the road.

ON THE TRAIL

Leave the parking area by heading west on the Issaquah–Preston Rail Trail. You'll follow this broad level track for about 0.7 mile before turning onto a well-marked trail heading uphill through lush forest. The broken canopy of the old second-growth forest allows a great deal of light to fall on the forest floor, encouraging a plethora of wildflowers to thrive here. Of course, that also brings a host of birds and animals, making this a great route on which to practice your bird-watching and wildflower identification skills.

The trail climbs for a good half mile before veering to the west on a long traverse around the ridge, with just enough small ups and downs along the way to keep your heart rate up for a quality workout. At the unmarked trail junction, stay right (left drops down to the Issaquah–Preston Rail Trail). At about 2.5 miles, the trail crosses a small road (30th Avenue Northeast) leading to a cluster of homes

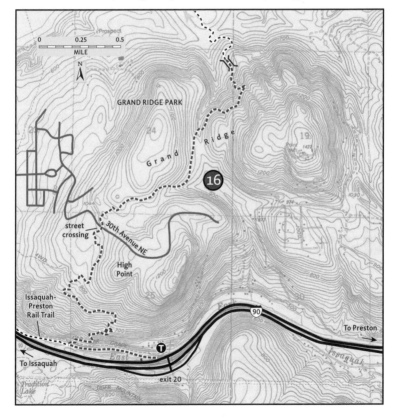

along High Point. Cross this road and get back into the forest so you don't lose your wild senses. At 3.5 miles, the trail forks. Stay to the right to descend into a lush green ravine filled with massive old western cedars. (Note: The left fork leads into a housing development, providing trail access for those residents.) This ravine is thick with birdsong most of the year, and frequented by local black-tailed deer and occasionally black bears.

The trail crosses a well-built footbridge over a gurgling creek at around 4.5 miles. This makes a great turnaround point. For a longer hike, you may continue north 2.2 miles from this bridge to Issaquah–Fall City Road.

17 Soaring Eagle Park

RATING/ DIFFICULTY	LOOP	ELEV GAIN/ HIGH POINT	SEASON
***/2	7.5 miles	150 feet/ 575 feet	Year-round

Map: King County Parks and Recreation, Soaring Eagle Park Map; **Contact:** King County Parks and Recreation; **GPS:** N 47 36.705, W 121 59.471

Soaring Eagle Regional Park, named by a contest-winning second grader from nearby Samantha Smith Elementary School, doesn't have a lot of soaring eagles overhead, but you will find a host of other birds—local Audubon members have counted more than forty species of avians in the park. The wildland park boasts more than 12 miles of trails looping through its 600 acres of somewhat dense second-growth forest. Visitors should make sure they grab a park trail map from the trailhead kiosk, or better yet (to ensure

they get one) from the King County Parks and Recreation website (see Appendix A).

GETTING THERE
From Seattle, drive east on I-90 to exit 15. Turn left (north) onto 17th Avenue Northwest, crossing over I-90. The road veers right, becoming Northwest Sammamish Road. Continue about 0.7 mile to a junction with East Lake Sammamish Parkway. Turn left (north) onto East Lake Sammamish Pkwy and drive 1.2 miles before turning right onto Southeast 43rd Way. Continue about 3.5 miles as this road loops around to the east before heading north (when it turns due north it becomes 228th Avenue Southeast). At about 5.6 miles from the I-90 off-ramp, turn right onto Southeast 8th Street. Follow Southeast 8th Street as it curves and becomes 244th Avenue Southeast. Turn right onto East Main Drive and follow it to the end. There is a parking area near the water tower.

ON THE TRAIL
We recommend that hikers stick mostly to the outermost trail loops, following close to the park edges, as the mountain bike riders seem to prefer the interior trails, and while bikes can be fun to ride on the trails, they aren't so much fun to run into unexpectedly. Head east from the trailhead on the Pipeline Trail and, at about 0.3 mile, turn left onto the Sleigh Ride Trail. A half mile from the trailhead, another junction is reached. You'll want to go left here on a short out-and-back leg. This quarter-mile side trail drops down to the northwestern park boundary and provides a stunning view of marshy wetland and grassy meadow. Birdlife abounds across this expansive clearing, where you may see

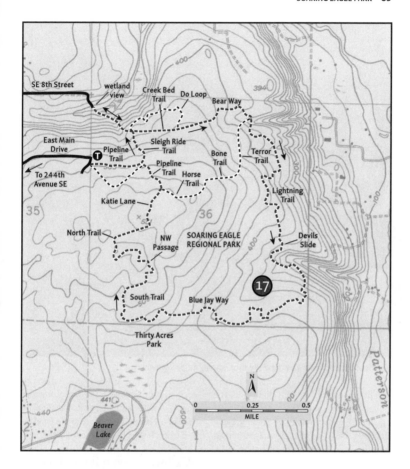

scores of redwing blackbirds, herons, and hawks. This is also your best opportunity to see the park's namesake bald eagles.

Head back up the quarter-mile side-track to the main trail and continue east on the Creek Bed Trail, which crosses Patterson Creek and continues east—staying straight at the next junction onto Bear Way. At about 1.6 miles into your hike (including

the half-mile out-and-back side trip to the wetland view), take the southeast fork at a trail junction to climb along the Lightning Trail. In a half mile, this heavily forested section reaches a junction with the Devils Slide Trail. Stay left to wind down into another creek basin and then, after a short climb back to a shallow ridgetop at about 3 miles out, stay left onto Blue Jay Way.

Northern park boundary wetland areas of Soaring Eagle Regional Park

You'll descend again, this time into the boggy bottomland of Thirty Acres Park—a small park encompassed by Soaring Eagle Regional Park. Continue straight ahead (westbound) at every trail junction until, at about 4.1 miles, you'll turn north onto South Trail and begin your rambling hike back toward the trailhead. At each junction pick the trail that best leads north (i.e., left onto Northwest Passage at 4.5 miles, right onto North Trail at 4.8 miles, and left onto Katie Lane at 5.1 miles).

As you skirt the cedar-rich bog on your left, though, and join Katie Lane, you'll want to stay on Katie rather than continue your northern rush. Katie Lane veers east at about 5.3 miles and intercepts the Pipeline Trail at 6.2 miles. Turn left onto the Pipeline and follow it west back to the trailhead.

18 Taylor Mountain–Holder Knob Loop

RATING/ DIFFICULTY	LOOP	ELEV GAIN/ HIGH POINT	SEASON
**/2	6 miles	600 feet/ 1100 feet	Year-round

Map: Green Trails Tiger Mountain No. 204S;
Contact: King County Parks and Recreation;

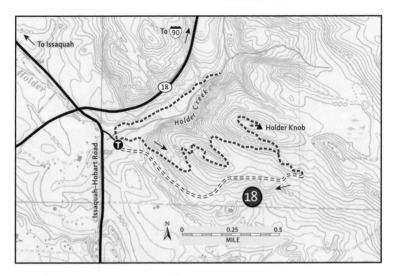

GPS: N 47 25.935, W 121 58.269

![icons] *Taylor Mountain represents an experiment in forest management. Over the decades, loggers took what they could from the 1700-acre forest, leaving behind a mess of scrub brush and second- (and third-) growth trees. But that young forest has filled in nicely, and nature is once more proving that, given the chance, it can recover on its own.*

GETTING THERE

From I-90 take exit 17 (Front Street), and turn right (south) onto Front Street and continue south through Issaquah. Front Street becomes Issaquah–Hobart Road as you leave town. Continue south along this road to its junction with State Route 18. Cross under SR 18 and drive another 0.25 mile, passing Holder Creek. At Southeast 188th Street, turn left into a new parking area to find the trail to Holder Creek on the left.

ON THE TRAIL

Start by venturing north along the trail leading out from the trailhead parking area to the left. In just 0.1 mile you'll see a side trail to your right. Ignore this for now and continue north to reach Holder Creek at about 0.2 mile. The route veers to the right here and follows Holder Creek upstream along an old logging road placed in the valley, below SR 18 (you can occasionally hear traffic through the forest above you).

The trail gains just 200 feet elevation as it climbs gradually along this small creek. At about 1.1 miles out, the way gets a bit brushy, and you will be forced to ford Holder Creek. We recommend turning around here. Make your way back down to the first trail junction (2.1 miles), and this time turn east (left) to climb the ridgeline above the trailhead.

The trail stays relatively flat for about a quarter mile, then climbs, steeply at times,

Open views from near the high point of Holder Knob on Taylor Mountain

to a ridge crest (nearly 2.9 miles into your trek) at 950 feet elevation. From here you'll descend nearly 200 feet over the next quarter mile before traversing around the southern slope of Holder Knob. At about 3.7 miles, the trail splits. Go left to climb a half mile, gaining 220 feet, to the summit of the knob. You'll return on the summit trail back to the junction below. Go a short distance farther down the trail to intersect a road. Follow the road to the right and continue another 1.3 miles back to the trailhead to close the loop on the road.

Opposite: The new trail leading to Kamakazi Falls (aka Teneriffe Falls) offers views southeast toward Mailbox Peak, Mount Washington, and beyond.

north bend

North Bend sits near the confluence of the three forks of the Snoqualmie River, and hikers have long enjoyed the wildland experiences found on the array of trails that weave through these river drainages. Many of the trails around North Bend draw more hikers on any given summer weekend than you would see in a year on similar trails a bit farther away. A good part of the reason for this is proximity to population centers. The North Bend area can be reached quickly and easily by hikers coming from the west (via I-90), from the south (via State Route 18), and from the north (via State Routes 202 and 203). The real key, though, to the area's popularity is the quality of the trails: from low river-valley hikes such as the Middle Fork Snoqualmie Trail to high climbs on rugged trails that make worthy destinations for peak baggers (Mount Si, for instance), the North Bend area offers some of the best hiking in the central Cascades, and much of it can be enjoyed year-round.

19 Bare Mountain

RATING/ DIFFICULTY	ROUNDTRIP	ELEV GAIN/ HIGH POINT	SEASON
***/5	8 miles	3250 feet/ 5353 feet	June–Oct

Maps: Green Trails Mount Si No. 174 and Skykomish No. 175; **Contact:** Mount Baker–Snoqualmie National Forest, Snoqualmie Ranger District, North Bend office; **Notes:** NW Forest Pass required; **GPS:** N 47 38.373, W 121 31.699

Hikers climbing up the last steep trail toward the summit of Bare Mountain

Any time you can hike to the site of an old fire-watch station, you know you'll have grand views—after all, those fire spotters needed a 360-degree panorama to be effective. Bare Mountain stands as one of those old fire tower sites and, nestled in the westernmost part of the Cascades, this trail offers a unique opportunity to enjoy a wild-country hike with views of the Puget Sound lowlands.

GETTING THERE
From Seattle drive east on I-90 to exit 31 (North Bend). Drive through North Bend on Main Street, then turn north onto Ballaratt Street and follow it out of town. This road becomes North Fork Road Southeast. About 4 miles after leaving the North Bend city limits, the road forks. Stay left and continue

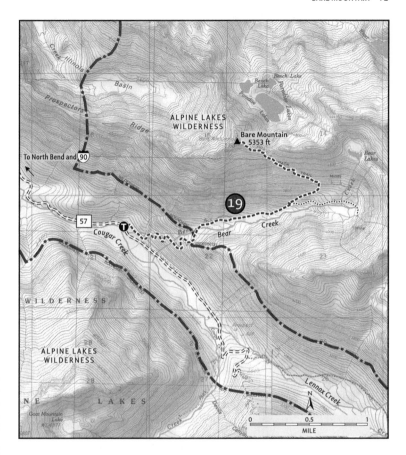

another 17 miles to the Forest Service boundary, where the road becomes Forest Road 57. Just after crossing Cougar Creek, stay right at the next junction to continue on FR 57. At mile 23 find the trailhead on the left.

ON THE TRAIL

The trail uses an old miners road for the first 2 miles as it climbs along the flank of Bare

Mountain and into the Bear Creek valley. You'll cross the creek about a half mile out, then cross it again just under a mile into your hike. At about 1 mile, you'll enter the Alpine Lakes Wilderness amid a moist meadow as the trail straightens out to parallel Bear Creek for the next mile.

At mile 2 you'll find a trail junction, where the trail leaves the old miners road. Turn

The beach areas along the Snoqualmie River in Tolt MacDonald Park

left and hike up the southern flank of Bare Mountain, winding upward through a long series of sweeping switchbacks.

After 2 miles of climbing, you'll find yourself atop the 5353-foot summit of Bare Mountain, with its grand views in all directions. To the south, Mount Rainier towers above the lesser Cascade peaks. To the west is the sprawling green world of the Snoqualmie Valley and the Puget Sound basin. North is mighty Mount Baker, and eastward lies the bulk of the Alpine Lakes Wilderness.

20 Tolt MacDonald Park

RATING/ DIFFICULTY	LOOP	ELEV GAIN/ HIGH POINT	SEASON
***/1	2.5 miles	100 feet/ 150 feet	Year-round

Map: King County Parks and Recreation, Tolt MacDonald Park Map, http://your.kingcounty.gov/ftp/gis/Web/VMC/recreation/BCT_Tolt Ames_brochure.pdf; **Contact:** King County Parks and Recreation; **GPS:** N 47 38.643, W 121 55.464

You'll find more than 12 miles of trails looping through the 574 acres of riverfront and highland parkland here, with access to another 27 miles on the Snoqualmie Valley Trail that pierces this park. Our recommended route sticks to the long stretch of fields and open forests lining the Snoqualmie River, leaving the remaining highland routes for you to explore on your own.

GETTING THERE

From Seattle, drive east on I-90 to exit 22 (Preston/Fall City). Turn left (north) and continue north to Fall City. At the first stop sign in the town of Fall City, turn right onto State Route 203 and continue to Carnation. Once in Carnation, stay on SR 203 to cross the Tolt River, then, just past the middle school, turn

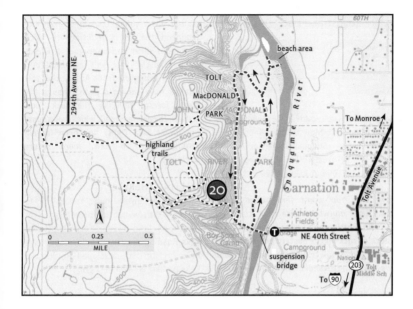

left onto Northeast 40th Street (signed as the access to Tolt MacDonald Park). Continue a half mile to the parking area.

ON THE TRAIL

From the parking area, cross the broad salmon-rich waters of the Snoqualmie River by way of the 500-foot-long suspension bridge just west of the parking lot. Once across the river, you'll find the broad rail trail underfoot. Turn right off of it and head north (downstream) along the riverbank. The trail meanders gently north, following along the meadows and small stands of forest that color this riverside trail. The wildflowers sparkle with color during spring bloom season. In the fall, the deciduous trees along the route—especially the maples—provide ample color of their own.

About a mile from the trailhead, the trail splits. Stay on the right fork (more straight ahead than a right-hand turn), and in a quarter mile you'll find yourself on a nice sand-and-stone beach along the river. Head back to the trail above and take the other branch (now on your right) to loop around and head back southward toward your starting point, passing along the foot of the bluff this time, with more opportunities to see and hear the resident bird populations and enjoy a bit more shade on a hot day.

At 2.4 miles (including the half-mile jaunt down to the beach and back) you'll be back on the old rail trail. If you seek more adventure, turn right and let that track take you up onto the highland trails, where you can wander for another 7 or 8 miles on looping trails at your leisure. Otherwise, turn left and recross the river on the bouncy bridge to end your outing.

21 Rattlesnake Ledge

RATING/ DIFFICULTY	ROUNDTRIP	ELEV GAIN/ HIGH POINT	SEASON
*****/3	4 miles	1160 feet/ 2078 feet	Mar–Nov

Map: Green Trails Rattlesnake Mountain No. 205S; **Contact:** Mount Baker–Snoqualmie National Forest, Snoqualmie Ranger District, North Bend; **Notes:** NW Forest Pass required; **GPS:** N 47 26.007, W 121 46.052

You won't find better views anywhere else this close to Seattle. Rattlesnake Ledge is a monolithic block of rock on the eastern end of Rattlesnake Ridge, towering high over the cool waters of Rattlesnake Lake and the Sno-qualmie River valley. Looking up from the trailhead, the site is daunting—the rock face looks sheer and impregnable. Fortunately, the cliff face isn't too broad, and hearty Washington Trails Association volunteers have carved a path through the steep forests flanking the rock face. Indeed, the original trail, which was daunting in its own right, has been largely replaced with a new, more secure pathway.

GETTING THERE
From Seattle drive 32 miles east on I-90 to exit 32 (436th Avenue Southeast). Turn right (south) on 436th Avenue Southeast (Cedar Falls Road Southeast) and drive about 2.4 miles to the well-developed Rattlesnake Lake parking area on the right.

Views of Mount Si rising above a fog-shrouded upper Snoqualmie Valley from the open areas of Rattlesnake Ledge

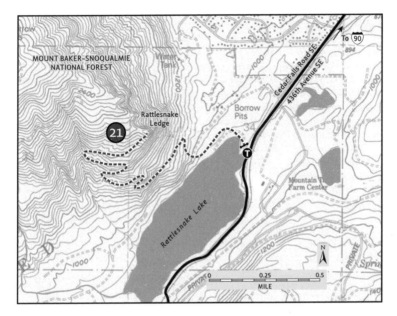

ON THE TRAIL

From the parking lot, round the gate and walk the old road 0.25 mile to a grassy swath on the west side of Rattlesnake Lake. A well-signed path leads off to the right. The rebuilt trail climbs steeply from the get-go, gaining more than 1000 feet in just over 1.5 miles. Of course, the old trail made that gain in just 1 mile, so please keep the complaints to a minimum as you slog up the switchbacks. Those new hairpin turns add a little distance to the hike, but they also level the trail a tad, making it a bit easier on the thighs.

After a seemingly endless upward march, you'll suddenly burst out of the forest onto the snout of the rock ledge. The views are unbelievable. Peer southeast into the rarely seen Cedar River watershed, with Chester Morse Lake dominating the close-in scenery. This big lake supplies Seattle with a significant portion of its drinking water. The rest of the watershed is filled with untrammeled forest—it is closed to most human access to ensure that the water remains uncontaminated. Look farther east and you'll see the peaks leading to Snoqualmie Pass and, of course, massive Mount Si just across the valley.

22 Rattlesnake Mountain

RATING/ DIFFICULTY	ROUNDTRIP	ELEV GAIN/ HIGH POINT	SEASON
****/3	4.5 miles	1600 feet/ 2530 feet	Mar–Nov

Map: Green Trails Rattlesnake Mountain No. 205S; **Contact:** Mount Baker–Snoqualmie National Forest, Snoqualmie Ranger District, North Bend; **Notes:** NW Forest Pass required; **GPS:** N 47 30.653, W 121 50.834

Though not a true wilderness trail, the Rattlesnake Mountain route comes as close to being one as you'll find this close to the urban center of Puget Sound. The relatively new (in trail years) trail climbs the western end of Rattlesnake Mountain, leading to some wonderful viewpoints and, for those who are looking for a real workout, all the way east to Rattlesnake Ledge. Great views, great workout, and great wildlife-viewing potential—all within minutes of downtown North Bend, and available March through November.

GETTING THERE

From Seattle drive east on I-90 to exit 27 and, after exiting, turn right. Continue about 0.5 mile to a large parking area and day-use picnic area. Park here.

ON THE TRAIL

The trail starts from the upper end of the parking area, leading into the forest. Around the half-mile mark you'll find your first views. Gaze north to the sprawling green Snoqualmie Valley at your feet and the jagged "foothill" peaks surrounding it.

Another quarter mile up the somewhat steep path brings you to a junction. The right fork drops a mere 100 yards to a pretty (in spring and early summer when it's running) creek in a rocky basin. Stay on the main trail to continue upward, passing through mixed forest of hemlocks, firs, and a few cedars. The forest floor is carpeted with a solid

Mount Si towers behind Snoqualmie and North Bend areas as seen from an overlook along the Rattlesnake Mountain Trail.

ground cover of salal, Oregon grape, and (in spring) western trilliums.

At 1 mile, the trail angles up to the right to start a steep traverse across an old logged-over area. Huge trees were left randomly throughout the clear-cuts to provide wildlife habitat. A few birds do rest in them, while the broad swathes of clearings are covered each spring and early summer with wildflower blooms. Views of Mount Si across the valley can be found at 1.2 miles, and just a quarter mile past that viewpoint the trail rolls under massive high-tension powerlines.

At 2.2 miles better views are found. A small way trail on the left drops you in just a few hundred feet onto a bench with stunning views of the North Bend area of the Snoqualmie Valley as well as of Mount Si, Mailbox

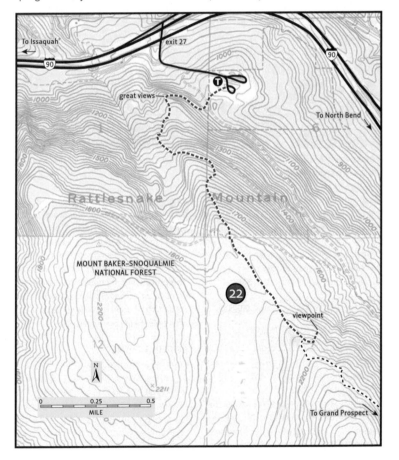

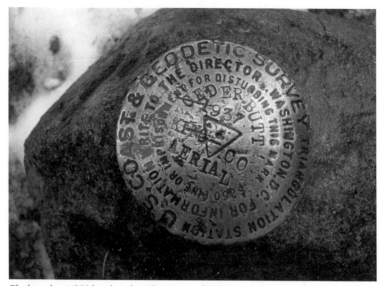

The legendary USGS benchmark on the summit of Cedar Butte . . . no, this isn't Ceder Butt, but it's worth a second look!

Peak, and all of the associated peaks of this area of the Cascades. There is even a picnic table here for a comfortable lunch.

Turn back here, or, if the views have you invigorated, turn left once back on the trail and continue another 2.5 miles to Grand Prospect—an even higher, grander viewpoint.

23 Cedar Butte

RATING/ DIFFICULTY	ROUNDTRIP	ELEV GAIN/ HIGH POINT	SEASON
***/3	5 miles	900 feet/ 1880 feet	Year-round

Map: Green Trails Rattlesnake Mountain No. 205S; **Contact:** Washington State Parks; **Notes:** Washington Discover Pass required; **GPS:** N 47 26.007, W 121 46.052

Cedar Butte may be the least-visited mountain in the Snoqualmie Pass corridor. The smallish butte stands between the popular Rattlesnake Lake and the remote Chester Morse Lake in the Cedar River watershed area. This butte's lack of popularity, though, has more to do with its lack of publicity than its dearth of scenery. Indeed, Cedar Butte offers plenty of scenic spectacle.

GETTING THERE

From Seattle drive east on I-90 to exit 32 (436th Avenue Southeast). Turn right (south) on 436th Avenue Southeast (Cedar Falls Road Southeast) and drive about 2.8 miles, passing the Rattlesnake Lake parking area, until you find the Iron Horse trailhead parking area on the left.

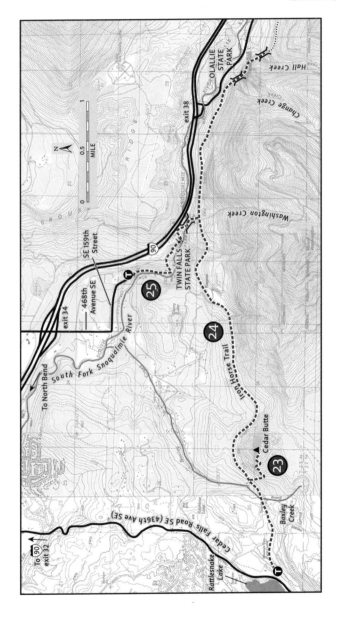

ON THE TRAIL

From the trailhead, start east along the wide ribbon of the Iron Horse Trail. When you reach Boxley Creek, you have another quarter mile or so before finding the start of the well-established path (about 1 mile from the parking area) up Cedar Butte. Turn right (south) onto the newly rebuilt Cedar Butte Trail.

The reconstructed trail offers better footing and routefinding, but signage can be a problem—the signs are installed and maintained by unauthorized volunteers rather than official agency staff. Still, even if the signs are down, the trail gets enough use and maintenance that it is easy to find if you look for it.

After leaving the Iron Horse, you'll cross an old logged-over area, then climb steeply up the face of Cedar Butte. At a half mile up the slope, you'll find a fork in the trail. The left branch leads steeply up to the summit (this is the old, original route). Stay right for a more gradual ascent of about a mile to the top. Once at the summit, enjoy broken views to the north—Mount Si, Mount Teneriffe, and Mailbox Peak stand tall on the horizon.

The trestle over Change Creek along the Iron Horse Trail

24 Iron Horse Trail– Change Creek

RATING/ DIFFICULTY	ROUNDTRIP	ELEV GAIN/ HIGH POINT	SEASON
***/2	12 miles	550 feet/ 1350 feet	Year-round

Maps: Green Trails Rattlesnake Mountain No. 205S and Mount Si NRCA No. 206S; **Contact:** Washington State Parks; **Notes:** Washington Discover Pass required; **GPS:** N 47 26.007, W 121 46.052

The Iron Horse Trail (officially known as the John Wayne Pioneer Trail) runs down the middle of the linear Iron Horse State Park. The trail utilizes the old rail line known as Milwaukee Road, which carried locomotives of the Chicago–Milwaukee–St. Paul & Pacific Railroad. The trail runs from Rattlesnake Lake to Idaho and is the only east-west cross-state trail.

GETTING THERE

From Seattle drive east on I-90 to exit 32 (436th Avenue Southeast). Turn right (south) on 436th Avenue Southeast (Cedar Falls Road Southeast) and drive about 2.8 miles, passing the Rattlesnake Lake parking area, until you find the Iron Horse trailhead parking area on the left.

ON THE TRAIL

From Rattlesnake Lake start up the old railroad bed—now the Iron Horse Trail—as it crosses Boxley Creek and heads east along the northern flank of Cedar Butte (Hike 23). The trail is relatively flat and wide enough for a family of four to walk side by side. Take your time and enjoy the walk along this historical route. At about 1 mile you'll see the side path to Cedar Butte summit. Bypass that and continue east on the broad Iron Horse Trail.

At 3 miles out, you'll find yourself crossing an unnamed creek. Continue the slow but steady climb east along the trail, enjoying the broad valley of the South Fork Snoqualmie. You'll occasionally see the hustle of cars on I-90 to the north, but don't let that modern intrusion detract from the natural and historical beauty around you.

At around 4.5 miles, pass the trail to Twin Falls (Hike 25) on your left, and in another 0.25 mile the road from the Mount Washington trailhead (Hike 43) on your left.

At about 6 miles up the trail, you'll find the towering trestles crossing Change and Hall creeks. This massive iron and wood structure offers those with acrophobia a chance to experience their fear, while the rest of you can experience the stunning views out over the lower South Fork Snoqualmie valley and its intersection with the broad Middle Fork Snoqualmie valley.

The fantail base of Twin Falls on the South Fork Snoqualmie River

Mount Si and Mailbox Peak stand tall to the north, marking the west and east flanks of the Middle Fork Snoqualmie valley.

25 Twin Falls

RATING/ DIFFICULTY	ROUNDTRIP	ELEV GAIN/ HIGH POINT	SEASON
****/2	3 miles	500 feet/ 1000 feet	Year-round

Map: Green Trails Rattlesnake Mountain No. 205S; **Contact:** Washington State Parks; **Notes:** Washington Discover Pass required; **GPS:** N 47 27.205, W 121 42.344

Twin Falls run year-round for one very good reason: the area around North Bend receives more than 90 inches of rain each year. Seattle—just 35 miles west—gets half that much. The South Fork Snoqualmie River takes that massive amount of rainfall and puts it to use entertaining hikers. The river squeezes into a narrow rocky gorge before tumbling over a very impressive stair-step falls. Then, when the water has been churned into a frothy torrent, it plunges over a 150-foot rock wall, creating the stunning cascade of the Lower Twin Falls.

GETTING THERE
From Seattle drive east on I-90 to exit 34. Turn right (south) on 468th Avenue Southeast (Southeast Edgewick Road) and proceed about a half mile. Immediately before the South Fork Snoqualmie River bridge, turn left (east) on Southeast 159th Street and drive a half mile to the trailhead parking lot at the road's end.

ON THE TRAIL
The first 0.7 mile of the trail passes through moss-laden forest along the shores of the South Fork Snoqualmie River. This flat mile provides kids plenty of opportunity to explore massive old nurse logs (fallen trees that act as nurseries for newly sprouted trees) and other interesting forest formations. Given the bounty of rain and the lush forest growth, this area feels almost like an Olympic Peninsula rain forest—just without the massive cedars and hemlocks.

After this long, flat run, the trail climbs gently up a series of long switchbacks. About

Views north of Mount Si's western cliffs seen from the summit of Little Si

1 mile out, you'll find a short spur trail on the right—this leads to a fantastic overlook of the lower falls, the mighty 150-foot cascade. Back on the main trail, you'll continue to climb another half mile or so to a bridge that takes you over the river gorge, directly between two of the stair-step falls. Turn back here or continue on another 0.2 mile to the junction with the Iron Horse Trail (Hike 24).

26 Little Si

RATING/ DIFFICULTY	ROUNDTRIP	ELEV GAIN/ HIGH POINT	SEASON
****/4	5 miles	1200 feet/ 1576 feet	Year-round

Maps: Green Trails Mount Si NRCA No. 206S and Snoqualmie Pass Gateway No. 207S; **Contact:** Department of Natural Resources, South Puget Sound Region; **Notes:** Washington Discover Pass required; **GPS:** N 47 29.267, W 121 45.378

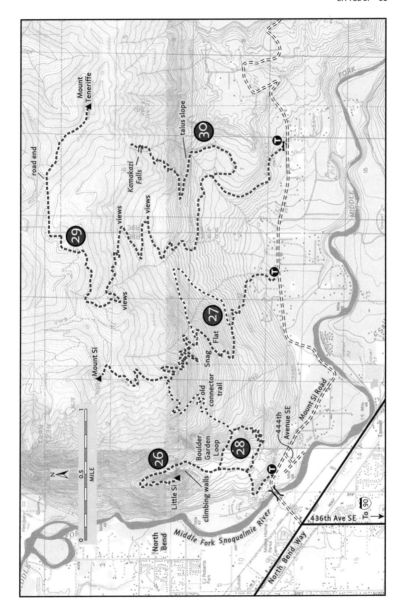

Mount, Teneriffe

road end

Kamakazi Falls

talus slope

30

29

views

views

views

Mount Si

27

Snag Flat

old connector trail

444th Avenue SE

Mount Si Road

26

Boulder Garden Loop

28

N

0.5

MILE

Little Si

climbing walls

To 90

436th Ave SE

North Bend

Middle Fork Snoqualmie River

North Bend Way

Rock climbers use the first half of this trail to get to the rock faces on the east end of Little Si. Hikers use the full trail to sweep around the west end and climb the tall knob on the easier (though still a bit rocky) route. Like its big sibling, Mount Si, Little Si offers phenomenal views of the Upper Snoqualmie Valley after a nice hike through forests and over rocks. The trail is steep initially, then mellow, then steep again as it scrambles straight up the northern spine to the 1576-foot summit.

GETTING THERE

From Seattle drive east on I-90 to exit 32 (436th Avenue Southeast). Turn left (north) over the freeway and drive 0.5 mile to North Bend Way. Turn left (west), and in 0.25 mile turn right (north) on Mount Si Road. Shortly after crossing the bridge, the road banks right. Just after this curve, look for a paved parking area on the left side of the road (if you get to the intersection with 444th Avenue Southeast, you've gone too far).

ON THE TRAIL

This area was logged extensively, but in the intervening decades the forest has regenerated nicely, and a diverse collection of evergreens and deciduous trees shade the trail.

The trail angles steeply up away from the back of the parking lot on open slope and enters the forest above. Once into the forest, at 0.3 mile, you come to Boulder Garden Trail on your right. Continue straight ahead to ascend Little Si. As you near the hulk of rocky bluff known as Little Si, the trail levels off in a swampy area. Small streams link bogs filled with trillium and skunk cabbage. The trail is generally high and dry, though you will encounter an area (or three) of mud.

At around 1.5 miles, views open up onto the high, craggy rock of the southeastern face of Little Si. You might see rock climbers crawling up the rock routes here. Continue along the trail as it loops north and then west to the gentler north face of Little Si.

The trail turns and runs straight up this northern spine, climbing steeply up the rocky ridge—you'll be forced to use your hands at times as you scramble up the biggest rocks—until finally capping out on the 1576-foot summit on the southern edge of the rocky prominence. Enjoy stellar views of the North Bend Valley before heading back the way you came.

27 Mount Si

RATING/ DIFFICULTY	ROUNDTRIP	ELEV GAIN/ HIGH POINT	SEASON
****/5	8 miles	3150 feet/ 3900 feet	May–Nov

Maps: Green Trails Mount Si NRCA No. 206S and Snoqualmie Pass Gateway No. 207S; **Contact:** Department of Natural Resources, South Puget Sound Region; **Notes:** Washington Discover Pass required; **GPS:** N 47 29.376, W 121 43.409

Mount Si should be experienced at least once by every hiker. In fact, a significant number of Puget Sound residents do just one hike per year, and these annual hikers almost invariably turn to Mount Si every time. In the early spring, mountain-loving backpackers and climbers use the trail as a tune-up for the coming season. Others come because the trail is one of few that becomes snow-free early in the year. Land managers estimate that Si draws between thirty thousand and fifty thousand visitors a year, making it the most heavily used trail in the state. As a result, on any sunny summer weekend the trail will be crowded—almost to the point of having to take a number and get in line. Really, it's not that bad, and the steep trail soon separates the serious hiker from the casual mall walker. And Si's payoff is incredible: views of the Upper Snoqualmie Valley, the Puget Sound basin, and far beyond.

GETTING THERE

From Seattle drive east on I-90 to exit 32 (436th Avenue Southeast). Turn left (north) over the freeway and drive 0.5 mile to North Bend Way. Turn left (west), and in 0.25 mile turn right (north) on Mount Si Road. Shortly after crossing the bridge, the road banks

right. The large trailhead parking lot is on the left, 2.5 miles down the road.

ON THE TRAIL

From the broad parking lot, the Mount Si Trail climbs moderately for 1 mile to the first views of the long hike. Here, at around 1600 feet, you'll find wonderful views from atop a rocky bluff on the side of the mountain. Hikers short on time and stamina could turn around here for a modest 2-mile outing.

As you near the 1.8-mile mark, you'll sweep alongside a small brook, with grassy banks on which to rest. This is Snag Flat—the site of an old burn, as evidenced by the blackened scars on the trunks of many of the old Douglas-firs in the area.

The trail then pushes on, never wavering from its steep ascent, until you finally crest the last slope and step out into the wildflower-filled meadow at the summit, or

A couple relaxes and enjoys the views of the Snoqualmie Valley from Mount Si.

Massive boulders and mossy trees on the Boulder Garden Loop

28 Old Si–Boulder Garden Loop

RATING/ DIFFICULTY	LOOP	ELEV GAIN/ HIGH POINT	SEASON
***/2	2.4 miles	800 feet/ 1350 feet	Year-round

Map: Green Trails Mount Si No. 206S; **Contact:** Department of Natural Resources, South Puget Sound Region; **Notes:** Washington Discover Pass required; **GPS:** N 47 29.267, W 121 45.378

If you want to enjoy the beauty of the Mount Si area without the thigh-burning experience of trekking to the top, jump onto this loop route. You'll find towering old second-growth forests, massive clusters of granite boulders, and mossy shrouds covering many of the rocks and trees. The loop provides a grand Northwest wildland escape without overworking you.

GETTING THERE
From Seattle drive east on I-90 to exit 32 (436th Avenue Southeast). Turn left (north) over the freeway and drive 0.5 mile to North Bend Way. Turn left (west), and in 0.25 mile turn right (north) on Mount Si Road. Shortly after crossing the bridge, the road banks right. Just after this curve, look for a paved parking area on the left side of the road (if you get to the intersection with 444th Avenue Southeast, you've gone too far).

ON THE TRAIL
Following the trail out of the far edge of the parking area, climb gradually through second-growth forest for about 0.3 mile to a junction. The main Little Si Trail continues

rather, the summit basin. The true summit of Si is atop the big rock "haystack" that towers over the edge of the meadow. The haystack does sport a scramble path to its summit, but the route is tricky, with incredible exposure (one slip and you'll plummet hundreds—thousands?—of feet). It's best not to attempt the Haystack, especially considering the added danger of other people kicking loose rocks down, creating deadly missiles from above. Besides, the views atop the rock are no better than those you'll enjoy from the meadows at its base.

straight from there. Turn right to start your adventure on the Boulder Garden Loop (moving counterclockwise through the loop).

The route continues in cool, dark forests, bringing you wonderful relief from summer heat and decent protection from the driving winter rains. As the trail steepens, the forest rapidly opens up onto jumbles of moss-laden boulders separated by lush strands of fern—sword ferns being most common, though you'll find several varieties including our own personal favorites, angel hair ferns.

At about 1.4 miles, a trail to the right leads steeply uphill. This is part of the old, original Mount Si Trail. Stay left to continue on the loop route, starting a gradual descent through more rock gardens and thick forest to a junction with Little Si Trail at about 1.8 miles. Turn left to return to the trailhead.

29 Mount Teneriffe

RATING/ DIFFICULTY	ROUNDTRIP	ELEV GAIN/ HIGH POINT	SEASON
****/5	14 miles	3800 feet/ 4788 feet	May–Nov

Map: Green Trails Mount Si No. 206S; **Contact:** Department of Natural Resources, South Puget Sound Region; **Notes:** Washington Discover Pass required; **GPS:** N 47 29.170, W 121 42.072

Typically, a moderate grade is one of the key benefits of hiking an old, closed road. Unfortunately, loggers and miners sometimes ignored the good health of their vehicles in the interest of enjoying expedited travel times—in these cases, roads pitched steeply upward. Mount

Views north from the open, rocky summit of Mount Teneriffe

Teneriffe sports one such truck-killing road. But a gradient that cripples trucks is a mere leg-stretcher for hikers. This road walk is not nearly as steep as the trail up adjacent Mount Si (Hike 27). And, unlike Si, Teneriffe is only lightly used, so you stand a good chance of enjoying a solitary adventure on this Si sibling.

GETTING THERE

From Seattle drive east on I-90 to exit 32 (436th Avenue Southeast). Turn left (north) over the freeway and drive 0.5 mile to North Bend Way. Turn left (west), and in 0.25 mile turn right (north) on Mount Si Road. Shortly after crossing the bridge, the road banks right. Continue past the Mount Si parking area (at 2.5 miles) to a wide turnaround area about a mile beyond. Park here, well clear of the road, and do not block any gates or driveways.

ON THE TRAIL

Start up the gated road on the left. Since you're hiking on an old logging road, you shouldn't be surprised that portions of the trek pass through old clear-cuts. But the logging took place in decades past, so even those areas scraped bare have sprouted fine young forests.

The two-track trail climbs through these young forest groves and stump-filled "meadows" for 2 miles, gaining a mere 500 feet in that distance. Then the angle increases and the road starts to switchback up another 2 miles. During this climb you'll pass through one massive forty-year-old clear-cut that has not regenerated well (its scar can still be seen from the freeway). You'll also witness the erosion that such land-clearing practices precipitate—small run-off streambeds have eroded into deep rock-rimmed gullies by the meltwaters that rush down treeless slopes.

At 4 miles (elev. 3200 feet) you can enjoy wondrous views, thanks in part to the above-bemoaned clear-cut: to the south lies the Cedar River watershed, Rattlesnake Ledge, and the long spine of Rattlesnake Ridge, not to mention Mailbox Peak and the summits of the Middle Fork Snoqualmie River valley. This makes a fine place to turn around if you want a shorter hike.

Shortly after you cross a creek, around 3600 feet, a side trail angles off toward Mount Si. Ignore it and stick to the road walk. About 2 miles after the viewpoint, you'll crest the ridge at 4200 feet. Standing here in a broad saddle below the true summit, you have a choice. Stop here to enjoy views that are even grander than those found below. Or leave the road and hike another 0.5 mile along a boot-beaten path up the ridge crest to the summit knoll at 4788 feet.

30 Kamakazi (Teneriffe) Falls

RATING/ DIFFICULTY	ROUNDTRIP	ELEV GAIN/ HIGH POINT	SEASON
***/3	6.5 miles	1300 feet/ 2400 feet	Mar–Nov

Map: Green Trails Mount Si No. 206S; **Contact:** Department of Natural Resources, South Puget Sound Region; **Notes:** Washington Discover Pass required; **GPS:** N 47 29.170, W 121 42.072

 A new trail up the side of Mount Teneriffe now brings the beautiful Kamakazi Falls (aka Teneriffe Falls) within reach. The route includes an easy climb on a broad old logging road, an exploration of a narrow dirt road being reclaimed by the forest, a stretch on a freshly built single-track trail through

a remarkable boulder field, and views of the south Cascades reaching from Mount Washington to Mount Rainier. Good stuff!

GETTING THERE

From Seattle drive east on I-90 to exit 32 (436th Avenue Southeast). Turn left (north) over the freeway and drive 0.5 mile to North Bend Way. Turn left (west), and in 0.25 mile turn right (north) on Mount Si Road. Shortly after crossing the bridge, the road banks right. Continue past the Mount Si parking area (at 2.5 miles) to a wide turnaround area about a mile beyond. Park here, well clear of the road, and do not block any gates or driveways.

ON THE TRAIL

Head up the gated road for an easy leg-stretching mile to get you warmed up for the hike. At the 1-mile mark, turn right at a road junction and follow this fainter road upward. Note the rapid reclamation the forest is making on this dirt track—the forest has overgrown much of the old road along the next mile. Note: At least one, and sometimes two—depending on wildlife traffic and brush growth—side trails lead off this road before the 2-mile mark. Avoid these dead-end options.

At 1.75 miles from the trailhead, the trail/reclaimed road traverses through a broad talus slope. This steep boulder field provides grand views south to Rattlesnake Ledge and the long ridge of Rattlesnake Mountain stretching west from the ledge. Even better views open up at 1.9 miles, with Mount Washington standing tall to the southwest.

At just over 2 miles, a new well-marked trail leaves the rough roadbed on the right, cutting steeply into the forest above. This path climbs through more rock gardens, dense forest, and sparse meadows before

Artistic masses of winter ice at the base of Kamakazi Falls (aka Teneriffe Falls)

reaching the forested foot of Kamakazi Falls (sources vary between this name and Teneriffe Falls). Use caution here, as the trail edge drops steeply away to the creek. A slip on the wet rock or mud of the trail could result in a fall of 5 to 10 feet onto the rocks at the base of the falls. During late fall through early spring, ice is also common here.

31 Granite Lakes

RATING/ DIFFICULTY	ROUNDTRIP	ELEV GAIN/ HIGH POINT	SEASON
****/4	12 miles	2100 feet/ 3075 feet	May–Nov

Maps: Green Trails Bandera No. 206 and Mount Si NRCA No. 206S; **Contact:** Mount Baker–Snoqualmie National Forest, Snoqualmie Ranger District, North Bend office;

Notes: NW Forest Pass required; **GPS:** N 47 28.171, W 121 40.132

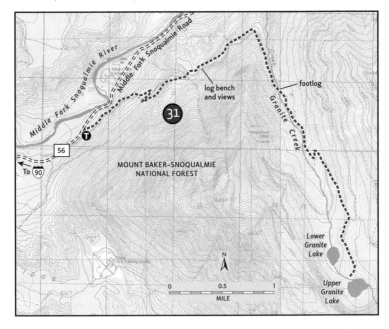 *This former "road hike" has been reclassified thanks to an ambitious "road-to-trail" reclamation project. The crews performed miracles with their machinery and muscles, completely obliterating the old roadway and leaving behind a seemingly pristine path through a beautiful wild area of forest.*

GETTING THERE

From Seattle, drive east on I-90 to exit 34 (Southeast Edgewick Road). Turn left (north) onto 468th Street Southeast and follow it to the junction with Middle Fork Snoqualmie Road (Forest Road 56). Turn right and continue up Middle Fork Snoqualmie Road, passing Valley Camp at 2.2 miles and the Mailbox Peak trailhead at 2.5 miles before reaching the Granite Lakes trailhead on the right at 2.7 miles. Park well clear of the road and all gates.

ON THE TRAIL

Leaving the parking area, start up the "old road" trail and you'll soon be on the newly rebuilt single-track wondering how vehicles ever made it up this way. At 1.1 miles, the trail loops into its first series of switchbacks, lifting you into open stands of alder as the trail climbs.

Tired hikers will find a respite beginning at about 2 miles, as the trail crews left several logs, with convenient "bench" cutoffs on which weary trekkers can rest. One of them, at 2.2 miles, features remarkable

Middle Fork Snoqualmie River

Middle Fork Snoqualmie Road

log bench and views

footlog

Granite Creek

31

T

56

To 90

MOUNT BAKER–SNOQUALMIE NATIONAL FOREST

Lower Granite Lake

Upper Granite Lake

N

0   0.5   1
MILE

At the junction reached just past 5.1 miles, stay right to descend gradually to the Granite Lakes basin, passing the lower lake before reaching Upper Granite Lake at around 6 miles. From here, the views of Mount Defiance are lovely.

32 Mailbox Peak

RATING/ DIFFICULTY	ROUNDTRIP	ELEV GAIN/ HIGH POINT	SEASON
*****/5	6 miles	4100 feet/ 4926 feet	May–Nov

Maps: Green Trails Bandera No. 206 and Mount Si NRCA No. 206S; **Contact:** Mount Baker–Snoqualmie National Forest, Snoqualmie Ranger District, North Bend office; **Notes:** NW Forest Pass required. Portions of this trail were in the process of being rebuilt during our research outing, so some of the descriptions below may change in the near future; **GPS:** N 47 28.045, W 121 40.491

A hiker taking in the autumn views around Lower Granite Lake

views across the Middle Fork Snoqualmie River valley to Bessemer Mountain and the Green Mountains. The views demand to be enjoyed from a seated position, so you have a grand excuse to plop down and rest while soaking them in.

Continuing on, the trail approaches Granite Creek at about 3.1 miles. Even when you can't see the creek, you'll hear its roar as it tumbles down the steep rocky slope. Cross the creek at 3.4 miles on a new log span—the old concrete road bridge that once crossed the creek was dismantled and removed by the earth-moving machinery used to rebuild the trail. No signs of that old road will remain in the not-too-distant future.

Wimpy hikers, turn the page. This trail offers nothing for you but pain and heartbreak. If you think you've got the goods to scramble up more than 1500 feet per mile, read on. Mailbox Peak brings a serious burn to the thighs of even the best-conditioned athletes, but the rewards make it all worthwhile. From the top of this jutting lump of rock, you'll enjoy spectacular views of the lower Snoqualmie River valleys. The entire Issaquah Alps range sprawls at your feet, with the rocky-topped Mount Si directly across the Middle Fork valley and the sheer wall of Rattlesnake Ledge just across the South Fork valley. After soaking in the views, pull the summit register out and leave your signature—you'll find the tattered pages of a notebook in an old metal mailbox wedged above the summit rocks.

GETTING THERE

From Seattle, drive east on I-90 to exit 34 (Southeast Edgewick Road). Turn left (north) onto 468th Street Southeast and follow it to the junction with Middle Fork Snoqualmie Road (Forest Road 56). Turn right and continue up Middle Fork Snoqualmie Road to the end of the pavement (about 2.5 miles from the Middle Fork turnoff). Turn right into the new trailhead parking area.

ON THE TRAIL

Start hiking by rounding the gate and walking up the road (avoiding all side roads). At around a half mile from your car, watch for a sign on the left marking the Mailbox Peak Trail. This trail is rough-hewn, since it was built by boots and only recently received any real trail work—and that done mostly by ad hoc volunteers. Volunteer work parties should have most if not all of the trail reconstruction completed by the end of September 2014.

The trail leaves the road and turns near-vertical, climbing ever more steeply over the next 2.5 miles—the first 0.5 mile of road walking gains only a few hundred feet of elevation, leaving about 3800 feet for the last 2.5 miles. That means you'll be climbing about 1500 feet per mile, and most hikers consider anything over 1000 feet per mile to be steep!

The first mile of climbing makes use of a few switchbacks—though a few more would moderate the pitch more reasonably. From there on, turns and twists become fewer and farther between. The trail climbs with ruthless focus—to get to the top in as direct a line as possible. As you move above 4000 feet, the forest falls away, the views open,

View across the Middle Fork Snoqualmie River valley at Mailbox Peak

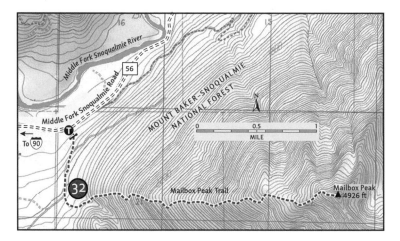

and all pretense of switchbacks disappears. You'll now be scrambling up steep, open hillsides. An old forest fire scoured the slope here, removing the tree cover but making space for a wonderful mix of heather, bear grass, and dense huckleberry thickets.

Finally, after one last scramble through the rocky crown around the summit, you're there, standing beside the battered mailbox on the top of Mailbox Peak. After you catch your breath, pat yourself on the back—because if you're on the summit, you've conquered perhaps the most difficult hike in this book!

33 CCC Road: Blowout Creek

RATING/ DIFFICULTY	ROUNDTRIP	ELEV GAIN/ HIGH POINT	SEASON
***/2	7 miles	620 feet/ 1520 feet	May–Nov

Maps: Green Trails Mount Si No. 174 and Mount Si NRCA No. 206S; **Contact:** Mount Baker–Snoqualmie National Forest, Snoqualmie Ranger District, North Bend office;

Notes: NW Forest Pass required; **GPS:** N 47 30.953, W 121 36.805

In the 1930s the Civilian Conservation Corps (CCC) took unemployed men out of America's cities and put them to work in the nation's forests. This jobs program helped get our country out of the Great Depression, as well as build some of the most impressive man-made features in our national parks and forests. The CCC Road isn't one of the program's most impressive accomplishments, but it is one of its lasting legacies. Originally built for logging in the Middle Fork Snoqualmie River valley, the road has become a primary recreational resource in this wonderland of the Middle Fork.

GETTING THERE

From Seattle, drive east on I-90 to exit 34 (Southeast Edgewick Road). Turn left (north) onto 468th Street Southeast and follow it to the junction with Middle Fork Snoqualmie Road (Forest Road 56). Turn right and continue up Middle Fork Snoqualmie Road 7.4 miles (or 2 miles after crossing a bridge over the Middle Fork) to a gated road on the left. Park here, well off the main road and without blocking the gated road. Start your hike by rounding the gate and starting up that side road.

ON THE TRAIL

Hiking up the gated road, you'll climb along-side Blowout Creek for nearly 1 mile before intersecting the CCC Road. About half of your total elevation gain will have been accomplished.

Once on the CCC Road (elev. 1300 feet), turn left and follow the twin-track trail west. Immediately upon your westward trek you will come to a crossing of Blowout Creek,

a bit of a trick at spring high water, as the creek cascades down through open alder/maple forest below you. Continuing on west from the creek, you'll find stunning panoramas between the trees periodically as you walk the gradually climbing trail.

At just under 3.5 miles from your car, you'll hear the sounds of falling water. Soon, you'll see it—Brawling Creek in its rough-and-tumble plummet down the rocky run of waterfalls.

EXTENDING YOUR TRIP

Brawling Creek is your turnaround point, though you can press on for added miles if you'd like toward the western end of the CCC Road.

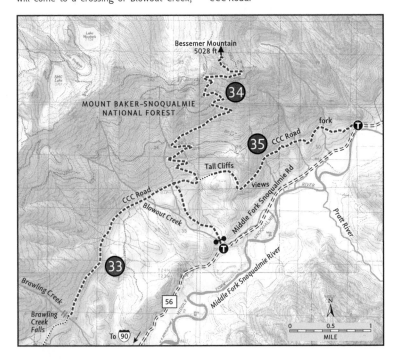

Blowout Creek tumbling down from the CCC Road

34 Bessemer Mountain

RATING/ DIFFICULTY	ROUNDTRIP	ELEV GAIN/ HIGH POINT	SEASON
***/4	12 miles	4100 feet/ 5028 feet	July–Oct

Maps: Green Trails Mount Si No. 174 and Mount Si NRCA No. 206S; **Contact:** Mount Baker–Snoqualmie National Forest, Snoqualmie Ranger District, North Bend office; **Notes:** NW Forest Pass required; **GPS:** N 47 30.953, W 121 36.805

The Middle Fork Snoqualmie River valley gives us hope. Once a waste-land of illegal trash dumping, rampant gunplay, and illicit drug manufacturing (and use), this area is now a premiere recreation destination. The Bessemer Mountain route is one of the valley's great success stories. On this old roadway built by folks eager to extract as much of the area's natural resources as possible, you'll discover that the greatest resource remains—the power of nature to heal itself. You'll explore fantastic mixed-age, diverse second-growth forests. You'll gawk at awesome views. And if you're lucky, you'll see and/or hear some of the native wildlife whose populations have rebounded.

GETTING THERE

From Seattle, drive east on I-90 to exit 34 (Southeast Edgewick Road). Turn left (north) onto 468th Street Southeast and follow it to the junction with Middle Fork Snoqualmie Road (Forest Road 56). Turn right and continue up Middle Fork Snoqualmie Road for 7.4 miles (or 2 miles after crossing a bridge over the Middle Fork) to a gated road on the left. Park here, well off the main road and without blocking the gated road. Start your hike by rounding the gate and starting up that side road.

ON THE TRAIL

Hike up the road, which parallels Blowout Creek (Hike 33) to its junction with the CCC Road. Turn right onto the CCC Road, and in less than 0.5 mile you'll encounter a fork in the path at about 1300 feet elevation. Turn left, rounding the gate in the road, and climb the steep two-track trail as it ascends the flank of Bessemer Mountain.

At about 3.5 miles, the road enters a wide clear-cut that clearly hasn't recovered from its shearing in the late 1970s. The road crosses this scar quickly, but stop and enjoy the one benefit such devastation offers—wide-open views. Look across the Middle Fork valley to the deep slash of the Pratt River as it carves its way steeply down the opposite side of the valley. Look east and enjoy the tall crowns of the Snoqualmie area peaks: Mount Garfield, Chimney Rock, Lemah, and others.

Continuing on, the road climbs ever more steeply, entering a series of switchbacks. At each fork, stick with the trail, which climbs ceaselessly upward. Finally, just over 5.5 miles out, you'll crest the ridge on a 4000-foot saddle. Grand views are found here, but don't stop now. Push on to the end of the road on a small bench—dubbed South Bessemer Summit—at 5028 feet.

35 CCC Road: Upper Trailhead

RATING/ DIFFICULTY	ROUNDTRIP	ELEV GAIN/ HIGH POINT	SEASON
***/2	4 miles	400 feet/ 1450 feet	Year-round

Map: Green Trails Mount Si No. 174; **Contact:** Mount Baker–Snoqualmie National Forest, Snoqualmie Ranger District, North Bend office; **Notes:** NW Forest Pass required; **GPS:** N 47 32.235, W 121 34.650

This old road built by workers in the Depression-era Civilian Conservation Corps (CCC) has been used to link lumber mills, provide miners easier access to their claims, and give loggers faster access to the big trees of

An open view across the Middle Fork Snoqualmie River valley toward Russian Butte from the hike up Bessemer Mountain

The CCC Road passes a mossy hillside near the moss cliffs region of the trail.

the lower Middle Fork Snoqualmie River. Today, closed to motors, the road provides a wonderful opportunity for hikers to explore the human and natural history of this region.

GETTING THERE

From Seattle, drive east on I-90 to exit 34 (Southeast Edgewick Road). Turn left (north) onto 468th Street Southeast and follow it to the junction with Middle Fork Snoqualmie Road (Forest Road 56). Turn right and continue up Middle Fork Snoqualmie Road for 9.6 miles (or 4.2 miles after crossing a bridge over the Middle Fork) to a parking area signed "CCC Road." Look for this section of trail on the left (north) side of the road, where the trail leads to the west (downvalley). Take that route.

ON THE TRAIL

Nature has largely reclaimed this roadway, leaving us to enjoy a wide single-track trail as it climbs gently away from the

Middle Fork Snoqualmie up onto the ridge above. The forest around the trail has recovered remarkably well from the savage clear-cutting that took place in the 1960s. This second-growth forest now sports massive trees, both evergreen and deciduous (maple and alder), giving the forest the diversity needed for true forest health.

After about a half mile of hiking, stay left as the road forks. You'll soon ford a stream (avoid this in spring when snowmelt raises the water level to a torrent) and continue steadily, though gradually, upward.

At 1.5 miles, the screen of trees opens enough to allow you uninterrupted views across the broad Middle Fork to the deep cut of the Pratt River, leading up the opposite valley, away from the Middle Fork. Over the next 0.5 mile, you'll have partial views of the pretty river and the valley around you.

At 2 miles out, sweep under Tall Cliffs, a moss-laden rock face towering over the trail. Enjoy the cool shade under this emerald face before returning to the trailhead.

EXTENDING YOUR TRIP

Hikers looking for more mileage can link this hike with the route up Bessemer Mountain, described in Hike 34.

36 CCC Road: Campground

RATING/ DIFFICULTY	ROUNDTRIP	ELEV GAIN/ HIGH POINT	SEASON
***/2	6 miles	400 feet/ 1350 feet	Year-round

Maps: Green Trails Mount Si No. 174 and Mount Si NRCA No. 206S; **Contact:** Mount Baker–Snoqualmie National Forest, Snoqualmie Ranger District, North Bend office; **Notes:** NW Forest Pass required; **GPS:** N 47 32.247, W 121 34.639

In the early part of the twentieth century, the Civilian Conservation Corps (CCC) built this route to help move logs out of the valley so they could be turned into lumber for the cities. In the early twenty-first century, volunteers and paid crews have turned the road into a trail to help people leave the cities and return— if only briefly—to the forests of this as happy hikers. This latest section of reclaimed trail explores the forests below Quartz Mountain.

GETTING THERE

From Seattle, drive east on I-90 to exit 34 (Southeast Edgewick Road). Turn left (north) onto 468th Street Southeast and follow it to the junction with Middle Fork Snoqualmie Road (Forest Road 56). Turn right and con-

The CCC Road's newest trail section toward the campground passes through mossy forest.

tinue up Middle Fork Snoqualmie Road for 9.6 miles (or 4.2 miles after crossing a bridge over the Middle Fork) to the parking area signed "CCC Road." Our trail starts a short 0.1 mile up the road from here on the left (north) side of the road and heads upstream (east).

ON THE TRAIL

Leaving the parking area, walk up Middle Fork Snoqualmie Road to find the trailhead, leading off the left side of the road into the forest. The new trail climbs very gradually to a creek crossing at 0.3 mile. Though named for the old Depression-era road, this trail actually avoids most of the old road grade, opting instead to utilize new routing roughly parallel to the old road, but at 0.5 mile, the new trail does roll down the old roadbed

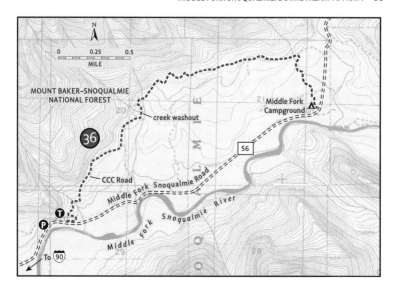

for a short way before moving away from the eroded road and into the pristine old second-growth forest.

After hiking just over a mile, the trail crosses a creek. Normally small and languid, this creek must rage in flood conditions, as it shows the scars of a massive blowout at some time in the recent past. The crossing is not difficult but does require care, as the rocks of the trail can shift underfoot. Fortunately, going slowly here makes sense. Stop between strides to enjoy the open views south to Russian Butte and the other peaks of the Middle Fork valley. From here, the trail climbs over a low bench, reaching its high point of 1350 feet before starting a gradual descent at around 2 miles. Here again the trail makes use of the original road right-of-way.

At 3 miles, the road turns south and drops into the newish Middle Fork Campground. Turn back here, or, if you'd rather add more miles, pass through the campground, cross

Middle Fork Snoqualmie Road, and use the Middle Fork footbridge to jump onto the Middle Fork Trail (Hikes 37 and 38).

37 Middle Fork Snoqualmie: Downstream to Pratt

RATING/ DIFFICULTY	ROUNDTRIP	ELEV GAIN/ HIGH POINT	SEASON
****/3	7 miles	200 feet/ 1100 feet	Mar–Nov

Maps: Green Trails Mount Si No. 174 and Skykomish No. 175; **Contact:** Mount Baker–Snoqualmie National Forest, Snoqualmie Ranger District, North Bend office; **Notes:** NW Forest Pass required; **GPS:** N 47 32.877, W 121 32.304

 The Middle Fork Sno-qualmie Trail has finally been extended from the stout footbridge

downstream to the nearly lost Pratt River Trail. This section of the trail explores some of the least-visited parts of the valley. As a result, birds and wildlife still thrive and opportunities to see untouched second-growth forest abound. This is a valley trail, but don't think it an easy flat hike to the Pratt—there are a lot of ups and downs, but never for too long or too steep.

GETTING THERE

From Seattle, drive east on I-90 to exit 34 (Southeast Edgewick Road). Turn left (north) onto 468th Street Southeast and follow it to the junction with Middle Fork Snoqualmie Road (Forest Road 56). Turn right and continue up Middle Fork Snoqualmie Road for 11.8 miles to the Middle Fork trailhead parking area on the right. Cross the river on the impressively large metal-and-wood footbridge.

ON THE TRAIL

After crossing the Gateway bridge, turn right and head downstream along the Pratt River Connector Trail. In less than a mile (0.7 mile to be precise) the path crosses a beautifully designed and built bridge over Rainy Creek. The seemingly ancient footlog crossing still visible below the new bridge from the old long-abandoned route shows how far this trail has advanced.

At 1.2 miles, after a quick climb and before the steep switchbacking descends again, enjoy a section of trail blasted out of a granite face and enjoy the roaring sounds of the river below. From here, another 1.3 miles puts you onto a very old roadway—heavily overgrown and reverted to a single track, but definitely identifiable as an old road piercing a jumble of boulders and salmonberry brambles.

The new bridge over Rainy Creek along the newly completed (2013) Pratt River Connector Trail

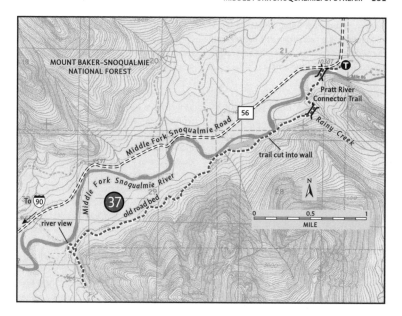

As the route levels out, you'll break out onto a flat plain at 3.2 miles as the trail nears the Middle Fork Snoqualmie River. The trail runs into a tight turn to the left at 3.5 miles—the start of the steep climb on a rough trail toward Pratt Lake. Save that for another day (preferably after the trail up to the lake gets rebuilt) and turn back here.

38 Middle Fork Snoqualmie: Upstream

RATING/ DIFFICULTY	ROUNDTRIP	ELEV GAIN/ HIGH POINT	SEASON
****/2	6 miles	200 feet/ 1100 feet	Mar–Nov

Maps: Green Trails Mount Si No. 174 and Skykomish No. 175; **Contact:** Mount Baker–Snoqualmie National Forest, Snoqualmie Ranger District, North Bend office; **Notes:** NW Forest Pass required; **GPS:** N 47 32.877, W 121 32.304

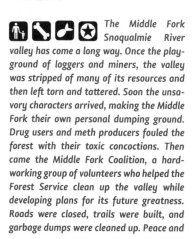

The Middle Fork Snoqualmie River valley has come a long way. Once the playground of loggers and miners, the valley was stripped of many of its resources and then left torn and tattered. Soon the unsavory characters arrived, making the Middle Fork their own personal dumping ground. Drug users and meth producers fouled the forest with their toxic concoctions. Then came the Middle Fork Coalition, a hardworking group of volunteers who helped the Forest Service clean up the valley while developing plans for its future greatness. Roads were closed, trails were built, and garbage dumps were cleaned up. Peace and

quiet were restored. Today, the Middle Fork Snoqualmie is a recreationist's dream, and the Middle Fork Trail is one of the best recreational resources in the valley.

GETTING THERE

From Seattle, drive east on I-90 to exit 34 (Southeast Edgewick Road). Turn left (north) onto 468th Street Southeast and follow it to the junction with Middle Fork Snoqualmie Road (Forest Road 56). Turn right and continue up Middle Fork Snoqualmie Road for 11.8 miles to the Middle Fork trailhead parking area on the right. Cross the river on the impressively large metal-and-wood footbridge.

ON THE TRAIL

The Middle Fork Snoqualmie River is a fast-moving, cold river that few hikers would care to cross on their own. But when

the Forest Service and a team of volunteers installed a bridge over the Middle Fork near the mouth of the Taylor River, hikers gained new trails to explore.

Walk across the bridge—stopping mid-span to enjoy the views up- and downstream, as well as to marvel at the beautiful bridge (circa 1993)—and turn left to hike upstream alongside the tumbling river. The trail rolls in and out of the trees, sometimes dropping down close to the water's edge and at other times pushing far into the forest. The Middle Fork is a trout-rich river, so it's not uncommon to see fish-eating birds along its banks. Blue herons and bald eagles are frequent visitors, so don't be surprised if a massive bird takes wing right before your eyes.

Around 0.75 mile into the hike, you'll pass under a tall granite wall, dubbed Stegosaurus Butte. These cliffs top out at 2000 feet (about 1100 feet above your head). Another

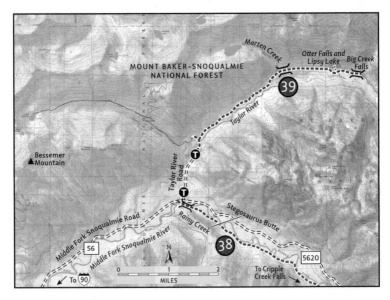

Northwestern view downstream from the trail along the Middle Fork Snoqualmie River

mile on and you'll find the narrow path opening up a bit as it takes advantage of an old railroad right-of-way—steam locomotives once used this route to pull railcars loaded with logs out of the forest.

The next 1.2 miles angle through the woods, finally dropping down to the riverside. Cool your feet in the icy waters—or maybe even wet a line if you're an angler (good fishing here at times)—before heading back down to the trailhead.

EXTENDING YOUR TRIP

For a 10-mile roundtrip hike, keep going east on the trail and at 5.1 miles reach a spectacular bridge and creek offering a stunning view of Cripple Creek Falls upstream.

39 Big Creek Falls

RATING/ DIFFICULTY	ROUNDTRIP	ELEV GAIN/ HIGH POINT	SEASON
***/3	10 miles	650 feet/ 1750 feet	Mar–Nov

Maps: Green Trails Mount Si No. 174 and Skykomish No. 175; **Contact:** Mount Baker–Snoqualmie National Forest, Snoqualmie Ranger District, North Bend office; **Notes:** NW Forest Pass required; **GPS:** N 47 32.877, W 121 32.304

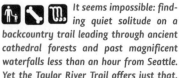 *It seems impossible: finding quiet solitude on a backcountry trail leading through ancient cathedral forests and past magnificent waterfalls less than an hour from Seattle. Yet the Taylor River Trail offers just that. While nearby Mount Si bristles with sweating hikers, and the Middle Fork Snoqualmie Trail hosts hordes of outdoor enthusiasts, the Taylor River Trail—an old road that's been reclaimed by the forest—goes largely unnoticed and unused.*

GETTING THERE

From Seattle, drive east on I-90 to exit 34 (Southeast Edgewick Road). Turn left (north) onto 468th Street Southeast and follow it to the junction with Middle Fork Snoqualmie Road (Forest Road 56). Turn right and continue up Middle Fork Snoqualmie Road for 12.5 miles to Taylor River Road (just past the Middle Fork trailhead parking area). Turn left onto Taylor River Road and drive to a wide parking area at its end, in about a half mile.

ON THE TRAIL

Start up the Taylor River Road/Trail, and in about 0.4 mile, when the road forks, stay right. Weave up the valley, and cross an old bridge structure at Marten Creek, about 3 miles up the track. Modern planking has been added to the bridge deck to ensure safe crossing. But once across, peer under the bridge to gain an appreciation of the type of timber harvested from this area. Huge cedar logs serve as the spanners that support the bridge.

From here, the trail rolls gently onto the Big Creek bridge at about 5 miles. This structure appears to be out of place here. The wide concrete bridge belongs on a highway—somewhere other than a backcountry trail—but it's a remnant of the old road and a developer's dream, a dream that fortunately died. The wide road that was planned into the headwaters of the Taylor River valley never progressed much beyond a logging road, and even that has largely disappeared, leaving this primitive trail.

The Big Creek bridge may be the first thing to grab your attention when you reach

Big Creek Falls

the creek, but it fades into the background as soon as you step onto its deck. Big Creek Falls tumbles off the hillside on the north side of the bridge—over a series of granite steps and down smooth granite faces to create a sparkling tapestry of watery jewels. A deep plunge pool lies at the foot of the falls, just below the bridge itself.

Big Creek Falls makes an ideal lunch stop—the sun streams down onto the bridge deck and the concrete curbing along its edges serves as a fine bench.

EXTENDING YOUR TRIP

Be sure to pause on your way back to the trailhead and take a side trip to Otter Falls. Watch for a small sign and a cairn (pile of rocks) about 0.25 mile from Big Creek. A side trail leads north through the woods for a few hundred yards, ending at a wide but shallow pool of water at the base of a huge vertical granite slab. A ribbon of water slides down the smooth gray rock face to splash into the pool. This is Lipsy Lake and Otter Falls.

In a normal snow year, the falls sparkles and crashes as the melting snowpack feeds

the creek, but even in a low-water year the falls is pretty, especially reflected in the calm waters of the lake, and especially when viewed in the quiet solitude that reigns along this valley trail from autumn through spring.

40 Rock Creek Falls

RATING/ DIFFICULTY	ROUNDTRIP	ELEV GAIN/ HIGH POINT	SEASON
***/3	11 miles	210 feet/ 3400 feet	July–Nov

Maps: Green Trails Snoqualmie Pass No. 207 and Skykomish No. 175; **Contact:** Mount Baker–Snoqualmie National Forest, Snoqualmie Ranger District, North Bend office; **Notes:** NW Forest Pass required; **GPS:** N 47 31.041, W 121 27.253

  Once upon a time, the Cascade Crest Trail rolled through the Rock Creek valley, carrying hikers down from the ridge above Snoqualmie Pass. That old scenic high route

An American dipper works the water near the confluence of Rock Creek and the Middle Fork Snoqualmie River.

later became the Pacific Crest Trail (PCT)—the brightest gem in the triple crown of the National Trails System (the PCT, the Continental Divide Trail, and the Appalachian Trail). While the PCT followed much of the old Cascade Crest route, this Rock Creek section was replaced when trail builders carved a new high route into the face of Kendall Peak (see Hike 60, Kendall Katwalk). The Rock Creek Trail was forgotten for many years, but hiking legends Harvey Manning and Ira Spring refused to let a good trail die, and they added the path to one of their last guidebooks. Here it is, in an abbreviated version, to ensure that this wonderful trail doesn't disappear.

GETTING THERE

From Seattle, drive east on I-90 to exit 34 (Southeast Edgewick Road). Turn left (north)

onto 468th Street Southeast and follow it to the junction with Middle Fork Snoqualmie Road (Forest Road 56). Turn right and continue up Middle Fork Snoqualmie Road for 12.5 miles to the junction with Taylor River Road. Pass that junction to continue east on Forest Road 5620 about 5 miles to the Dingford Creek trailhead.

ON THE TRAIL

Start the hike by dropping down from the trailhead and crossing a large metal bridge over the Middle Fork Snoqualmie River. Enjoy views of the scenic river from here. Once over the river, you'll head off through the woods. Head left onto the well-graded Middle Fork Snoqualmie Trail and travel upstream 2.5 miles. Just after crossing Rock Creek, turn right onto the Cascade Crest Trail and start a climb up a tight series of switchbacks alongside Rock Creek.

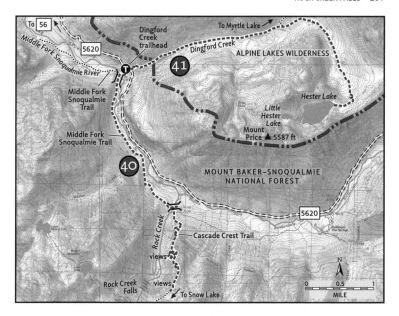

The trail can be rough and a bit brushy at times. Persevere, and soon (near the 3-mile mark) the trail levels out briefly as it skirts along an old railroad right-of-way. Then the climbing begins in earnest again. Over the next mile or so, the views behind you begin to open up as you climb out of the dense forest of the valley and into a more open, view-friendly forest. Since the best views are back over the valley behind you, you'll have good reason to pause and rest—uh, I mean, enjoy the views—frequently. The grandest views start at 4 miles, where you can stare out over the valley at the massive face of Mount Garfield.

This is a good turnaround point, though if you really want to experience the best this route has to offer, push on. The trail continues to weave upward through the creekside forests.

Finally, at about 5.5 miles, you'll find a stunning view up through the headwater basin of Rock Creek. Before you stands the steep rocky slope of the valley headwall, and the bright white ribbon of a waterfall pouring down its face.

HOW TO HELP THIS TRAIL

The best way to help protect this trail is to hike it, and then let the local ranger district know that you have visited and think the trail is a valuable part of the backcountry trail network in this area. But don't just call: put it in writing. Send a letter, describing your experience and where you see need for improvements (e.g., reconstruction of trail tread, brush cutting, log removal, etc.). Send the letter to the ranger and to the good folks at the Washington Trails Association,

The very wet forest floor supports a multitude of fungus growth.

the leading volunteer trail-maintenance organization in the state.

EXTENDING YOUR TRIP

If you're really serious about your scrambling (and bushwhacking), push on up the trail. It gets rougher and harder to follow, but in another 2 miles you'll find yourself on the shores of Snow Lake, which is typically accessed from the Alpental trailhead at Snoqualmie.

41 Dingford Creek–Hester Lake

RATING/ DIFFICULTY	ROUNDTRIP	ELEV GAIN/ HIGH POINT	SEASON
****/4	12 miles	2600 feet/ 3900 feet	July–Oct

Map: Green Trails Skykomish No. 175; **Contact:** Mount Baker–Snoqualmie National Forest, Snoqualmie Ranger District, North Bend office; **Notes:** NW Forest Pass required; **GPS:** N 47 31.041, W 121 27.253

 Pack a fishing pole and a camera. There are many meal-sized trout in this basin's lakes, and there are endless views to enjoy, both on the trail and at the trail's end. The route pierces the old-growth forest in the valley as it enters the Alpine Lakes Wilderness and leads to glorious examples of the wilderness's namesake lakes. Hester Lake sprawls below Mount Price, and short scrambles are possible to Little Hester Lake and the scenic ridges around the basin.

GETTING THERE

From Seattle, drive east on I-90 to exit 34 (Southeast Edgewick Road). Turn left (north) onto 468th Street Southeast and follow it to the junction with Middle Fork Snoqualmie Road (Forest Road 56). Turn right and continue up Middle Fork Snoqualmie Road for 12.5 miles to the junction with Taylor River Road. Pass that junction to continue east on Forest Road 5620 about 5 miles to the Dingford Creek trailhead.

ON THE TRAIL

The Dingford Creek Trail climbs from the banks of the Middle Fork Snoqualmie River, heading north up the creek valley. The forest path immediately starts a sweat-popping climb, with a long series of switchbacks over the first mile. At the

top of the last switchback, the trail ducks into the Alpine Lakes Wilderness and the grade levels out a bit. The surrounding forest, young second growth near the trailhead, slowly transitions to native old growth as the trail penetrates deeper into the wilderness.

At 3.5 miles the trail—and the creek—split. To the left the trail continues due north another 2.5 miles to Myrtle Lake, while the right fork heads due south to Hester Lake in just 2.5 miles. Both lakes are enjoyable and both hold pan-sized trout. Hester, however, offers somewhat better views, with the jagged peak of Mount Price looming above it.

The last couple of miles to Hester are rough and poorly maintained, making the final walk into the lake basin all the more rewarding. Stop and rest along the shores of the blue-water lake, enjoying views of Mount Price and Big Snow Mountain.

EXTENDING YOUR TRIP

If you feel the need for more miles, detour off your return trip to make the 5-mile roundtrip to Myrtle Lake. It is nestled in a deep rocky cirque at the end of a 2.5-mile trail that is just as rough and steep as the one leading to Hester.

42 Upper Middle Fork Snoqualmie

RATING/ DIFFICULTY	ROUNDTRIP	ELEV GAIN/ HIGH POINT	SEASON
***/4	12 miles	1600 feet/ 4600 feet	Aug–Oct

Lush forest ground cover dominates most all of the very wet Middle Fork Snoqualmie region's lower elevations.

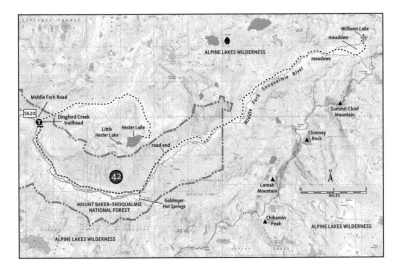

Maps: Green Trails Skykomish No. 175 and Stevens Pass No. 176; **Contact:** Mount Baker–Snoqualmie National Forest, Snoqualmie Ranger District, North Bend office; **Notes:** NW Forest Pass required. High-clearance vehicle required for last few miles to trailhead; **GPS:** N 47 31.041, W 121 27.253

⚙️🥾❌ *All you have to do to enjoy this trail is survive perhaps the worst road in the Cascades. But the long, slow drive (crawl) is worth it. You'll ramble through groves of ancient forests, cross massive avalanche chutes choked with slide alder and salmonberries, and enjoy endless views of the stunning peaks of the upper Snoqualmie River watershed. Reap maximum benefit by visiting in late summer through early fall: (1) because by September most of the mosquitoes are dead and gone; (2) because cooler nights add brilliant color to the vine maples and slide alders; and (3) because ripe huckleberries await at the upper end of the valley.*

GETTING THERE

From Seattle, drive east on I-90 to exit 34 (Southeast Edgewick Road). Turn left (north) onto 468th Street Southeast and follow it to the junction with Middle Fork Snoqualmie Road (Forest Road 56). Turn right and continue up Middle Fork Snoqualmie Road for 12.5 miles to the junction with Taylor River Road. Pass that junction to continue east on Forest Road 5620 about 5 miles to the Dingford Creek trailhead. Park here. The road beyond Dingford Creek has been closed to motor vehicles. Start hiking up the old rutted jeep track beyond the gate.

ON THE TRAIL

Head east past the road gate, hiking the old, rough road as it follows the north side of the river east into the Alpine Lakes Wilderness. This two-track trail pierces cool old

HIKE WITH KIDS

School just let out for summer and the kids are already bored and restless. What do you do? Take a hike!

This book features many scenic-but-gentle trails laced throughout state lands and national forests and parks, offering wilderness adventures perfect for families with young kids. With the abundance of these easy-to-moderate hiking trails, there is no reason for anyone to miss out on the enjoyment of hiking. This pastime has grown to be truly a sport for people of all ages, all abilities.

The woods are full of things kids of all ages find fascinating. Besides bugs, birds, and animals there are all sorts of relics of human history to discover and explore, from rusting railroad spikes and mining equipment to old fire lookouts and foresters' cabins to Native American petroglyphs and rock art. There are fascinating geologic formations and countless forms of water bodies—streams, creeks, seeps, marshes, tarns, ponds, lakes, and bays.

Before heading out to discover your own great trail experiences, though, there are some things to consider. First and perhaps most important are the ages of the kids and their physical condition (not to mention your own). If you are new to hiking, or have been away from it for a while (like, since the kids were born), or if your kids are under fourteen years old, stick to trails shorter than 2 or 3 miles initially. Both you and the kids will find this to be long enough, and many of the trails in that range offer plenty to see and experience.

Once the trip is planned, parents can do a few things to make sure their kids have fun—for instance, never hike with just one child. Kids need companions to compete with, play with, and converse with. One child and a pair of adults makes a hike seem too much like work for the poor kid. But let your child bring along a friend or two and all will have the time of their lives.

When starting out on the trail, adults need to set goals and destinations that are attainable for everyone. Kids and adults alike are more likely to enjoy the hike if they know there is a specific destination rather than just an idea of "going until we feel like turning back."

Then, when hiking, make sure to take frequent breaks and offer the kids "energy food" consisting of a favorite cookie or tasty treat. These snacks serve two purposes. The kids will be motivated to make it to the next break site, knowing they will get a good-tasting treat, and the sugar will help keep the kids fueled up and energized on the trail. For maximum benefit, make the energy foods a special treat that the kids especially like but maybe don't get as often as they'd like. Pack plenty of water, too, to wash down the snacks and to replace what is lost as sweat.

Finally, let the kids explore and investigate the trail environment as much as they like. Patience is more than a virtue here—it's a necessity. Take the time to inspect the tadpoles in trailside bogs, to study the bugs on the bushes, and to try spotting the birds singing in the trees. Just let the kids be kids. If you can then share in their excitement and enthusiasm, everyone will have a great time on the trail.

second-growth forest for 6 miles, with frequent views of the Middle Fork Snoqualmie River. To get to the true single-track trail quicker, you may prefer to use a mountain bike to roll up this lower section. At the end of the old road, the route narrows to a hiking path (no bikes allowed here) and continues east, climbing steadily but gently.

The long, straight trail crosses several small side creeks (some are seasonal—dry in late summer—others are raging trickles year-round). As you hike you'll find your eyes constantly drawn upward. The slopes on both sides are a patchwork of bright white granite, green forest, and (in autumn) brilliantly colored bands of vine maples.

The trail meanders in and out of forest, sliding through meadows, skirting the base of alder-clogged avalanche chutes, and hopping over small creeks and gullies. Turn around at the road end for a 12-mile hike.

EXTENDING YOUR TRIP

The varied terrain and gentle climbing continues for another 7 miles until the trail reaches a stunning little valley-bottom meadow dotted with small ponds and laced with wandering streams. Low-bush huckleberries fill the grassy meadows. If the berries aren't ripe, you can feast on the view of Summit Chief Mountain. This massive rock looms to your right (east), casting a remarkable reflection in the meadow ponds.

This is a great place for lunch before heading back downvalley for that long drive home.

HOW TO HELP THIS TRAIL

The best way to help protect this trail is to hike it, and then let the local ranger district know that you have visited and think the trail is a valuable part of the backcountry trail network in this area. But don't just call: put it in writing. Send a letter, describing your experience and where you see need for improvements (e.g., reconstruction of trail tread, brush cutting, log removal, etc.). Send the letter to the ranger and to the good folks at the Washington Trails Association, the leading volunteer trail-maintenance organization in the state.

*Opposite: McClellan Butte with a fresh dusting of snow seen
to the south from Dirty Harry Balcony*

snoqualmie pass
corridor: west

Savvy hikers know that the western side of the Snoqualmie Pass corridor means steep climbs and grand views. Not all trails in the region boast thigh-burning climbs, but the walls of the South Fork Snoqualmie valley are brutally steep and very tall. Few other parts of the Cascade Range offer such a collection of near-vertical trails and stellar views. Hike up the Ira Spring Trail with its 2500 feet of elevation gain in 3 miles, and you'll think it can't get much steeper than that—until you go over to Granite Mountain and push up 3800 feet in 4 miles! Yes, you'll get a workout on these trails, but you'll also get phenomenal payoffs. The lakes nestled in deep bowls among these peaks are stunning, and the views from the high, craggy mountaintops are simply out of this world.

43 Mount Washington

RATING/ DIFFICULTY	ROUNDTRIP	ELEV GAIN/ HIGH POINT	SEASON
***/5	8 miles	3200 feet/ 4405 feet	June–Nov

Maps: Green Trails Bandera No. 206 and Mount Si NRCA No. 206S; **Contact:** Washington State Parks; **Notes:** Washington Discover Pass required; **GPS:** N 47 26.519, W 121 40.332

Grand views, spectacular spring wildflowers, and easy access make this a great after-work outing or an early spring escape. The route follows an old logging road-turned-trail up a rock-rimmed mountain, providing hikers a good workout absent crowds.

GETTING THERE
From Seattle drive east on I-90 to exit 38. Turn right (south) onto old US Highway 10 and after crossing the South Fork Snoqualmie River, turn right again into the Ollalie State Park/Twin Falls trailhead parking area, just a few hundred yards after exiting I-90.

ON THE TRAIL
Find the access trail near the restroom building. This short spur trail cuts up to an

Looking out over the South Fork Snoqualmie valley at Mount Si and the North Bend vicinity from the summit of Mount Washington

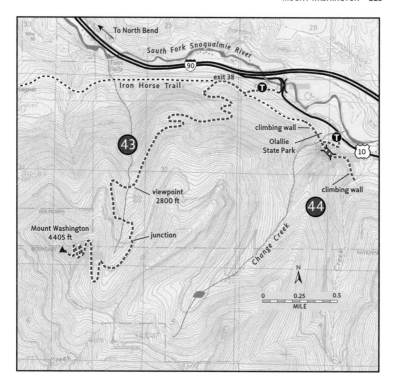

old roadbed, which leads in turn to the Iron Horse Trail. Follow the Iron Horse Trail west a few hundred yards before turning left (south) onto the trail, which is actually a faint, old gravel logging road. This trail leads upward in long switchbacks, climbing the northern face of Mount Washington.

Much of the landscape has been logged at some distant point in the past, but as you climb, the cleared areas—now thick with green growth—offer grand views. The road/trail winds up the steep face of the mountain, over and around rocky bluffs, craggy cliffs, and deep ravines. On sunny summer weekends you might find superhero wannabes doing Spiderman impersonations on many of the rock walls.

Your route climbs continuously from the Iron Horse. Any time you encounter a spur trail, stick to the main trail and continue up, up, up. At 2 miles you'll find grand views from a broad bench on the flank of the mountain. This area provides the best views found anywhere on the lower mountain. Continue upward, and at the next trail junction above the bend, go right onto a newly built trail that leads to an intersection with another old road just below the summit. Another 1.5 miles leads to a bench just below the summit rocks at 4 miles. Enjoy the views here, then head back the way you came.

44. Deception Crags

RATING/ DIFFICULTY	ROUNDTRIP	ELEV GAIN/ HIGH POINT	SEASON
**/1	1 mile	250 feet/ 1450 feet	Apr–Nov

Maps: Green Trails Bandera No. 206 and Mount Si NRCA No. 206S; **Contact:** Washington State Parks; **Notes:** Washington Discover Pass required; **GPS:** N 47 26.285, W 121 39.666

This easy walk provides some unique opportunities to view the local wildlife—Craggius rattius, better known as crag rats. These human creepy crawlers can be found hanging from their fingertips all along the rocky walls towering over the Iron Horse Trail near the Change Creek canyon. Of course, rock walls draw more than vertically oriented humans. An assortment of birds call these cliff faces home as well—swallows and swifts, hawks and falcons. Indeed, some of the most exciting wildlife moments come from swallows diving and swirling around the heads of climbers (who frequently will suck up close to the wall to avoid the "bombs" dropped by these small flyers).

GETTING THERE
From Seattle drive east on I-90 to exit 38. Turn right (south) onto old US Highway 10 and, after crossing the South Fork Snoqualmie River, continue on this road as it veers left. About 0.7 mile from the freeway, find a parking area just before crossing Change Creek (if you find yourself on a rickety old bridge, you've gone a bit too far).

ON THE TRAIL
No multiday assaults on multipitch, big-wall routes here. The most common form of climbing you'll see is actually bouldering, or climbing "low." In bouldering, climbers stick to the rock and seldom get more than 10 feet off the flat ground. Instead, they'll plaster themselves onto the rock face, then traverse along it, staying a few feet above the ground. It's a great sport to watch, and a great way to practice climbing without the fear of falling from heights.

The trail follows Change Creek, climbing steeply from the road to the Iron Horse Trail. Once on the Iron Horse, you'll immediately

On the way up to the Deception Crags area, Change Creek trestle rises above the trail.

be in the midst of the climbing world. Before you is Change Creek Wall. This tall face is usually streaked with white chalk scuffs, and on close inspection you'll see it is marred by countless steel bolts—climbers have drilled the wall and installed these permanent anchors into which they clip their ropes. The bolts improve safety, but are somewhat controversial among climbers, since they turn natural rock into gymlike, man-made climbing routes. Still, hikers will barely notice the bolts (unless you hear a purist climber howl in protest).

Hike east to cross Change Creek on a rustic trestle for views out over the South Fork Snoqualmie (I-90) valley. After visiting the trestle, head back west and continue past the trail you came up on to explore the base of several climbing walls along this short 0.5-mile stretch of trail as well as views down into Olallie State Park.

45 Dirty Harry

RATING/ DIFFICULTY	ROUNDTRIP	ELEV GAIN/ HIGH POINT	SEASON
***/3	5 miles	1300 feet/ 2600 feet	June–Oct

Maps: Green Trails Bandera No. 206 and Mount Si NRCA No. 206S; **Contact:** Mount Baker–Snoqualmie National Forest, Snoqualmie Ranger District, North Bend office; **Notes:** NW Forest Pass required; **GPS:** N 47 26.030, W 121 37.952

Go ahead, hike this way. Okay, Clint Eastwood I'm not. But this hike is more entertaining than any Dirty Harry movie you'll see. It follows an old logging road up to a high bench overlooking the central section of

McClellan Butte dominates the southern view from Dirty Harry Balcony.

the South Fork Snoqualmie River valley. The walking is fairly easy on this wide road-turned-trail, and the views are breathtaking. This previously unnamed peak was given its Hollywood-sounding name by wilderness advocate (and guidebook legend) Harvey Manning. The name is a backhanded memorial to Harry Gault, the logger who carved so many roads and clear-cuts into the mountains (including this one) of the Snoqualmie Valley. Dirty Harry indeed!

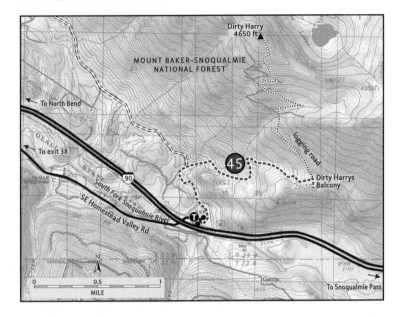

GETTING THERE

From Seattle drive east on I-90 to exit 38. After exiting, turn right, cross the Snoqualmie River, and follow Southeast Homestead Valley Road east about a mile, following signs to "State Fire Training Center." This will lead you under the freeway to roadside parking and a gate. Parking is not allowed beyond this gate, so park in the paved lot.

ON THE TRAIL

After you park outside the gate, walk a half mile up the road, crossing the South Fork Snoqualmie River, to the "Dirty Harry Logging Road" on the right—you'll find it in the middle of a left-hand curve. (Note that by walking up to this true starting point, you're far less likely to miss it.)

The next 1.5 miles of road walking is a little more exciting than the initial road, but

not much. Roadside trees limit the views until you get higher, so just enjoy the exercise as you climb to 2500 feet elevation.

About 2 miles from the gate (and your car), look for a faint path on the right just at the apex of a switchback to the left. This 0.1-mile-long boot trail climbs 100 feet to a rocky ledge Mr. Manning dubbed Dirty Harrys Balcony. Marvelous views sweep across the rugged mountains to the south and east. Big Mac (McClellan Butte) rises to the south. On your east flank is Bandera Mountain, while to the west Mount Washington rises into the sun.

EXTENDING YOUR TRIP

Turn your 5-mile hike into an 11-mile trek (with an additional 2000 feet of elevation gain) by continuing up the road-turned-trail route to the 4650-foot summit of Dirty Harry Peak.

46 McClellan Butte

RATING/ DIFFICULTY	ROUNDTRIP	ELEV GAIN/ HIGH POINT	SEASON
***/5	9 miles	3700 feet/ 5162 feet	June–Oct

Maps: Green Trails Bandera No. 206 and Snoqualmie Pass Gateway No. 207S; **Contact:** Mount Baker–Snoqualmie National Forest, Snoqualmie Ranger District, North Bend office; **Notes:** NW Forest Pass required. Avalanche danger when slopes are snow-covered; **GPS:** N 47 24.851, W 121 35.305

Sometimes, you hike the steep trails to get the best possible views. Other times, you hike the steep trails just because they are steep. McClellan Butte hikers generally fall into this latter category. The trail is steep and physically demanding, while the views are less spectacular than you'll find on other nearby trails. But folks flock to this wonderful trail, using it as a warm-up for more serious alpine adventures later in the year. And unlike other "training" hills (Mount Si and Granite Mountain, for instance), McClellan Butte doesn't draw hundreds of people every day in the spring and summer. You're not going to hike in solitude, of course (every trail in the I-90 corridor draws weekend boot traffic), but you might see only a few other people as you sweat your way to the summit.

GETTING THERE
From Seattle drive east on I-90 to exit 42 (West Tinkham Road). Turn right from the off-ramp and continue past the Department of Transportation office. The parking lot and

Summit block on McClellan Butte

trailhead are just past the office driveway on the right (west) side of the road.

ON THE TRAIL
Like much of the west side of the South Fork Snoqualmie valley (the I-90 corridor), loggers got to this mountain before you. The trail leaves the parking area and ascends through dense second-growth timber for about a mile, crossing the Iron Horse Trail (rail-to-trail route) about a half mile up the Alice Creek valley.

About a half mile past that broad trail, the trail to McClellan pokes out onto a rough old logging road. You might find vehicles

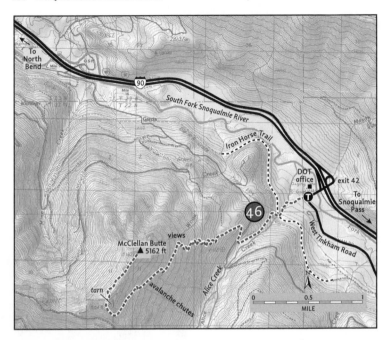

here, but don't worry. It's much better to park low and hike this far than to beat your vehicle to death on the long, roundabout, rough road.

After that first warm-up mile, the trail turns steep while the forest opens up a bit, with a few majestic old-growth behemoths still gracing this mountain retreat. The trail climbs ever steeper, winding through an endless series of tight switchbacks. Finally, about 2.5 miles into your hike, the trail levels a bit and rolls southwest to a very steep avalanche chute. Caution: This area can be covered in snow until well into July some years. If there is snowpack on the steep slope, come back when the way is clear, since the snow can slide at any time.

Beyond that potential hazard zone, the trail gets back to the business of climbing, offering you more switchbacks to enjoy. At 4.1 miles you'll crest the mountain's southern ridge (elev. 4500 feet). Stop here (as if you had a choice after that blistering climb!) and enjoy the views. Peer down into the deep, green wilderness of the Cedar River watershed (off-limits to most humans) and across the way to Kent Mountain.

The next 0.5 mile of trail rolls down to a small tarn, then up along the ridge spine toward the summit. Grand views can be had from the ridgetop viewpoints, and anyone without well-honed rock scrambling skills should consider stopping here. The last 100 vertical feet to the top of the mountain

Upper meadows open up views toward Mount Defiance on the Ira Spring Trail.

requires the use of hands and feet to move cautiously up to the 5162-foot summit.

47 Ira Spring Trail

RATING/ DIFFICULTY	ROUNDTRIP	ELEV GAIN/ HIGH POINT	SEASON
***/4	6 miles	2550 feet/ 4750 feet	June–Oct

Maps: Green Trails Bandera No. 206 and Snoqualmie Pass Gateway No. 207S; **Contact:** Mount Baker–Snoqualmie National Forest, Snoqualmie Ranger District, North Bend office; **Notes:** NW Forest Pass required; **GPS:** N 47 25.543, W 121 35.057

 *Hikers owe an incredible debt of thanks to Ira Spring. This soft-spoken man and his trail-loving photography did more for trail protection in Washington than any other person in hiking history. Ira was a tireless advocate for trails, working both behind the scenes and as one of the most recognizable trails spokesmen in the country. He lobbied Congress, influenced local land-management decisions,*

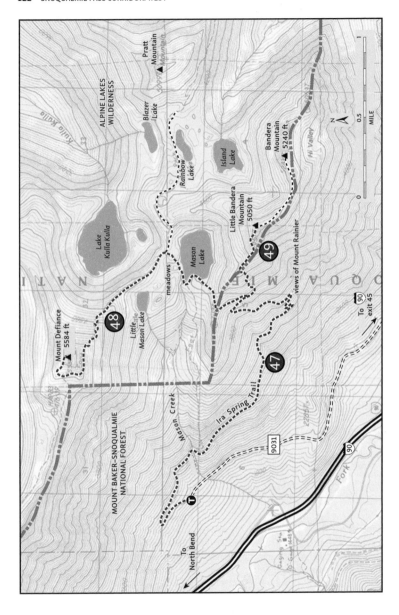

and introduced several generations of hik-ers to the wonders of Washington's trail network through the hiking guide series he created with Mountaineers Books. It is only fitting that this rehabilitated trail to Mason Lake bears his name. The fact that his namesake trail leads to a beautiful mountain lake is also appropriate, as Ira loved lakes of all kinds and sizes.

GETTING THERE

From Seattle drive east on I-90 to exit 45 (Forest Road 9030). Turn left over the freeway then left on FR 9030. About 0.8 mile from the freeway, you'll encounter a fork. The right fork leads to Talapus/Olallie trail-head. Stay straight on FR 9031, and in about 3 miles you'll come to a large parking lot.

ON THE TRAIL

Start up the road and in just 0.5 mile cross Mason Creek. You'll enjoy a couple of miles of walking on this old roadbed-turned-trail, giving you ample time to stretch and loosen up your muscles before starting the real climbing. The road ends at around 2 miles, and the new trail leads upward into the forest.

You'll find a trail junction near the Alpine Lakes Wilderness boundary at 2.9 miles out. Stay left here and continue climbing through the dense, young forest (regrowth that sprouted after a fire many decades ago). In 0.6 mile you'll crest the ridge (elev. 4750 feet) and start a short but steep descent (losing 500 feet in elevation) to the forested basin of Mason Lake.

Mason Lake is a deep pool, home to some fine—though hard to hook—trout. Enjoy a dip in the cool waters, if you don't want to try your angling skills, and then relax under the shady forest fringe and reflect on the man who helped save these mountains for hikers.

48 Mount Defiance

RATING/ DIFFICULTY	ROUNDTRIP	ELEV GAIN/ HIGH POINT	SEASON
*****/5	11 miles	3384 feet/ 5584 feet	Aug–Oct

Maps: Green Trails Bandera No. 206 and Snoqualmie Pass Gateway No. 207S; **Contact:** Mount Baker–Snoqualmie National Forest, Snoqualmie Ranger District, North Bend office; **Notes:** NW Forest Pass required; **GPS:** N 47 25.543, W 121 35.057

Defiance is futile! This peak and its stunning views will amaze you. The long ridge spine to the north of the South Fork Snoqualmie River (the I-90 cor-ridor) offers some of the steepest hiking trails in the Cascades, but also some of the best views. Mount Defiance gives you both, and lakeside rest areas make the thigh-burning climb well worth the effort. Plan your trip when the atmosphere is clear (right after or a few days before a storm— look for barometric pressure changes to clue in to weather changes). With clear skies and clean air around you, views will stretch across the breadth of Washing-ton—from Mount Baker near the Canadian border to Mount Adams (and very faintly, Mount Hood) near the Columbia River and the Oregon border.

GETTING THERE

From Seattle drive east on I-90 to exit 45 (Forest Road 9030). Turn left over the freeway then left on FR 9030. About 0.8 mile from the freeway, you'll encounter a fork. The right fork leads to Talapus/Olallie trail-head. Stay straight on FR 9031 and in about 3 miles you'll come to a large parking lot.

ON THE TRAIL

Start climbing the Ira Spring Trail, following it toward Mason Lake (Hike 47) as it ascends the old logging road and then becomes a true trail. At about 3.5 miles, as you skirt above the shore of Mason Lake, turn left at a trail fork. Right leads down alongside Mason Lake and on toward Rainbow and Pratt lakes.

This left-hand path climbs for 2 miles, running through forest and open slopes to an elevation of 5240 feet. You'll find yourself in a broad meadow packed with wildflowers and views. Those with no desire or skill to scramble can enjoy this wonderful wilderness garden, but those looking for a little more can push on.

A rough path runs steeply up the ridge to the summit of Mount Defiance at 5584 feet. From here, the views are as good as you'll find anywhere. Look due north for the snow-capped cone of Mount Baker, and to its right and a little closer in, Glacier Peak. Turn and face west to see the South Fork Snoqualmie valley running down into the Puget Sound lowlands and, beyond, the sawtooth ridges of the Olympic Mountains. Face south and enjoy the massive mountain that is Rainier, and behind it, Mount Adams. To the west of these you might see the abbreviated summit of Mount St. Helens, and in the gap between Adams and St. Helens, look for the faint outline of Mount Hood (count yourself lucky if you see it). Finally, look east and take in the long ridge to Bandera and Pratt mountains.

Lake Kulla Kulla and Mason Lake seen from Mount Defiance

49 Little Bandera Mountain

RATING/ DIFFICULTY	ROUNDTRIP	ELEV GAIN/ HIGH POINT	SEASON
***/4	7 miles	2850 feet/ 5050 feet	June–Oct

Maps: Green Trails Bandera No. 206 and Snoqualmie Pass Gateway No. 207S; **Contact:** Mount Baker–Snoqualmie National Forest, Snoqualmie Ranger District, North Bend office; **Notes:** NW Forest Pass required; **GPS:** N 47 25.543, W 121 35.057

Bandera may be the most overlooked mountain in the Snoqualmie Pass region. Granite Mountain, Mount Defiance, and McClellan Butte all get more traffic, though the climb to Bandera offers all of the same great features you'll find on those routes—with far fewer people to crowd you off the trail. Grand views, beautiful wildflowers, delicious berries, and a wonderful path through the wilderness await you here.

GETTING THERE
From Seattle drive east on I-90 to exit 45 (Forest Road 9030). Turn left over the freeway then left on FR 9030. About 0.8 mile from the freeway, you'll encounter a fork. The right fork leads to Talapus/Olallie trailhead. Stay straight on FR 9031 and in about 3 miles you'll come to a large parking lot.

ON THE TRAIL
Start climbing the Ira Spring Trail, following it as it ascends the old logging road. Continue as it traverses the slope until about the 2-mile mark, where the way turns steep. You'll find a trail junction near the Alpine Lakes Wilderness boundary at 2.9 miles out. The left trail leads to Mason Lake. Stay right to continue climbing up the open grassy meadow slopes to the ridge spine above.

View from Little Bandera Mountain down at I-90 and across the South Fork Snoqualmie valley

THE BEAR ESSENTIALS

Usually a bear encounter will involve only catching a glimpse of the bear's behind. But occasionally the bruin may actually want to get a look at *you*. In very rare cases a bear may act aggressively. If you did everything right (see "Bear in Mind" in the Introduction) and Yogi appears to be agitated, heed the following advice:

- **Respect a bear's need for personal space.** If you see a bear in the distance, make a wide detour around it, or if that's not possible (i.e., if the trail leads close to the bear) leave the area.
- **If you encounter a bear at close range, remain calm.** Do not run, as this may trigger a predator/prey reaction from the bear.
- **Talk in a low, calm manner** to the bear to help identify yourself as a human.
- **Hold your arms out from your body,** and if you are wearing a jacket, hold open the front so you appear to be as big as possible.
- **Don't stare directly at the bear**—the bear may interpret this as a direct threat or challenge. Watch the animal without making direct eye-to-eye contact.
- **Slowly move upwind of the bear** if you can do so without crowding it. The bear's strongest sense is its sense of smell, and if it can sniff you and identify you as human, it may retreat.
- **Know how to interpret bear actions.** A nervous bear will often rumble in its chest, clack its teeth, and "pop" its jaw. It may paw the ground and swing its head violently side to side. If the bear does this, watch it closely (without staring directly at it). Continue to speak low and calmly.
- **A bear may bluff-charge**—run at you but stop well before reaching you—to try to intimidate you. **Resist the eager desire to run from this charge,** as that would turn the bluff into a real charge and you will *not* be able to outrun the bear (black bears can run at speeds up to 35 miles per hour through log-strewn forests).
- **If you surprise a bear and it does charge from close range, lie down and play dead.** A surprised bear will leave you once the perceived threat is neutralized. However, if the bear wasn't attacking because it was surprised—if it charges from a long distance, or if it has had a chance to identify you and still attacks—you should fight back. A bear in this situation is behaving in a predatory manner (as opposed to the defensive attack of a surprised bear) and is looking at you as food. Kick, stab, and punch at the bear. If it knows you will fight back, it may leave you and search for easier prey.
- **Carry a 12-ounce (or larger) can of bear spray.** The spray—a high concentration of oils from hot peppers—should fire out at least 20 or 30 feet in a broad mist. Don't use the spray unless a bear is actually charging and is in range of the spray.

Once on the ridge, the trail rolls up the spine through high alpine forest and across granite slopes to the summit of Little Bandera at 5050 feet, nearly 3.5 miles out. Stop here for a long pause and enjoy the panoramic views. These are views equal to any you'll find in the region, sweeping in the entire western face of the Cascades north to south.

EXTENDING YOUR TRIP

If you're not a summit bagger, turn back at Little Bandera, satisfied that you've seen the best views of the route. Otherwise, continue about another mile of forested walking along the rolling ridgeline, reaching the true summit of Bandera Mountain at 5240 feet—don't expect views from the timbered summit, however.

50 Talapus and Olallie Lakes

RATING/ DIFFICULTY	ROUNDTRIP	ELEV GAIN/ HIGH POINT	SEASON
***/2	4 miles	1220 feet/ 3780 feet	May–Oct

Maps: Green Trails Bandera No. 206 and Snoqualmie Pass Gateway No. 207S; **Contact:** Mount Baker–Snoqualmie National Forest, Snoqualmie Ranger District, North Bend office; **Notes:** NW Forest Pass required; **GPS:** N 47 24.041, W 121 31.137

These two easy-to-reach lakes receive a lot of visitors every sunny summer weekend, but don't let that keep you away. All those people can't be wrong—even if it means sharing. In fact, bring the kids—by mid-August the snow-fed lakes have warmed enough that you can take a swim without turning blue. Even if cool mountain lake swimming isn't your bag, there's still a lot to keep kids occupied. There are some trout (though they get a lot of fishing pressure), and other critters abound. Deer are frequent visitors, and

Logs collect near the outlet of Talapus Lake.

gray jays (aka camp robber jays) have learned to congregate wherever hikers travel en masse. Indeed, these beautiful birds can be downright pesky. Keep a close eye on your gorp bag, or you might find a camp robber carrying it off.

GETTING THERE

From Seattle drive east on I-90 to exit 45 (Forest Road 9030). Turn left to cross over the freeway then left on FR 9030. About 0.8 mile from the freeway, you'll encounter a fork. Turn right onto Talapus Road and drive to the Talapus/Olallie trailhead at the road's end.

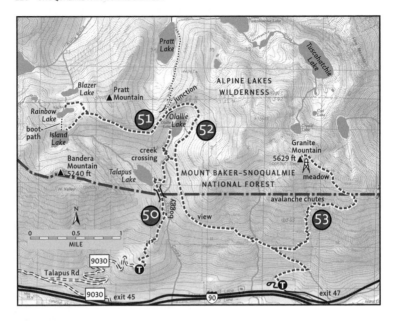

ON THE TRAIL

From the parking area, head up the broad trail as it climbs through easy switchbacks for the first mile. As you cross into the Alpine Lakes Wilderness the route levels out through a broad bench that boasts a bit of a bog. As you move through this wet section, try to stay on the trail even if it's a bit muddy—better to dirty your boots than to erode more land around the trail.

The trail soon sweeps across a small bridge (crossing the lake's outlet) just below Talapus Lake, then climbs the last few yards to the lakeshore at 3250 feet. Forests push in along the shores of this pretty lake, with talus tapering down to the water's edge on the far side. Anglers can wet their lines in this lake first, and families can find fine swimming opportunities along its banks.

The trail climbs away from Talapus before traversing the valley wall, heading up the valley to Olallie. About 0.7 mile from Talapus, stay left at a small trail junction and proceed upvalley to the outlet of Olallie Lake. This pretty lake sits in a nice alpine basin, providing plenty of opportunities to enjoy cooling shade under the boughs of towering firs. It also offers sun lovers a chance to get warm while catching a few rays on the rocks along the shore.

51 Island and Rainbow Lakes

RATING/ DIFFICULTY	ROUNDTRIP	ELEV GAIN/ HIGH POINT	SEASON
****/4	10 miles	2000 feet/ 4400 feet	June–Oct

Maps: Green Trails Bandera No. 206 and Snoqualmie Pass Gateway No. 207S; **Con-**

tact: Mount Baker–Snoqualmie National Forest, Snoqualmie Ranger District, North Bend office; **Notes:** NW Forest Pass required; **GPS:** N 47 24.041, W 121 31.137

🦴 🐾 🐾 *If you want to shed the crowds while still exploring the wonderful routes of the western Snoqualmie Pass region, this might be the destination to consider. Sure, you'll have to share the first section of the route with the hordes, but most of the casual hikers will drop out at Talapus or Olallie lake. By pushing on, you get higher and quieter country to explore as well as a much more scenic lake basin to enjoy.*

GETTING THERE

From Seattle drive east on I-90 to exit 45 (Forest Road 9030). Turn left over the freeway then left on FR 9030. About 0.8 mile from the freeway, you'll encounter a fork. Turn right onto Talapus Road and drive to the Talapus/Olallie trailhead at the road's end.

ON THE TRAIL

Head up the trail toward Talapus and Olallie lakes (Hike 50), looping through a couple of long switchbacks before crossing into the Alpine Lakes Wilderness at about 1 mile.

In a long 0.25 mile past that boundary you'll find yourself at Talapus Lake (elev. 3250 feet), and in another mile you'll swing around the Olallie Lake basin. Avoid the trail to the lakeshore of Olallie. Instead, turn right and cross the creek, then turn left at the next trail junction (just above the creek) to stay on the high trail as it sweeps along the hillside to the east of the lake.

The trail curves to the west along the headwall of the lake basin, and at 3.6 miles from the trailhead it reaches another trail

An osprey leaves its fishing perch along the lakeshore to check out the photographer.

junction. Stay left (Hike 52, Pratt Lake Basin, is to the right). Skirt the flank of Pratt Mountain for 1 mile to a high point above Island and Rainbow lakes. Turn left here and drop 0.4 mile to Island Lake, or stay right and drop 0.5 mile to Rainbow. A small boot-beaten path through the woods links the two lakes.

52 Pratt Lake Basin

RATING/ DIFFICULTY	ROUNDTRIP	ELEV GAIN/ HIGH POINT	SEASON
****/4	8 miles	2300 feet/ 4100 feet	June–Oct

Maps: Green Trails Bandera No. 206 and Snoqualmie Pass Gateway No. 207S; **Contact:** Mount Baker–Snoqualmie National Forest, Snoqualmie Ranger District, North Bend office; **Notes:** NW Forest Pass required; **GPS:** N 47 23.874, W 121 29.163

🦴 🐾 ⭐ *The path to Pratt Lake was once a braided super highway, at times more than 10 feet wide.*

Hardly the stuff of wilderness. But Washington Trails Association (WTA) volunteers stepped in and rebuilt the trail. Not only did they rebuild the tread to channel all hikers onto the proper path, they decommissioned all of the unauthorized secondary trails, creating a new single track worthy of a pristine wild area. Hikers can now stroll easily up this picturesque trail to the pretty Pratt Lake basin.

GETTING THERE

From Seattle drive east on I-90 to exit 47 (Asahel Curtis/Denny Creek). Turn north over the freeway, turn left at the T, and drive to the nearby Pratt Lake–Granite Mountain parking area.

ON THE TRAIL

The first mile of trail is busy. You're sharing this section with crowds headed for Granite Mountain (Hike 53). But don't worry: at the 1-mile mark most of your fellow hikers will peel off to the right as you push on straight ahead to Pratt Lake.

At around 2.5 miles out you'll find a fine viewpoint at 3400 feet. Pause to take pictures of the Snoqualmie Valley and the peaks above the Olallie, Talapus, and Pratt lake basins. Just beyond you'll enter the Alpine Lakes Wilderness, and then you'll encounter a side trail at 3.8 miles leading down to forest-rimmed Talapus Lake.

A scant 0.25 mile past this junction you'll reach a low saddle (elev. 4100 feet)

Kaleeten Peak from the approach to Pratt Lake

separating the higher Pratt Lake basin from the Talapus and Olallie basins. This is a great place to stop for a rest and, in late August (most years), to harvest the abundant huckleberries. Turn around here unless you really need to reach the lake.

EXTENDING YOUR TRIP

If you're a lake bagger, push on the final 1.6 miles as the trail swings around the basin walls. Turn right at the ridgetop and slowly angle down to the shores of Pratt Lake (elev. 3400 feet).

53 Granite Mountain

RATING/ DIFFICULTY	ROUNDTRIP	ELEV GAIN/ HIGH POINT	SEASON
*****/5	8 miles	3800 feet/ 5629 feet	July–Oct

Map: Green Trails Snoqualmie Pass Gateway No. 207S; **Contact:** Mount Baker–Snoqualmie National Forest, Snoqualmie Ranger District, North Bend office; **Notes:** NW Forest Pass required. Avalanche danger when slopes are snow-covered; **GPS:** N 47 23.874, W 121 29.163

One look at the parking lot midday on any summer weekend, and the obvious will jump out and bite you: the Granite Mountain Trail is the most heavily traveled summit path in the Snoqualmie Pass corridor. Of course, there is a good reason for that: it's spectacular. But it's also steep. Mind-numbingly, thigh-burning steep. You'll climb a heel-blistering 3800 feet in 4.3 miles to an old fire lookout at the 5629-foot summit, with awesome views in all directions. Pack

The lookout at the summit of Granite Mountain on a day socked in the clouds

plenty of water, as there is no good source along the trail.

GETTING THERE

From Seattle drive east on I-90 to exit 47 (Asahel Curtis/Denny Creek). Turn north over the freeway, turn left at the T, and drive to the nearby Pratt Lake–Granite Mountain parking area.

ON THE TRAIL

The trail starts out climbing. You'll hike away from the trailhead parking area through a lush old forest and gain a solid 800 feet in the first mile. At 1 mile the trail forks. Turn right off this relatively flat trail for some serious climbing (Hike 52 to Pratt Lake basin goes left).

In the next 0.5 mile the switchbacks are easy, if a bit steeper. But as you near 2 miles the switchbacks get tighter, the trail gets steeper, and the breathing gets more difficult. At 4000 feet elevation you'll get a breather as the trail angles across a tricky avalanche chute.

Caution: Early in the year the upper mountain is covered in snow and ice, and the upper slopes are very avalanche prone. If you're here anytime before mid-June (most years), pause before crossing the chute and look up the gully. If there is still snow above you, be extremely careful—slides can happen at any time.

Once across, the trail starts climbing again. If you time your trek just right, you'll find huckleberries alongside the trail all the way to the ridgetop. You'll also break out of the trees and start exploring wide, steeply slanted meadows. Bulbous bear grass fills these meadows in early summer, and when those white blooms disappear, lupine and paintbrush color the slopes red and blue.

At 5200 feet you'll crest the summit ridge,

getting a brief reprieve from the ruthless climbing as you cross a meadow. You still have another half mile or so to cover along the ridge crest and then up the summit crown, but the hardest work is behind you. Note: Early season hikers, be aware that many years this north-side basin holds snow well into July, and routefinding can be a bit confusing. Use caution. Once at the top enjoy the 360-degree views from the lookout—on some weekends, volunteers open it up to visitors.

54 Denny Creek

RATING/ DIFFICULTY	ROUNDTRIP	ELEV GAIN/ HIGH POINT	SEASON
***/2	4 miles	700 feet/ 3000 feet	June–Oct

Map: Green Trails Snoqualmie Pass Gateway No. 207S; **Contact:** Mount Baker–Snoqualmie National Forest, Snoqualmie Ranger District, North Bend office; **Notes:** NW Forest

Lower section of Denny Creek

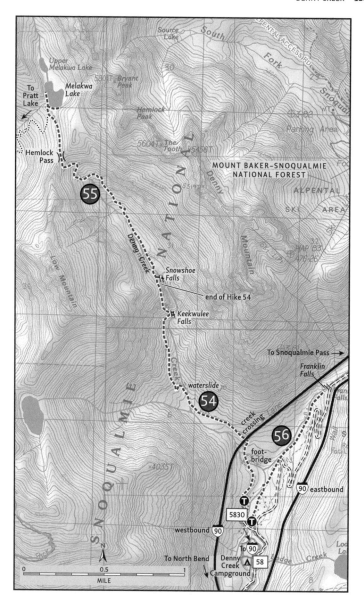

Source Lake

South

Fork

Snoqua

Upper
Melakwa Lake

To
Pratt
Lake

Melakwa
Lake

5801T

Bryant
Peak

30

Hemlock
Peak

4400

Parking Area

Hemlock
Pass

5604T The
Tooth 5456T

55/9?6T

Denny

MOUNT BAKER–SNOQUALMIE
NATIONAL FOREST

ALPENTAL

55

SKI AREA

Denny Creek

Low Mountain

36

Snowshoe
Falls

end of Hike 54

Keekwulee
Falls

Creek

Mountain

SKI LIFTS

32
HAP 83

476-26

NATIONAL

To Snoqualmie Pass →

Franklin
Falls

54

waterslide

creek
crossing

56

foot-
bridge

4035T

90 eastbound

T
5830

T

S
N
O
Q
U
A
L
M
I
E

westbound 90

To North Bend

Denny
Creek
Campground

To 90

58

Creek

N

0   0.5   1

MILE

Pass required. In spring 2009 the bridge at the 1.3-mile-mark crossing of Denny Creek washed out. Now it is possible to cross there safely only in late summer's low water; **GPS:** N 47 24.903, W 121 26.593

 Denny Creek may be the most family-friendly trail in the region. The popular path leads to a series of waterfalls and to a smooth natural waterslide—a massive rock face over which the creek flows, providing a slippery summertime escape from the heat of the lowlands. Just beyond, hikers will find a couple more falls—most notably the beautiful Keekwulee Falls.

GETTING THERE

From Seattle drive east on I-90 to exit 47 (Asahel Curtis/Denny Creek). Turn left over the overpass and proceed to a T. Turn right and travel 0.25 mile to Denny Creek Road (Forest Road 58). Turn left and drive 2.5 miles, passing the Denny Creek Campground. Just past the campground, turn left onto FR 5830. The trailhead is at the road's end.

ON THE TRAIL

Head up the trail as it rolls north under the high viaduct that carries I-90 traffic west. The trail crosses a creek at about a half mile, then winds through the forested valley before recrossing the creek at base of the waterslide rock at about 1.3 miles.

Come mid-August, you'll certainly find hikers—young and old—sporting in the cold water of Denny Creek as it slides over the granite slabs. The creek is shallow enough to be safe, but strong enough to be fun. You'll want to stick close to the kids, though, as there is a small plunge pool at the end of the slab, and the cold water can be shocking.

After cooling off, keep moving up the trail. Just above the waterslide at 1.4 miles is a small stair-step falls, Keekwulee Falls. In another 0.5 mile (2 miles from the trailhead) is the small Snowshoe Falls. Turn around here for a 4-mile hike. Be sure to stop at the waterslide on your way out—it's worth another round of water play before driving home.

EXTENDING YOUR TRIP

Should your waterplay leave you rejuvenated and energized, you can press on from Snowshoe Falls all the way to Melakwa Lake for a 9-mile roundtrip (see Hike 55).

55 Melakwa Lake

RATING/ DIFFICULTY	ROUNDTRIP	ELEV GAIN/ HIGH POINT	SEASON
***/4	9 miles	2300 feet/ 4600 feet	June–Oct

Map: Green Trails Snoqualmie Pass Gateway No. 207S; **Contact:** Mount Baker–Snoqualmie National Forest, Snoqualmie Ranger District, North Bend office; **Notes:** NW Forest Pass required. In spring 2009 the bridge at the 1.3-mile-mark crossing of Denny Creek washed out. Now it is possible to cross there safely only in late summer's low water. **GPS:** N 47 24.903, W 121 26.593

Crowds disappear once you are past Denny Creek's waterfalls (Hike 54)—the hordes thinning to a respectable number of serious hikers looking for an alpine lake experience. And what an experience! The trail finally crests Hemlock Pass and descends moderately to Melakwa Lake, a broad alpine wonder with rocky slopes leading straight down into the crystal water. Those bright waters also

reflect the craggy peaks that ring the lake:
most notably Chair and Kaleetan peaks.

GETTING THERE

From Seattle drive east on I-90 to exit 47 (Asahel Curtis/Denny Creek). Turn left over the overpass and proceed to a T. Turn right and travel 0.25 mile to Denny Creek Road (Forest Road 58). Turn left and drive 2.5 miles, passing the Denny Creek Campground. Just past the campground, turn left onto FR 5830. The trailhead is at the road's end.

ON THE TRAIL

Hike up the trail as it rolls under the I-90 westbound viaduct to the Denny Creek waterslide at 1.3 miles. You'll pass Keekwulee Falls and Snowshoe Falls at 1.4 and 2 miles and will then climb the long, steep valley of Denny Creek. The path crosses the creek

Melakwa Lake

periodically and ambles through dense forest and across rocky avalanche chutes.

At about 3 miles the trail gets serious about climbing and weaves up a series of switchbacks to Hemlock Pass at 3.5 miles (elev. 4600 feet). Note: Use caution if you are here early in the summer, when solid snowpack still covers the ground from Hemlock Pass to the lake. It is easy to lose your sense of direction here and end up dropping down westward into the Pratt River basin. Many search-and-rescue missions have occurred here in recent years. The trail slides through the forested pass (yes, it's largely a hemlock forest), before dropping gradually over the next mile, then comes to a trail junction where going right takes you to the shores of Melakwa Lake.

Avoid walking though the fragile meadows as much as possible—there's enough rock and established trail that you won't need to further damage the already trampled heather and wildflower fields around the lake.

EXTENDING YOUR TRIP

The left path from the trail junction near the lake continues another 3 miles, descending along the lake's outlet stream to Lower Tuscohatchie Lake, and at 3.5 miles from Melakwa Lake, reaches Pratt Lake (Hike 52). This is a rough trail with far less traffic than the path to Melakwa.

56 Franklin Falls

RATING/ DIFFICULTY	ROUNDTRIP	ELEV GAIN/ HIGH POINT	SEASON
***/1	2 miles	400 feet/ 2600 feet	June–Nov

Map: Green Trails Snoqualmie Pass Gateway No. 207S; **Contact:** Mount Baker–Snoqualmie

Deer fern fonds uncurling in the spring

National Forest, Snoqualmie Ranger District, North Bend office; **Notes:** NW Forest Pass required; **GPS:** N 47 24.780, W 121 26.493

👨‍👧 📖 🏠 *Settlers heading for the Puget Sound lowlands had few route options: they could float down the Columbia River (portaging around the falls near The Dalles), take a ship through the Pacific—either from California, or all the way around from the Atlantic—or take Snoqualmie Pass Wagon Road. This road was originally a trading path used by Native Americans, and later a mule trail used by fur traders. Eventually, settlers and traders carried goods on wagons over this lowest of the Cascade passes. Today's interstate uses parts of the old wagon track, but in the Denny Creek area, where the interstate splits, the old wagon trace is still visible.*

GETTING THERE
From Seattle drive east on I-90 to exit 47 (Asahel Curtis/Denny Creek). Turn left over the overpass and proceed to a T. Turn right and travel 0.25 mile to Denny Creek Road (Forest Road 58). Turn left and drive 2.5 miles, passing the Denny Creek Campground. Just past the campground, turn left onto FR 5830 and park before crossing the bridge.

ON THE TRAIL
The trail is well marked as it follows the old wagon track along the South Fork Snoqualmie River. There's also a continuation of Denny Creek Road as it follows the old highway route up to the pass. If the kids get footsore on the mile-long hike up to the falls, let them skip down the road on the way back. But the trail is the better option, as it climbs through the mossy forest, periodically crossing the old carved ruts of the wagon road—those steel-shod wooden wagon wheels cut deep.

The path reaches Franklin Falls at 1 mile, with the last 100 yards climbing steeply on rocky trail to the base of the falls. The tall falls pounds down a sheer rock face, providing a refreshing spray to cool hot hikers. Don't venture out into the falls water, however. It's coming down hard and frequently carries loose rocks down with the tumbling water.

57 Asahel Curtis Nature Trail

RATING/ DIFFICULTY	LOOP	ELEV GAIN/ HIGH POINT	SEASON
***/1	0.5 mile	180 feet/ 2000 feet	June–Nov

Map: Green Trails Snoqualmie Pass Gateway No. 207S; **Contact:** Mount Baker–Snoqualmie

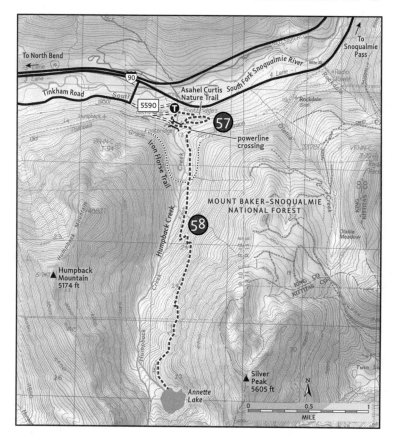

National Forest, Snoqualmie Ranger District, North Bend office; **Notes:** NW Forest Pass required; **GPS:** N 47 23.560, W 121 28.465

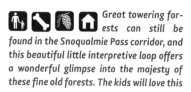 Great towering forests can still be found in the Snoqualmie Pass corridor, and this beautiful little interpretive loop offers a wonderful glimpse into the majesty of these fine old forests. The kids will love this

walk through the woods. They can scamper over massive fallen logs, marvel at towering trees, and listen to the flitterings and callings of birds. The trail is named for perhaps the most renowned photographer in Washington history.

GETTING THERE

From Seattle drive east on I-90 to exit 47 (Asahel Curtis/Denny Creek). Turn right

The Asahel Curtis Trail winds past massive old-growth trees.

from the off-ramp and continue 0.25 mile, then turn left on Forest Road 5590. You'll find the parking area in 0.3 mile.

ON THE TRAIL

Minnesota-born Asahel Curtis moved to Washington in 1888 at the age of fourteen and started working in a family-owned photo studio when he was twenty. He soon became the preeminent photographer in the Seattle area, documenting the natural landscape, the native people, and the historical elements

of the Pacific Northwest right up until his death in 1941. The Washington State History Museum holds more than sixty thousand of his photographic images.

This trail named for Curtis gives a taste of what inspired him. It first meanders away from the trailhead, following Humpback Creek through the refreshingly cool old forest. This moss-laden woodland felt the bite of axes in the early part of the twentieth century, but today the scars of logging are limited to old stumps—many now nursing new trees in the old, rotting cores. The short path loops through these old forests, exploring both natural and human history while providing a wonderfully peaceful walk through the forest primeval.

58 Annette Lake

RATING/ DIFFICULTY	ROUNDTRIP	ELEV GAIN/ HIGH POINT	SEASON
***/3	7.5 miles	1700 feet/ 3600 feet	June–Oct

Map: Green Trails Snoqualmie Pass Gateway No. 207S; **Contact:** Mount Baker–Snoqualmie National Forest, Snoqualmie Ranger District, North Bend office; **Notes:** NW Forest Pass required; **GPS:** N 47 23.560, W 121 28.465

  *Dense forest drapes the lower trail, keeping hik-*ers cool on the hottest August afternoons. At trail's end, a deep lake waits to kill off the last of the summer heat—for those brave enough to dive into its icy waters. Between the thick second-growth-forest stands and the high alpine lake, the trail rolls along Humpback Creek, offering tantalizing views now and again of pretty waterfalls along the tumbling creek.

GETTING THERE

From Seattle drive east on I-90 to exit 47 (Asahel Curtis/Denny Creek). Turn right from the off-ramp and continue 0.25 mile, then turn left on Forest Road 5590. You'll find the parking area in 0.3 mile.

ON THE TRAIL

The trail begins alongside the Asahel Curtis Nature Trail (Hike 57) but continues to climb

Silver Peak rises from the eastern shores of Annette Lake.

to the right when the loop goes left. You'll follow an old logging road (mostly reclaimed by the fertile forest).

At about 1 mile out, you'll pass under a high-tension powerline and 0.25 mile later will cross the wide track of the Iron Horse Trail (the old railroad right-of-way). From this point, the trail gets serious—serious about scenery, and serious about climbing.

The path switchbacks up the Humpback Creek valley for more than 1.5 miles until the last steep pitch puts you at about 3600 feet elevation. For the next mile, you'll traverse the slope above Humpback Creek, with occasional views across the valley to Humpback Mountain. The trail ends at the shores of Annette Lake, which lies in the cirque between Humpback Mountain, Abiel Peak, and Silver Peak.

Opposite: Denny Mountain reflects in the calm, glass-like waters of Lodge Lake.

snoqualmie pass area

Say "Snoqualmie Pass" to just about anyone in Washington, and they'll think "Interstate 90." This low pass in the center of the Cascade Range has a long history. Native tribes used the path through the pass as a trade route. Early settlers upgraded the trail to a wagon road. Later, a railroad track was added to the wagon road, and the wagon road was upgraded into a motorway. Today, the freeway represents the core use of the Snoqualmie Pass corridor. But fast travel from east to west reveals only the veneer most people see when they look at Snoqualmie Pass. A closer look uncovers the pass as a gateway to one of the most spectacular wilderness areas in the country. The Alpine Lakes Wilderness, found just north of Snoqualmie Pass, draws backcountry recreationists like flies to honey—for good reason. High craggy peaks, crystal-clear alpine lakes, and lush forests and meadows await you in the Alpine Lakes and in the surrounding mountains and valleys.

wild heart of the Cascades with minimal driving and easy hiking. The trail starts just off the most heavily used highway in the Cascades, yet you'll soon find yourself caught deep in the wilderness experience as you stride into the fragrant forests, scrambling over the tumbling creeks of crystal-clear snowmelt waters and climbing through the rocky meadows in this mountain valley.

GETTING THERE
From Seattle drive I-90 to exit 52 (signed for Snoqualmie Pass west). At the bottom of the exit ramp, turn left (north) and cross under the freeway. In about 100 yards, turn right

Guye Peak above the trail into Commonwealth Basin

59 Commonwealth Basin

RATING/ DIFFICULTY	ROUNDTRIP	ELEV GAIN/ HIGH POINT	SEASON
****/4	10 miles	2700 feet/ 5350 feet	July–Oct

Map: Green Trails Snoqualmie Pass Gateway No. 207S; **Contact:** Mount Baker–Snoqualmie National Forest, Snoqualmie Ranger District, North Bend office; **Notes:** NW Forest Pass required; **GPS:** N 47 25.722, W 121 24.806

There's nothing common about Commonwealth Basin. This deep canyon nestled in the shadows of Red Mountain and Kendall Peak offers a great opportunity to explore the

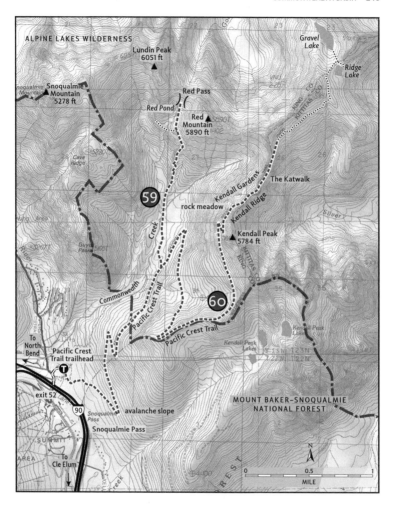

onto a dirt road leading to the Pacific Crest Trail (PCT) trailhead.

ON THE TRAIL

Start up the PCT as it climbs into the trees above the parking lot and makes a long, lazy sweep southeast before rounding a hairpin turn to return northwest across the lower end of an avalanche slope. The jumble of trees piled around the trail illustrates how powerful a little snow can be when it starts to slide downhill. The trail stays in the trees for 2.5 miles before reaching a fork. The PCT continues to climb (Hike 60), while your path angles off left, slicing up into the valley of Commonwealth Creek.

The trail continues up the creek for the next mile, climbing moderately to the headwall of the basin. Here, the going gets tough as the trail runs upward through a long series of tight, steep switchbacks. At nearly 4 miles the route levels a bit as the forest finally gives way to heather meadows.

At 4.5 miles you'll pass above Red Pond (elev. 4860 feet)—a short spur trail drops down to it. Huckleberries can be found in season around the pond basin, and a variety

Kendall Katwalk, a section of the PCT blasted into the side of a cliff, is an attraction all to its own.

of wildflowers color the meadows above and below the pond.

The final 0.5 mile of trail gains 500 feet as it rises up to the saddle of Red Pass on the ridge between Red Mountain and Lundin Peak. Grand views can be enjoyed from here.

60 Kendall Katwalk

RATING/ DIFFICULTY	ROUNDTRIP	ELEV GAIN/ HIGH POINT	SEASON
*****/4	11 miles	2700 feet/ 5400 feet	July–Oct

Map: Green Trails Snoqualmie Pass Gateway No. 207S; **Contact:** Mount Baker–Snoqualmie National Forest, Snoqualmie Ranger District, North Bend office; **Notes:** NW Forest Pass required; **GPS:** N 47 25.722, W 121 24.806

The Katwalk offers a remarkable hiking experience—striding on a narrow shelf hundreds of feet in the air. The trail, blasted into the cliff face by dynamite crews hanging suspended from ropes, is perfectly safe once the winter's snow has completely melted off. If snow lingers, don't attempt to cross—it's not the place to slip and fall. There is, of course, more to this hike than just the Katwalk. The Pacific Crest Trail (PCT) climbs from Snoqualmie Pass through old-growth forests, dances through a log-littered avalanche slope (a perfect place to see just how powerful an avalanche can be), and traverses broad, steep-sloped wildflower meadows.

GETTING THERE
From Seattle drive I-90 to exit 52 (signed for Snoqualmie Pass west). At the bottom of the exit ramp, turn left (north) and cross

under the freeway. In about 100 yards, turn right onto a dirt road leading to the PCT trailhead.

ON THE TRAIL

Climbing moderately for the first 2.5 miles, the trail runs through forests on the flank of Kendall Peak. At the junction with the Commonwealth Basin Trail (Hike 59), go right and continue up the PCT. Just past that junction, the trail steepens into a series of long switchbacks.

The forest thins as the trail gains elevation, and about 3.5 miles into the hike the forest starts to break up as small clearings and meadows appear. Soon, the trail angles across the open meadows below Kendall Ridge. Red Mountain fills the skyline ahead while wildflowers color the ground around your feet.

These wildflower fields—known to some as Kendall Gardens—continue as the trail crests the ridge and angles north through a jumble of boulders on the ridgetop. Finally, at 5.5 miles, the gardens narrow to a mere path, and the path suddenly disappears onto a broad shelf on the east face of the ridge. This is the Katwalk. The timid can turn back on the near side, but most hikers prefer to cross the Katwalk before heading back to the gardens for a leisurely lunch and the return hike to the trailhead.

EXTENDING YOUR TRIP

Those who want to spend the night can continue another 2 miles on relatively level trail to a pair of lakes that border the trail just below Alaska Mountain—the best campsites are just south of Ridge Lake, but Gravel Lake (on the north side of the trail) also has a few good spots.

Snow Lake

61 Snow Lake

RATING/ DIFFICULTY	ROUNDTRIP	ELEV GAIN/ HIGH POINT	SEASON
****/3	6 miles	1400 feet/ 4400 feet	July–Oct

Map: Green Trails Snoqualmie Pass Gateway No. 207S; **Contact:** Mount Baker–Snoqualmie National Forest, Snoqualmie Ranger District, North Bend office; **Notes:** NW Forest Pass required; **GPS:** N 47 26.725, W 121 25.381

If there's such a thing as a wilderness superhighway, this is it. The Snow Lake Trail is Washington's most heavily used trail within a designated wilderness area. On any given summer weekend, you can expect to share the area

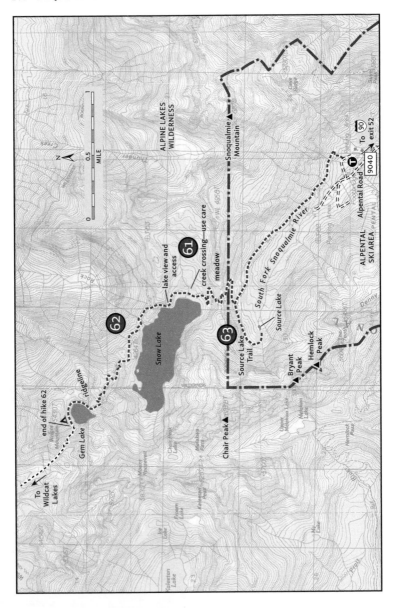

with upward of two hundred hikers. Fortunately, midweek the route is virtually deserted, and after Labor Day the number of weekend hikers drops to more reasonable levels. Why is it so popular? It's a combination of easy-to-access wilderness trail and a route to one of the most picturesque lakes in the water-rich Alpine Lakes Wilderness. Snow Lake is surrounded by high granite peaks and is visited by deer, mountain goats, and a host of small critters and birds. What's more, the lakeshores are lined with wildflowers in early summer and juicy huckleberries later in the year. All in all, the crowds are justified—few places that are so easy to reach offer such a stunning wilderness experience.

GETTING THERE

From Seattle drive east on I-90 to exit 52 (signed for Snoqualmie Pass west). Turn left (north), crossing under the freeway. Go 100 yards past the turnoff for the Pacific Crest Trail (PCT) on the right, then turn right onto Alpental Road (Forest Road/9040) and continue to the end of the road at the Alpental Ski Area parking lot.

ON THE TRAIL

Find the trail at the northeastern corner of the broad parking area (directly across from the ski lodge), and start up the long trail as it climbs a series of crib steps. These wooden "cribs" backfilled with dirt earn curses from some hikers, but they were necessary improvements. Volunteers added them in the late 1990s to reverse the ravages of erosion that plagued the trail. As you walk up the steps over the first half mile or so, take time to admire the workmanship and intensive effort that went into rescuing this trail from destruction. The steps may not match

your stride perfectly, but the alternative would be a lost trail.

After that first 0.5 mile, the trail traverses the slope above the upper South Fork Snoqualmie River, rolling through forest and occasional alder-filled avalanche chutes for nearly 1.5 miles to a trail junction at that headwall of the valley. A secondary path (Hike 63) leads off to the left, contouring around the headwall and leading to Source Lake, the headwaters of the South Fork Snoqualmie River that flows to North Bend.

The trail to Snow Lake goes right and climbs long, steep switchbacks up the headwall to a high saddle between Snoqualmie Mountain and Chair Peak. As you climb, you'll enjoy increasingly fine views of the craggy peaks of the Snoqualmie Pass area. The long ridge to the southwest starts with Chair Peak at the end of the ridge you're climbing, and south from there is Bryant Peak, The Tooth, and Denny Mountain.

At about 2.5 miles, you'll crest the meadow-covered ridge (elev. 4400 feet) and start a moderately steep descent over the last 0.5 mile to the lakeshore. You can stroll all the way around the steep northeastern shore of the sprawling lake on the boot-beaten trail, but please don't create new paths—or widen any of the other faint way trails that have been kicked into the heather by hikers' boots.

62 Gem Lake

RATING/ DIFFICULTY	ROUNDTRIP	ELEV GAIN/ HIGH POINT	SEASON
*****/4	10 miles	2200 feet/ 4927 feet	July–Oct

Map: Green Trails Snoqualmie Pass Gateway No. 207S; **Contact:** Mount Baker–

Wright Mountain, to the north of sapphire-colored Gem Lake

Snoqualmie National Forest, Snoqualmie Ranger District, North Bend office; **Notes:** NW Forest Pass required; **GPS:** N 47 26.725, W 121 25.381

![icons] *Sometimes you have to work a little harder to get what others can't reach. Such is the case here. As stunning as the deep blue basin of Snow Lake is, the little jewel nestled high above it is even more stunning. And far less crowded. While the hordes stop at Snow Lake, savvy (and fit!) hikers will push on, climbing steeply another 2 miles from the southern end of Snow to reach the shoreline of Gem, cradled in a meadow-filled basin atop the ridge to the north of the more popular lake.*

GETTING THERE

From Seattle drive east on I-90 to exit 52 (signed for Snoqualmie Pass west). Turn left (north), crossing under the freeway. Go 100 yards past the turnoff for the Pacific Crest Trail (PCT) on the right, then turn right onto Alpental Road (Forest Road/9040) and continue to the end of the road at the Alpental Ski Area parking lot.

ON THE TRAIL

Hike the popular trail from the Alpental parking lot to Snow Lake (Hike 61). At 3 miles, you'll be standing just above the lakeshore near a small inlet stream. Continue hiking north along the eastern shore (usually high above it) of the lake, before angling upward more steeply at about 3.4 miles.

The trail climbs a rock-strewn ridge snout, then bisects a couple of flower-filled—and usually mosquito-filled—marshy meadows before making the final ascent up a steep talus slope to crest the ridge above the Gem basin at 4.5 miles. Drop down to the shoreline for a relaxing break at the water's edge. There are some camps high in the tree-speckled meadows to the north and east of the lake.

Anglers should note that a strong population of brook trout thrives in Gem, and they can frequently be enticed to nibble on small dry flies. Nonanglers might be tempted to cool off in the crystal clear waters of Gem, but before diving in they should dip in a toe: The lake water is seldom much above 42 degrees Fahrenheit!

EXTENDING YOUR TRIP

Those looking for more adventures can continue past Gem, climbing through more talus to ascend the ridge to the north. Once atop this ridge, the trail becomes fainter and rougher as it drops a series of steep switchbacks into the deep forested valley to the north. Once in the valley bottom, the trail runs through forest and meadow to the boggy shores of Lower Wildcat Lake. A faint trail turns left then and climbs westward to Upper Wildcat, a high lonesome lake teeming with trout about 7.6 miles from the trailhead. There are only two small campsites on the steep and brushy shores here, though, so if others get there first, campers risk being homeless when venturing out this far.

63 Source Lake

RATING/ DIFFICULTY	ROUNDTRIP	ELEV GAIN/ HIGH POINT	SEASON
***/3	4 miles	700 feet/ 3800 feet	July–Oct

Map: Green Trails Snoqualmie Pass Gateway No. 207S; **Contact:** Mount Baker–Snoqualmie National Forest, Snoqualmie Ranger District, North Bend office; **Notes:** NW Forest Pass required; **GPS:** N 47 26.725, W 121 25.381

Chair and Bryant peaks tower above Source Lake.

It all starts at Source Lake—the mighty Snoqualmie River flows from this humble pond. But if the pond is humble and less than remarkable, the mountains surrounding it are anything but. The craggy peaks that form a granite fence around the headwaters of the South Fork Snoqualmie make an impressive skyline.

GETTING THERE

From Seattle drive east on I-90 to exit 52 (signed for Snoqualmie Pass west). Turn left (north), crossing under the freeway. Go 100 yards past the turnoff for the Pacific Crest Trail (PCT) on the right, then turn right onto Alpental Road (Forest Road/9040) and continue to the end of the road at the Alpental Ski Area parking lot.

ON THE TRAIL

The trail starts from the northeastern corner of the broad parking area (directly across from the ski lodge). Head up the Snow Lake Trail (Hike 61), taking a moment to silently thank the volunteers who worked countless hours to save this route from years of neglect. The trail winds upward through a long series of crib steps before turning north on a long, climbing traverse of the lower flank of Snoqualmie Mountain. The trail stays well above the South Fork Snoqualmie River but crosses many seasonal creeks and seeps as it angles up the valley. Cool fir forest gives way to heat-drenched, alder-clogged avalanche chutes.

At about 1.5 miles, as the trail sweeps across the headwall of the South Fork basin, stay left on the secondary trail as the main path leads upward to Snow Lake. The Source Lake Trail continues to swing around the headwall, climbing gently for another 0.5

mile. Enjoy a dip in the lake's cool waters while gazing out over the spires and peaks above: Chair Peak, Bryant Peak, The Tooth, Denny Mountain, and Snoqualmie Mountain tower overhead.

64 Lodge Lake

RATING/ DIFFICULTY	ROUNDTRIP	ELEV GAIN/ HIGH POINT	SEASON
**/2	3 miles	500 feet/ 3500 feet	July–Oct

Map: Green Trails Snoqualmie Pass Gateway No. 207S; **Contact:** Mount Baker–Snoqualmie National Forest, Snoqualmie Ranger District, North Bend office; **Notes:** NW Forest Pass required; **GPS:** N 47 25.640, W 121 25.226

Snoqualmie Pass grows ever more developed each year. Condos go up left and right, the ski area plans new ski lifts (or replacements for existing chairs), and hotels pop up east and west. But even with the development, these are still mountains and there is still stunning mountain scenery to enjoy, even on the fringes of the developed areas. Lodge Lake stands as proof.

GETTING THERE

From Seattle drive east on I-90 to exit 52 (signed for Snoqualmie Pass west). Turn right (south) and right again onto the dirt road leading around the westernmost parking lot of the ski area. Park at the far western end of the road, near the sign marking the Pacific Crest Trail.

ON THE TRAIL

The trail climbs gradually through scrubby forest for 0.5 mile as it makes its way from

THIS IS COUGAR COUNTRY

While eastern Washington is clearly cougar country (home to Washington State University), so are the central Cascades. But the cougars that roam these hills don't don red and gold—they're wild cats. And they're proliferating. Cougar populations throughout the state have been increasing. No surprise—so have sightings. Cougar encounters are still rare. But it's important to know how to react just in case you do have a run-in with this elusive predator.

Cougars are curious animals. They may appear threatening when they are only being inquisitive. By making the cougar think you are a bigger, meaner critter than it is, you will be able to avoid an attack (the big cats realize that there is enough easy prey out there that they don't have to mess with something that will fight back). Keep in mind that fewer than twenty fatal cougar attacks have occurred in the United States since the early twentieth century (on the other hand, more than fifty people are killed, on average, by deer each year—most in auto collisions with the deer).

If the cat you encounter acts aggressively:
- **Don't turn your back or take your eyes off the cougar.**
- **Remain standing.**
- **Throw things**, provided you don't have to bend over to pick them up. If you have a water bottle on your belt, chuck it at the cat. Throw your camera, wave your hiking stick, and if the cat gets close enough, whack it *hard* with your hiking staff (I know of two cases where women delivered good, hard whacks across the nose of aggressive-acting cougars, and the cats immediately turned tail and ran away).
- **Shout loudly.**
- **Fight back aggressively.**

You can minimize the already slim chances of having a negative cougar encounter by doing the following:
- **Don't hike or run alone** (runners look like fleeing prey to a predator).
- **Keep children within sight and close at all times.**
- **Avoid dead animals.**
- **Keep dogs on leash and under control.** A cougar may attack a loose, solitary dog, but a leashed dog next to you makes two foes for the cougar to deal with—and cougars are too smart to take on two aggressive animals at once.
- **Be alert to your surroundings.**
- **Use a walking stick.**

the freeway corridor. Abruptly, the path erupts out of the trees onto the smooth grassy slopes of the ski runs.

For the next 0.25 mile or so, the trail runs through the sun-filled slopes, crossing under ski lifts and around lift towers before cresting the ridge near the 3500-foot level, about 0.75 mile from the start of the hike.

The trail drops off the ridge in a gentle traverse to a photogenic pond, Beaver Lake,

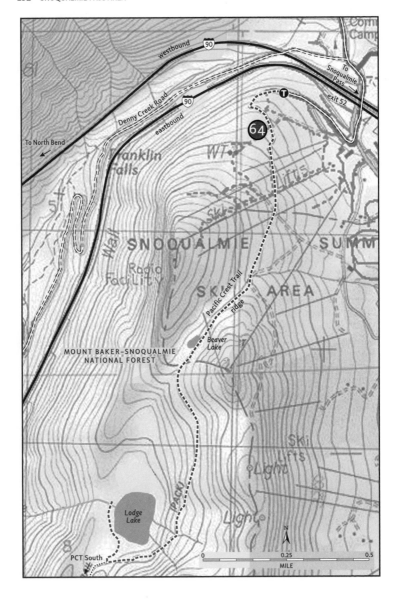

65 Iron Horse Trail Tunnel

RATING/ DIFFICULTY	ROUNDTRIP	ELEV GAIN/ HIGH POINT	SEASON
***/3	6 miles	0 feet/ 2500 feet	May–Oct

Map: Green Trails Snoqualmie Pass Gateway No. 207S; **Contact:** Washington State Parks; **Notes:** Discover Pass required. Tunnel is closed November 1 through May 1; **GPS:** N 47 23.581, W 121 23.568

Here's a trivia question to toss out during your next trail party: The Iron Horse Trail and Washington's other cross-state trail, the Pacific Crest Trail (PCT), intersect but never touch. Why not? Answer: Because the Iron Horse Trail runs through the 2.3-mile-long Snoqualmie Tunnel, while the PCT rolls up and over the peaks south of Snoqualmie Pass. When you head out to explore this dark Iron Horse section, be sure you bring a flashlight—and a headlamp. In fact, make sure every person in your party has a primary light and a backup: this is not a hike you want to do without light. The tunnel is long enough that you'll be in deep, total darkness much of the way. And it's easy to get turned around inside. I've seen savvy hikers bouncing around like pinballs inside the tunnel because they couldn't get themselves headed straight down the tunnel after losing their light.

A happy pooch cools off in the tranquil waters of Lodge Lake.

which makes a grand reflecting pool for the surrounding mountain peaks. From Beaver, the trail continues downhill, ending at 1.5 miles on the shores of the tree-lined Lodge Lake. The namesake lodge is long gone (it was a cabin built by The Mountaineers in the early 1900s), but the lake remains a place for kids and dogs to play while parents enjoy the surrounding mountain scenery, including a lovely reflection of Denny Mountain in the water when you look north on a calm day.

GETTING THERE

From Seattle drive east on I-90 to exit 54. Turn right, then take an immediate left on State Route 906, and in 0.5 mile turn right on Keechelus Lake Boat Launch Road. In about

200 feet, turn right to access the trailhead parking area.

The sun shines at the end of the Snoqualmie Tunnel on the Iron Horse Trail.

ON THE TRAIL

Find the trail on the south side of the parking area, and turn west to hike along the open railroad trail until you reach the eastern portal to the tunnel. Stop and recheck your flashlight batteries before diving into the darkness.

You might also want to pull on your sweater before you go in so you don't have to fumble in the darkness. It can be 100 degrees Fahrenheit outside on a bright, sunny day, but underground the temperature drops into the 50s. The dampness makes it feel even colder.

Also, note that the tunnel is gated November 1 through May 1 for safety reasons. Giant icicles form in the tunnel during the cold winter months, creating massive spears that could threaten the unwary.

66 Silver Peak

RATING/ DIFFICULTY	ROUNDTRIP	ELEV GAIN/ HIGH POINT	SEASON
****/3	8.5 miles	1900 feet/ 5495 feet	July–Oct

Map: Green Trails Snoqualmie Pass Gateway No. 207S; **Contact:** Okanogan–Wenatchee National Forest, Cle Elum Ranger District; **Notes:** NW Forest Pass required; **GPS:** N 47 22.2080, W 121 26.658

  The Pacific Crest Trail (PCT) south of Snoqualmie Pass lacks the glamorous reputation of the

more northern sections, but there are some gems to be found around this top-of-the-world route, including Silver Peak. The PCT provides easy access to one of the most view-rich summits of the Snoqualmie region, getting you up into meadows and panoramic splendor quickly and relatively easily. Keep an eye skyward during your hike as well, since this area has a large gaggle of turkey vultures in residence.

GETTING THERE

From Seattle, drive east on I-90 to exit 54 (signed "Hyak"). At the bottom of the ramp take a right, followed by a left onto a gravel road leading into a broad parking lot at the base of the Hyak Ski Area. Stay left as you cross the parking lot and find a road (signed "Hyak Estates Drive") leading east out of the center of the parking lot. Continue east through a series of vacation homes and public works buildings. The road soon turns to gravel and becomes Forest Road 9070. Continue up the road about 6 miles to a broad ridge saddle—Windy Pass—in a fairly recent clear-cut. Park in the broad pullout and find the PCT South trailhead on the left side of the road.

ON THE TRAIL

Begin hiking south through the open clear-cut along the PCT, and you'll soon enter a stand of second growth that gives way to an older clear-cut area. Though not the most picturesque of settings, these types of clear-cuts are great habitat for deer, as the absent forest canopy means lots of sun reaching the ground plants, bringing them into lush growth for the deer to munch on. Just consider the cut areas broad meadows!

Sweeping views of Annette Lake and the surrounding basin from the summit of Silver Peak

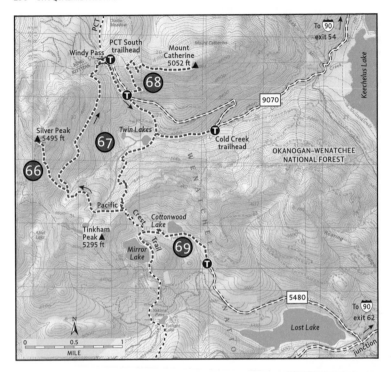

Continue south on the PCT—it does enter more substantial stands of forest at 0.2 mile, and you'll skirt the flank of Silver Peak as the trail curves southeast.

At 2 miles you'll find a modest trail junction. A lesser-used trail to the right heads westward and upward. Take this path and start climbing. Most of your elevation gain—well over 1100 feet of it, comes in the next mile as the trail slices steeply upward. The final 0.25-mile scramble to the top of the mountain requires some routefinding skills, as it climbs through stands of forest and rocky meadows to the 5495-foot summit. The upper slopes of the peak are carpeted with colorful wildflowers, and the views are wonderful from the top.

Enjoy the 360-degree views before returning the way you came.

67 Twin Lakes–Tinkham Loop

RATING/ DIFFICULTY	LOOP	ELEV GAIN/ HIGH POINT	SEASON
****/3	8 miles	2600 feet/ 4500 feet	July–Oct

Map: Green Trails Snoqualmie Pass Gateway No. 207S; **Contact:** Okanogan–Wenatchee National Forest, Cle Elum Ranger District; **Notes:** NW Forest Pass required; **GPS:** N 47 21.804, W 121 25.347

🐾⚙️🔪 *Be prepared for animal encounters: the forest and dense underbrush along the lower sections of this route are perfect cover for a host of critters, from raccoons and possums to bobcats, coyotes, badgers, weasels, martens, mink, and more. Pretty alpine meadows also await you on the flanks of rocky Tinkham Peak; sparkling alpine tarns dot the ridgeline. And if you venture up the side trip to Silver Peak, glorious views from the grassy summit spread out like a picnic buffet before your feet—a veritable feast for the eyes as you look south to the Norse Peak Wilderness, north to the Alpine Lakes Wilderness, west through the gap of Snoqualmie Pass to Granite Mountain, and east into the receding Cascade foothills.*

GETTING THERE

From Seattle, drive east on I-90 to exit 54 (signed "Hyak"). At the bottom of the ramp check your odometer, then turn right, followed by a left onto a gravel road leading into a broad parking lot at the base of the Hyak Ski Area. Stay left as you cross the parking lot and find a road (signed "Hyak Estates Drive") leading east out of the center of the parking lot. Continue east through a series of vacation homes and public works buildings. The road soon turns to gravel and becomes Forest Road 9070. Continue up the road to a hairpin turn to the right, found about 3.5 miles from the interstate ramp (where you checked your mileage, remember?). There is parking at the apex of the corner, or you can move farther above or below the corner to park along the road. The Cold Creek Trail begins at the corner.

At Windy Pass, the PCT looks out on Snoqualmie Pass–area peaks.

ON THE TRAIL

The trail angles off into a tight bramble of slide alder, fireweed, and lupine before climbing slowly into a stand of second-growth forest. The trail stays mostly in the shady forest for the next mile as it climbs gradually to Twin Lakes. The trail splits at the lake basin and you go left. The first 0.5 mile past the lakes leads into a steeply angled tangle of devil's club and stinging nettles. The trail stays above the worst of the pricking weeds, but it's a good idea to resist reaching out for handholds along this trail.

At 2.5 miles from the trailhead, the route reaches a junction with the Pacific Crest Trail (PCT) on the flank of Tinkham Peak. The PCT drops left (south) a mile to reach Mirror Lake, but you should go right and traverse through small meadows and past tiny tarns filled with skunk cabbage in early summer for a little more than 0.5 mile to reach a climbers path leading to the summit of Silver Peak.

The open summit of Mount Catherine

Continue north around the loop on the PCT to Windy Pass, 5.3 miles from the trailhead. The last 0.2 mile of the route to Windy Pass slices through a relatively fresh clearcut: the replanted trees are barely taller than most (two-legged) hikers. These types of clear-cuts are great habitat for deer, as the absent forest canopy means lots of sun reaching the ground plants, bringing them into lush growth for the deer to munch on.

At Windy Pass the PCT strikes a road. Turn right onto this road and hike 0.6 mile to a trail that drops off the right side of the road across from where the Mount Catherine Trail leads east away from the road. The trail descends the steep slope on a long traverse.

The path is brushy for the first 0.5 mile before dropping into trees to roll another 0.6 mile to Twin Lakes and the junction with the Cold Creek Trail, which leads you back to the trailhead in 1 mile.

68 Mount Catherine

RATING/ DIFFICULTY	ROUNDTRIP	ELEV GAIN/ HIGH POINT	SEASON
**/3	3 miles	1300 feet/ 5052 feet	July–Oct

Map: Green Trails Snoqualmie Pass Gateway No. 207S; **Contact:** Okanogan–Wenatchee National Forest, Cle Elum Ranger District;

Notes: NW Forest Pass required; **GPS:** N 47 22.2080, W 121 26.658

🚫 ⛷ *Cross-country skiers and snowshoers have long enjoyed Mount Catherine, but hikers have pretty much ignored this Snoqualmie Pass peak since the middle of the twentieth century. The route is short, and the close-in views encompass sprawling clear-cuts, so perhaps hikers simply decided it wasn't worth a visit—even map makers have neglected to include the trail on their maps. But when the masses wrote off this route as unworthy, they actually made it more enjoyable for the rest of us. You'll find fine views from Mount Catherine once you lift your eyes above the logging scars on the slopes below. You'll also find broad thickets of huckleberries and an array of birds and animals that take advantage of that abundant juicy fruit.*

GETTING THERE

From Seattle, drive east on I-90 to exit 54 (signed "Hyak"). At the bottom of the ramp check your odometer, then turn right, followed by a left onto a gravel road leading into a broad parking lot at the base of the Hyak Ski Area. Stay left as you cross the parking lot and find a road (signed "Hyak Estates Drive") leading east out of the center of the parking lot. Continue east through a series of vacation homes and public works buildings. The road soon turns to gravel and becomes Forest Road 9070. Continue up the road past the Twin Lakes–Tinkham Loop (Hike 67) about 1.8 miles to a pull-out parking area 5.3 miles total from the freeway.

ON THE TRAIL

The trail climbs east up the flank of Mount Catherine, utilizing an old logging track

for the first 0.5 mile. After crossing an old berry-filled clear-cut, the trail runs into the forest before climbing switchbacks for 0.7 mile. Most of the elevation gain comes with these hairpin turns. Visit in early August most years and you'll find a rich crop of huckleberries in the trail's first mile.

Once on the ridgetop, the trail turns and runs steeply up the spine to the summit of the mountain. Along this section the trail pops in and out of forest, providing grand views as you hike. Tinkham Peak and Silver Peak can be seen to the south and, once atop Catherine, you can look north to see the peaks of Snoqualmie Pass and southeast to views of I-90 and Keechelus Lake.

69 Mirror Lake

RATING/ DIFFICULTY	ROUNDTRIP	ELEV GAIN/ HIGH POINT	SEASON
**/2	3 miles	800 feet/ 4200 feet	July–Oct

Map: Green Trails Snoqualmie Pass Gateway No. 207S; **Contact:** Okanogan–Wenatchee National Forest, Cle Elum Ranger District; **Notes:** NW Forest Pass required. High-clearance vehicle recommended for last 0.5 mile to the true trailhead, or park and walk; **GPS:** N 47 20.645, W 121 25.477

🚫 ⛷ *Mirror, mirror, in the mountains: where's the fairest lake of all? Truth be told, the answer isn't Mirror Lake; there are far finer lakes in these lake-rich mountains. But Mirror Lake is arguably the fairest lake of all in the area south of Snoqualmie Pass. This region has been ravaged by logging, and the few pockets of undisturbed wildlands generally are unremarkable. But Mirror Lake sits in a* deep basin alongside the Pacific Crest Trail (PCT). Forests line much of the water's edge, but there are plenty of clear banks where you can sit in the sunshine and enjoy the marvelous views over the lake and beyond to the mountains ringing the basin. Sit quietly and you might see kingfishers in the trees or diving on the resident trout. There's also a host of deer living in the region, and they make frequent visits to the lake basin for water and rich forage.

GETTING THERE

From Seattle drive east on I-90 to exit 62 and, after exiting, turn right. Continue 1.1 miles before turning right onto gravel Forest Road 5480. Drive 5.2 miles from the freeway exit ramp (stay straight past a junction with FR 5483 at 2.8 miles) to Lost Lake and a three-way road junction. Take the middle option, nearly straight ahead, and drive 2.7 miles to the trailhead at the road's end.

ON THE TRAIL

From the parking area walk 0.5 mile up the gently climbing rough road to the true trailhead, found at the switchback in the road. The trail contours away from the road, climbing gradually through brushy forest and old clear-cuts for 0.5 mile before reaching the wading pond called Cottonwood Lake (this lake is too shallow for fish, but perfect for mosquito breeding—don't linger if you value your blood).

From Cottonwood continue upward, pushing west another 0.5 mile to a junction with the PCT at the shores of Mirror Lake. Turn left onto the PCT to walk the shoreline and to find the best reflections in the calm waters. Standing near the outlet stream, you'll see Tinkham Peak in the lake's mirror finish.

Mirror Lake, not so mirror-like here, tries to reflect Tinkham Peak.

EXTENDING YOUR TRIP

From Mirror Lake, the PCT continues north for another 200-plus miles. Hike as far north along the PCT as necessary to get your desired mileage in before returning the way you came.

70 Stirrup Lake

RATING/ DIFFICULTY	ROUNDTRIP	ELEV GAIN/ HIGH POINT	SEASON
***/3	4 miles	600 feet/ 3630 feet	June–Oct

Map: Green Trails Snoqualmie Pass Gateway No. 207S; **Contact:** Okanogan–Wenatchee National Forest, Cle Elum Ranger District; **Notes:** NW Forest Pass required; **GPS:** N 47 21.851, W 121 21.490

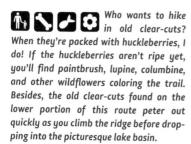 *Who wants to hike in old clear-cuts? When they're packed with huckleberries, I do! If the huckleberries aren't ripe yet, you'll find paintbrush, lupine, columbine, and other wildflowers coloring the trail. Besides, the old clear-cuts found on the lower portion of this route peter out quickly as you climb the ridge before dropping into the picturesque lake basin.*

GETTING THERE

From Seattle drive east on I-90 to exit 62 and, after exiting, turn right. Continue 1.1 miles before turning right onto gravel Forest Road 5480. At 2.8 miles from the freeway exit ramp, turn left onto FR 5483 and continue 2.9 miles (continue straight ahead through one junction in this section) before turning left on FR 5484. Drive 0.2 mile (for a total of 5.9 miles from I-90) to a small parking area at the Stirrup Lake trailhead.

ON THE TRAIL

The hike starts up the Stirrup Creek valley in lovely old-growth and very old second-growth forest, which helps keep you cool as you climb nearly 500 vertical feet in the first 0.7 mile. At this point, the trail leaves the forest in an old clearing and crosses the Pacific Crest Trail.

From this point on, the trail weaves upward through an old, wildly overgrown clear-cut. There are thickets of huckleberries, and frequently herds of elk wandering through (note that during berry season, this area is also visited by black bears in search of the succulent

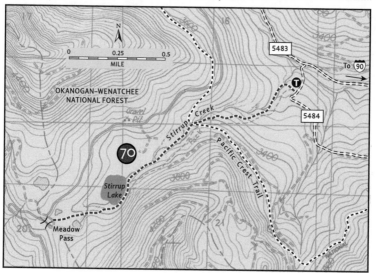

purple fruit). At 1.2 miles, the trail delivers hikers to the shores of Stirrup Lake. For the best lake access, continue a quarter mile around to the western side of the basin, where you can dip your toes and, if you are so inclined, cast a fishing line into the trout-friendly lake while enjoying the views back downvalley.

From the west end of the lake, you may continue to push west another half mile to Meadow Pass, which offers some slightly improved views and access to a refreshing breeze.

71 Gold Creek Pond Loop

RATING/ DIFFICULTY	LOOP	ELEV GAIN/ HIGH POINT	SEASON
**/1	1 mile	100 feet/ 3000 feet	May–Oct

Map: Green Trails Snoqualmie Pass Gateway No. 207S; **Contact:** Okanogan–Wenatchee National Forest, Cle Elum Ranger District; **Notes:** NW Forest Pass required; **GPS:** N 47 24.068, W 121 22.426

Lush shorelines surround Stirrup Lake as Meadow Mountain rises to the north.

North of Gold Creek Pond, the Alpine Lakes Wilderness beckons.

This trail proves that not all hikes have to be epic outings to be enjoyable. Though short, this loop is a great learning adventure for folks of all ages. Preteen kids will especially love exploring its watery world of lakes and creeks, as well as diving deep into century-old forests. It's hard to believe, but in the 1970s and early 1980s this was a gravel pit created and used for building I-90. Since then, agencies have worked together to reclaim the area, and they've done a remarkable job.

GETTING THERE

From Seattle drive east on I-90 to exit 54 (signed "Hyak"). Turn left (north) under the freeway and right on the frontage road (FR 4832) marked "Gold Creek." After about 1 mile (from the off-ramp), turn left on Gold Creek Road (sometimes labeled as Road 144, signed for Gold Creek Pond), and in another 0.5 mile reach a junction. Turn left into the Gold Creek Pond parking area.

ON THE TRAIL

Hiked counterclockwise, the first part of this trail winds through willow and wildflowers along a creek to the junction with the Gold Creek Trail—that path leads up the Gold Creek Valley for several miles toward Alaska Lake, but quickly becomes brushy and hard to follow. Keeping to the loop, hikers will soon leave the pavement and begin on a well-maintained boardwalk. This takes you above a marshy area until you cross over the creek at the north end of the pond. The views open up here as you look across the

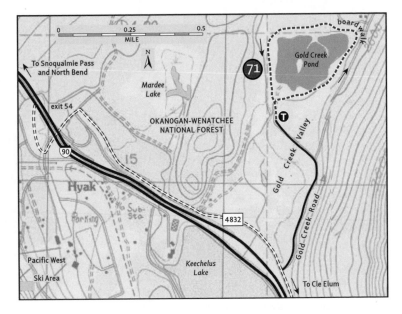

pond to the south. The pond (which looks more like a lake) beckons: crystal-clear, blue, and very deep. You don't need to scramble down to its banks, because a paved spur trail leads hikers down to it. Kids will enjoy throwing rocks in the water and exploring.

After enjoying the pond, head back to the trail, where in a short way you will end at a picnic area. Numerous picnic tables are on this beach, though in midsummer none is in the shade. While picnicking, enjoy the view into the Alpine Lakes Wilderness looking north—it's a stunner.

72 Margaret Lake

RATING/ DIFFICULTY	ROUNDTRIP	ELEV GAIN/ HIGH POINT	SEASON
***/3	6 miles	1500 feet/ 5100 feet	June–Oct

Map: Green Trails Snoqualmie Pass Gateway No. 207S; **Contact:** Okanogan–Wenatchee National Forest, Cle Elum Ranger District; **Notes:** NW Forest Pass required; **GPS:** N 47 21.851, W 121 21.490

Logging paid for most of the trails in the Cascades, so sometimes hikers must expect to hike the terrain that provided that rich stock of timber. This trail starts on an old logging road, leads through old clear-cuts—now nicely regrown as lush berry meadows and forest stands—and enters lush old second-growth forest. It's a great way to experience both the natural and human history of the area, while enjoying some remarkable wild country around a pristine alpine lake.

Margaret Lake feels mystical on foggy days.

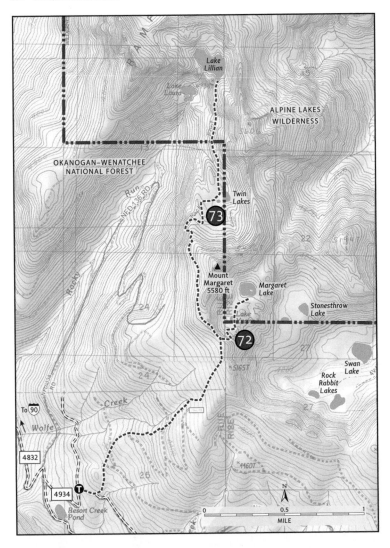

GETTING THERE

From Seattle drive east on I-90 to exit 54 (signed "Hyak"). Turn left (north) under the freeway and right on the frontage road (FR 4832) signed "Gold Creek." After about one mile, pass the turn for Gold Creek Road

(Hike 71) and continue straight on Forest Road 4832, driving east, briefly parallel to the interstate, before the road angles upward. At 3.9 miles from the freeway turn left onto FR 4934, and in 0.25 mile look for the parking lot on the left.

ON THE TRAIL

Head up the gravel road leading past the parking lot and in 0.25 mile veer left onto a small dirt road. Hike around an old cable gate and climb the dirt road as it slants steeply upward into an old clear-cut. Don't let the ugly connotations of that label fool you, however. This field of stumps has been reclaimed by native flora—acres of huckleberries punctuated by an array of wildflowers. Bear grass, lupine, paintbrush, tiger lilies, fireweed, and more grace these slopes.

The road peters out in 0.5 mile and the narrow trail weaves upward, providing great views south over Keechelus Lake and back up toward Snoqualmie Pass. As you near the ridge Mount Rainier comes into view far to the south, too.

About 1.5 miles from the trailhead, the trail enters forest and, at 2 miles, reaches a junction near the ridgeline. To the left is Lake Lillian (Hike 73). Turn right instead to cross the ridge and descend a steep mile to Margaret Lake. The lake is a wonderful place to relax and enjoy a refreshing dip after lunch before heading back up and over the ridge.

EXTENDING YOUR TRIP

Campsites ring the lake, and on the ridge below the pool you can see other small jewels glittering in the sun: Stonesthrow, Rock Rabbit, and Swan lakes perch precariously on the slope under Margaret. Rough, boot-beaten trails lead down to these colorfully named alpine ponds.

A tree blaze on an old-growth tree along the trail to Lake Lillian

73 Twin Lakes and Lake Lillian

RATING/ DIFFICULTY	ROUNDTRIP	ELEV GAIN/ HIGH POINT	SEASON
***/4	9 miles	1500 feet/ 5300 feet	June–Oct

Map: Green Trails Snoqualmie Pass Gateway No. 207S; **Contact:** Okanogan–Wenatchee National Forest, Cle Elum Ranger District;

Notes: NW Forest Pass required; **GPS:** N 47 21.851, W 121 21.490

🔪 ⚙️ 🥾 🌱 You'll run the gamut of scenery here, from clear-cuts to ancient forests to huckleberry fields to alpine lakes. The route climbs up and over a forested ridge, rolls past an assortment of lakes, and provides great opportunities to see birds of prey hunting overhead and small mammals browsing underfoot. The best wildlife viewing comes in the clear-cuts thanks to the abundance of huckleberries growing in those man-made meadows. The lake basin also offers wildlife viewing, as beasts and birds flock to the pools to drink and to graze on the lakeside vegetation. The lakes themselves are marvelous alpine wonders. The Twin Lakes sparkle blue amid green and red heather, while Lake Lillian is a deep gem set in a granite cirque.

GETTING THERE

From Seattle drive east on I-90 to exit 54 (signed "Hyak"). Turn left (north) under the freeway and right on the frontage road marked "Gold Creek." After about a half mile, pass the turn for Gold Creek Road (Hike 71) and continue straight on Forest Road 4832, driving east, briefly parallel to the interstate, before the road angles upward. At 3.9 miles from the freeway turn left onto Forest Road 4934, and in 0.25 mile look for the parking lot on the left.

ON THE TRAIL

Walk up the road leading past the parking lot and then, at 0.25 mile, veer left onto the dirt road, around an old cable gate, and climb as the road slants steeply upward into an old clear-cut. The road peters out in 0.5 mile and the narrow trail weaves upward, providing great views south over Keechelus Lake and back up toward Snoqualmie Pass. As you near the ridge Mount Rainier comes into view far to the south.

About 1.5 miles from the trailhead, the trail enters forest and, at 2 miles, reaches a junction near the ridgeline. To the right is Margaret Lake (Hike 72).

Go left and continue north 1.2 miles to Twin Lakes (elev. 4700 feet). These dual pools are shallow and sandy-bottomed. They are popular with birds of all kinds, but look especially for nutcrackers and small songbirds—the shallow lakes and vegetation-rich meadows are full of insects for these birds to feed on.

From Twin Lakes the trail drops steeply, losing 150 feet in elevation, then climbs just as steeply back up 250 feet to reach the shores of Lake Lillian at 4.5 miles.

Opposite: The final approach to the summit of Hex Mountain offers this hiker a moment to take in the views.

snoqualmie pass
corridor: east

One highway, one mountain pass, two different worlds. Few places in the country sit so closely together yet offer such stark contrasts. The wet west side of the Snoqualmie Pass corridor is filled with musky cedar, hemlock, and Douglas-fir forests. Ferns and mosses abound. Just east of the Cascade crest, though, you enter a new world. Pines and larches fill the forests. The lush greenery of ferns and moss mostly disappears and hardier sun-loving plants such as huckleberries and heathers replace them. The trails east of Snoqualmie Pass offer sun-filled hikes on ridgetops and into fragrant pine forests. You'll find broad swathes of berry brambles and stunning views from high, open mountaintops.

74 Rachel Lake

RATING/ DIFFICULTY	ROUNDTRIP	ELEV GAIN/ HIGH POINT	SEASON
****/4	8 miles	1600 feet/ 4600 feet	July–Oct

Maps: Green Trails Snoqualmie Pass No. 207 and Kachess Lake No. 208; **Contact:** Okanogan–Wenatchee National Forest, Cle Elum Ranger District; **Notes:** NW Forest Pass required; **GPS:** N 47 24.071, W 121 17.086

The condition of the trail to Rachel Lake and the lake's environs exhibit what can happen when too many nature-loving hikers are unleashed on a fragile landscape. Though you'll enjoy spectacular views at the lake and en route, closer examination reveals a web of way trails stomped into the fragile meadows around the lake. And heavy use and poor trail planning have left the trail in rough condi-

tion. You'll splash up a track marred by mud and water, with seasonal streams running down the middle of the trail at times. You'll also fight crowds for the right to that sloppy trail, which receives unbelievably heavy use every weekend in the summer. For maximum benefit visit midweek or after Labor Day.

GETTING THERE
From Seattle take I-90 east to exit 62 (signed "Kachess Lake"). Turn left from the exit ramp and drive northeast on Kachess Lake Road (Forest Road 49) toward Kachess Lake. Follow the signs to Lake Kachess Campground. Turn left on Forest Road 4930, which leads in about 4 miles to a large parking lot and the trailhead at the road's end.

ON THE TRAIL
The trail runs into the forest of Box Canyon Creek, climbing gradually for the first mile, entering the Alpine Lakes Wilderness before leveling out for another 1.5 miles. The path stretches along the flank of Hibox Mountain, with occasional views up the face of Hibox and across the valley to Alta Mountain. Mostly, though, the trail stays under the trees, keeping you cool and well shaded as you hike toward the head of Box Canyon.

There, at about 2.5 miles, the trail starts upward, climbing steeply as it gains more than 1300 feet in the next mile. That cruel pace is made all the more difficult because of the trail's poor condition. Seasonal streams spring from the headwall slope, trickling down onto the trail until they merge into a muddy stream. Effort has been made to divert the water off the trail tread, but just as soon as one ribbon of water is siphoned off, another streams down to take its place.

At about 3.5 miles out, just as your legs are getting weak and your lungs are burning from the climb, the trail levels out and rolls through the splashing spray at the foot of a gorgeous and refreshingly cool fantail waterfall. Stop for pictures and a moment of rest before tiptoeing along the logs that cross the creek below the falls.

The next 0.5 mile of trail climbs more moderately before thrusting you out onto the sunlit shores of Rachel Lake. Try to stay on the primary trail around the lake—too many boots have stomped across the fragile heather and moss meadows, creating a web of way trails that are slow to heal.

Find a suitable rock on which to relax while enjoying the views of the broad lake and the towering wall of Rampart Ridge beyond.

HOW TO HELP THIS TRAIL

The best way to help protect this trail is to hike it, and then let the local ranger district know that you have visited and think the trail is a valuable part of the backcountry trail network in this area. But don't just call: put it in writing. Send a letter, describing your experience and where you see need for improvements (e.g., reconstruction of trail tread, brush cutting, log removal, etc.). Send

Fall colors surrounding the Rampart Lakes basin

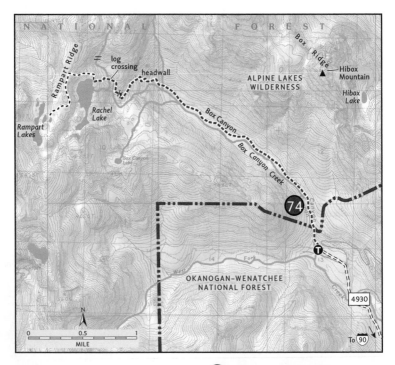

the letter to the ranger and to the good folks at the Washington Trails Association, the leading volunteer trail-maintenance organization in the state.

EXTENDING YOUR TRIP

If you haven't worked enough, push on past Rachel Lake. The trail continues straight along the north shore of the lake, climbing 0.5 mile through a steep series of switchbacks to a saddle on Rampart Ridge (elev. 5100 feet). Once on the ridge, turn left and ramble along the ridgetop for a bit over 1 mile to enter the pothole country of Rampart Lakes—a series of cool blue ponds nestled in depressions in the granite basin atop the ridge.

75 Kachess Ridge

RATING/ DIFFICULTY	ROUNDTRIP	ELEV GAIN/ HIGH POINT	SEASON
****/4	6 miles	2200 feet/ 4600 feet	June–Oct

Map: Green Trails Kachess Lake No. 208; **Contact:** Okanogan–Wenatchee National Forest, Cle Elum Ranger District; **Notes:** NW Forest Pass required; **GPS:** N 47 16.032, W 121 10.424

 *Starting a hike with a serious climb is a good way to limber up your muscles and*

shake off any casual hikers. But crowds don't pose a problem on this route—few hikers, it seems, know about this trail. It's just minutes off the interstate, with grand views of the three big lakes of the eastern Snoqualmie Pass corridor (Keechelus, Kachess, and Cle Elum). You'll also find panoramic views that encompass the peaks of the Cle Elum Valley and reach south to Mount Rainier.

GETTING THERE

From Seattle drive I-90 over Snoqualmie Pass to exit 70. After exiting, turn left over the interstate and then turn left onto the frontage road. Continue a short distance before turning right onto Forest Road 4818 (signed "Kachess Ridge and Easton Ridge"). Drive about 1 mile, then turn right at the next road junction and continue another 0.5 mile to the trailhead.

ON THE TRAIL

From the trailhead, hike the trail a short ways to the junction. Here, the trail to Kachess Ridge climbs to the left while a second path drops off to the right (south) along Easton Ridge (Hike 76). The trail wastes no time in starting to climb, running steeply up the nose of the tall face of Kachess Ridge. As you climb, the forest opens periodically to provide views south to Mount Baldy, Domerie Peak, and Easton Ridge.

Rather than continue straight up to the

A spot near the beacon site on Kachess Ridge looks down on Kachess Lake.

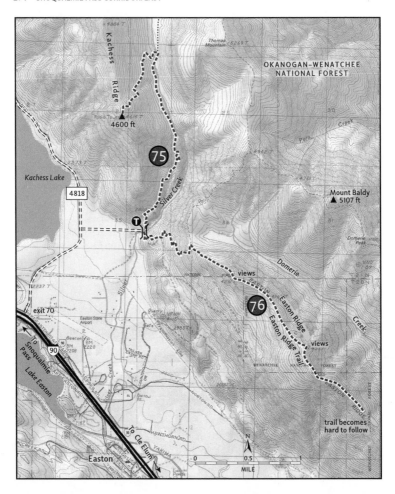

ridgetop, the trail angle moderates just past 1 mile, running almost level for the next 0.75 mile as it follows the tumbling waters of Silver Creek upstream.

At 1.9 miles (elev. 3800 feet) the trail splits. The main trail continues right, up Silver Creek, paralleling the long spine of Kachess Ridge. Our route goes left, climbing through a couple of gentle switchbacks away from the creek.

The trail then straightens out for a long, climbing run up the ridge to a high knob (elev. 4600 feet) at the southern end of Kachess Ridge. This unnamed peak was

Spectacular open views toward Kachess Lake from along Easton Ridge

used in the past as a base for an air-traffic beacon. Outstanding views await you, looking out on the deep basin of Kachess Lake, south to Mount Baldy, and west to Ambilis Mountain. The open ridge areas near the beacon offer stunning wildflowers in May and June for early enjoyment when the high country might still be buried under snow.

HOW TO HELP THIS TRAIL

The mile-long spur trail from the Kachess Ridge Trail to the Kachess beacon site is rough and poorly maintained. After hiking it, write the Forest Service and ask them to devote some trail-maintenance resources to this endangered trail, and send a copy of your letter to the good folks at the Washington Trails Association, the leading volunteer trail-maintenance organization in the state.

76 Easton Ridge

RATING/ DIFFICULTY	ROUNDTRIP	ELEV GAIN/ HIGH POINT	SEASON
***/4	6 miles	2270 feet/ 4470 feet	June–Oct

Map: Green Trails Kachess Lake No. 208; **Contact:** Okanogan–Wenatchee National Forest, Cle Elum Ranger District; **Notes:** NW Forest Pass required; **GPS:** N 47 16.032, W 121 10.424

Easton Ridge once sported a wonderful trail along its entire length. Hikers can still enjoy that long, high route, but the trail disappears in the middle, and the southern end is hard to access. Fortunately, the best of the trail is the northern end, where you'll find grand views, rich huckleberry brambles, and endless opportunities to enjoy wildlife—especially the feathered variety. The Easton area is home to one of the largest populations of turkey vultures in the state, and the massive birds of prey (or birds of opportunity, if you prefer) soar en masse over the thermal-producing faces of Easton and Kachess ridges. Of course, those big birds of opportunity are here for a reason—the region has healthy populations of mammals, big and small, from marmots to mountain goats, beavers to bull elk. Keep your eyes open and you'll see a wide range of critters.

GETTING THERE

From Seattle drive east on I-90 to exit 70. After exiting, turn left over the interstate and then turn left onto the frontage road. Continue a short distance before turning right onto Forest Road 4818 (signed "Kachess Ridge and Easton Ridge"). Drive about 1 mile, then turn right at the next road junction and continue another 0.5 mile to the trailhead.

ON THE TRAIL

Find the trailhead near the parking area. Hike the trail a short ways, and where the Kachess Ridge Trail goes left, go right to drop down to Silver Creek. Cross the creek on the bridge. Now climb steeply to the southeast, plunging straight up the steep face of the wall above Silver Creek. The trail switchbacks for more than 0.75 mile, gaining 1000 feet, to reach the junction with the Domerie Divide Trail (elev. 3400 feet).

Turn right at the trail junction to head south along the ridgeline. In the next 2 miles you'll climb gradually to a 4470-foot viewpoint on the ridge. Peer down to the small

community of Easton alongside Easton Lake. On the other side (to the east) look across the Domerie Creek valley to Domerie Peak and Mount Baldy.

HOW TO HELP THIS TRAIL

The best way to help protect this trail is to hike it, and then let the local ranger district know that you have visited and think the trail is a valuable part of the backcountry trail network in this area. But don't just call: put it in writing. Send a letter, describing your experience and where you see need for improvements (e.g., reconstruction of trail tread, brush cutting, log removal, etc.). Send the letter to the ranger and to the good folks at the Washington Trails Association, the leading volunteer trail-maintenance organization in the state.

77 Thorp Lake

RATING/ DIFFICULTY	ROUNDTRIP	ELEV GAIN/ HIGH POINT	SEASON
***/4	7 miles	1300 feet/ 4800 feet	June–Oct

Map: Green Trails Kachess Lake No. 208; **Contact:** Okanogan–Wenatchee National Forest, Cle Elum Ranger District; **Notes:** NW Forest Pass required; **GPS:** N 47 22.399, W 121 9.466

 This route offers many outstanding rewards but demands serious effort in payment. The trail has suffered years of neglect, leaving the route rough. Add the strenuous climbs and you have a hike that taxes even the toughest hikers. In return, though, hikers will find views that are unmatched in this part of the state. From

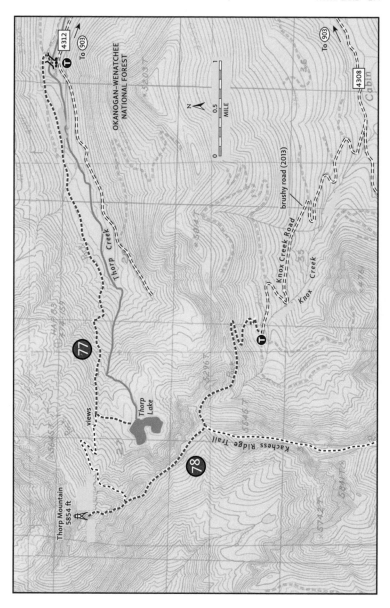

The unique shape of Thorp Lake is best seen from above.

the fire lookout cabin atop the heather-carpeted peak you can scan the horizon in every direction, picking out peaks and valleys throughout the Alpine Lakes Wilderness and south all the way to Mount Rainier (on clear days). The ridges rolling away from Thorp Mountain sport colorful flower meadows, and the blue pool of Kachess Lake sparkles in the deep valley at its foot.

GETTING THERE

From Seattle drive east on I-90 to take exit 80 (signed "Roslyn/Salmon la Sac"). Head north on Bullfrog Road, and at the round-about junction with State Route 903, go left into Roslyn on SR 903 and continue through town and up the valley. At mile 13 (from the roundabout), turn left onto French Cabin Road (Forest Road 4308). Drive 3.25 miles up FR 4308 to FR 4312 on the right. Go right and drive 1.5 miles to another road junction, with FR 4312-121. This road is typically gated, so park here (don't block the gate).

ON THE TRAIL

Round the gate and walk 0.1 mile to a bridge over Thorp Creek. Cross the creek and turn left. The true trail starts 0.25 mile up this road on the left. The trail climbs steadily but modestly as it parallels tumbling Thorp Creek. Keep your eyes wide open and you might spot a lot of wildlife along the lower trail, especially as the path leaves the stands of forest and pops briefly into old, overgrown clear-cuts. These transition zones are popular places for deer to hang out, since they provide good cover (the forest) as well as close proximity to good browse (in the clear-cuts).

About 1.5 miles from the gate, the trail starts to climb more steeply, angling upward away from the creek. The forest thins with increasing elevation, providing more sun breaks and viewpoints. At nearly 3 miles a small side trail drops left 0.5 mile to Thorp Lake. Take this path to descend to the lake shore at 4800 feet elevation. Enjoy the cool waters, and, if you are so inclined, cast a line out in pursuit of the lake's abundant trout.

HOW TO HELP THIS TRAIL

The best way to help protect this trail is to hike it, and then let the local ranger district know that you have visited and think the trail is a valuable part of the backcountry trail network in this area. But don't just call: put it in writing. Send a letter, describing your experience and where you see need for improvements (e.g., reconstruction of trail tread, brush cutting, log removal, etc.). Send the letter to the ranger and to the good folks at the Washington Trails Association, the leading volunteer trail-maintenance organization in the state.

78 Knox Creek–Thorp Mountain

RATING/ DIFFICULTY	ROUNDTRIP	ELEV GAIN/ HIGH POINT	SEASON
****/3	4.4 miles	1800 feet/ 5854 feet	June–Oct

Map: Green Trails Kachess Lake No. 208;
Contact: Okanogan–Wenatchee National

The meadow-covered summit of Thorp Mountain, complete with the beautiful Thorp Mountain lookout building

Forest, Cle Elum Ranger District; **Notes:** NW Forest Pass required; **GPS:** N 47 21.413, W 121 11.263

⬤⬤⬤ *Starting in steep hillside meadows awash in colorful wildflowers, this route offers incredible wilderness experiences that include stunning flora, fauna, scenic panoramas, and a touch of history, with its stop atop a peak hosting a historic fire lookout station.*

GETTING THERE
From Seattle drive east on I-90 to take exit 80 (signed "Roslyn/Salmon la Sac"). Head north on Bullfrog Road, and at the roundabout junction with State Route 903 go left into Roslyn on SR 903 and continue through town and up the valley. At mile 13 (from the roundabout), turn left onto French Cabin Road (Forest Road 4308). Drive 5 miles up FR 4308 to a brushy road on the right signed "Knox Creek: 2." Take this road 2 miles to a wide spot in the road. This is your parking area. The trail leads uphill on the right.

ON THE TRAIL
The hike begins with a lovely switchback trail leading up through a lush wildflower meadowland. These flowers are generally at their prime bloom in mid-July. After numerous long switchbacks in the first 0.9 mile, the trail leaves the hillside meadows, but before entering pine and fir forest the route passes a picturesque rock band overflowing with wildflowers, including rock penstemon, scarlet gilia, and tiger lilies.

At 1.3 miles reach a junction with the Kachess Ridge Trail. Stay right now on the Kachess Ridge Trail to continue upward to the top of Thorp Mountain and in another 0.2 mile you'll find your first grand views of the lookout-topped peak.

Passing through a couple of forest clearings and more fragrant forest, you'll reach the bottom of the final steep pitch to the summit at 1.9 miles. Go left, off the Kachess Ridge Trail, and reach the summit at 2.2 miles—you'll gain 450 feet in this last 0.3 mile of climbing, but the rewards are stellar: 360-degree views from the former lookout tower.

79 No Name Ridge– Thorp Mountain

RATING/ DIFFICULTY	ROUNDTRIP	ELEV GAIN/ HIGH POINT	SEASON
****/3	9 miles	1000 feet/ 5854 feet	June–Oct

Map: Green Trails Kachess Lake No. 208; **Contact:** Okanogan–Wenatchee National Forest, Cle Elum Ranger District; **Notes:** NW Forest Pass required; **GPS:** N 47 24.605, W 121 12.525

⬤⬤⬤⬤ *The northern portion of Kachess Ridge is very lightly traveled, and what lovelier way to do one of the best early summer wildflower hikes to Thorp Mountain than to come in through the "back door"?*

GETTING THERE
From Seattle drive east on I-90 to take exit 80 (signed "Roslyn/Salmon la Sac"). Head north on Bullfrog Road and at the roundabout junction with State Route 903, go left into Roslyn on SR 903 and continue through town and up the valley. At mile 15 (from the roundabout), turn left onto Forest Road 4600 to cross the Cle Elum River. Continue

4.7 miles to Cooper Lake and the Pete Lake trailhead access on the right; here the road turns gravel. Continue straight ahead on FR 4600 and at 7 miles veer left onto FR 4617 with a sign indicating "Kachess Ridge Trail." At 1.2 miles up FR 4617 stay left at a junction signed "Kachess Ridge Trail: 2" and in 3 miles (yes, the sign is wrong) come to the end of the road in an old clear-cut, 4.2 miles up from FR 4600 and 11.2 miles from the main road. The trail leaves the road-end parking area on the east side of road.

ON THE TRAIL

Before leaving on your adventure, pause and enjoy the stunning views from the trailhead! To start your hike, follow the trail (old roadbed) as it climbs across the center of a clear-cut area, and at 0.15 mile enter the old forest to the south. You'll start to gradually climb here, slowly warming your muscles as you go gently up the ridge before you.

In a half mile, you'll find the first of many great views to the southwest, sweeping in many peaks of the south Cascades, including the stunning presence of Mount Rainier in the far distance. As you near the 1-mile mark, the route rolls onto an open rocky slope full of wildflowers and open views to the north, including the snowcapped summit of Mount Daniel.

The route continues to gradually amble up and down along the ridge, and at 2.4 miles the trail becomes rather faint as it runs through a lush hillside meadow—the flora here tends to grow quickly, and the trail

Views from the northern Kachess Ridge area of No Name Ridge offer open views toward Mount Daniel and Mount Hinman.

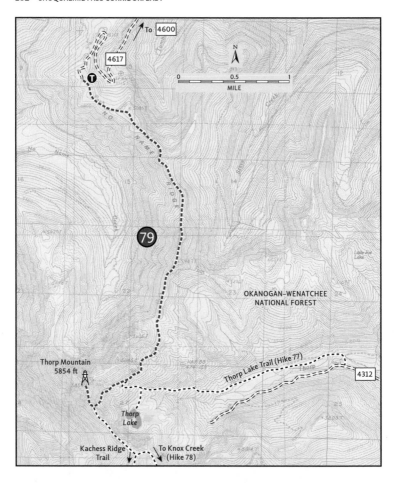

can be hidden if crews haven't gotten in and brushed it out. While picking out your path, enjoy all of the wildflowers at your feet.

A junction at 3.7 miles offers the option of a descent to Thorp Lake or a climb to Thorp Mountain. Go right to choose the climb, and at 4.2 miles reach another junction with the summit trail (to the left is the Knox Creek–

Thorp Mountain access, Hike 78). Turn right once more and start the serious climb to the top of the peak.

The Thorp Mountain Lookout remains one of the finest old fire lookouts in the Cascades, with stunning views in all directions: down upon Kachess Lake to the south and southwest, Mount Daniel and Mount

WHOSE LAND IS THIS?

All of the hikes in this book are on public land. That is, they belong to you and me and the rest of the citizenry. As fellow guidebook writer Craig Romano points out in *Day Hiking: Olympic Peninsula*, what's confusing is just who exactly is in charge of this public trust. Several different governing agencies manage the lands described in his guide and in this one as well.

The largest of the agencies, and the one managing most of the hikes in this book, is the US Forest Service. A division of the Department of Agriculture, the Forest Service strives to "sustain the health, diversity, and productivity of the Nation's forests and grasslands to meet the needs of present and future generations." The agency purports to do this under the doctrine of "multiple-use"—the greatest good for the greatest number, frequently resulting in conflict. Supplying timber products, managing wildlife habitat, and developing motorized and nonmotorized recreation options have a tendency to conflict with one another. Some of these uses may not exactly sustain the health of the forest either.

The Mount Baker–Snoqualmie and Wenatchee national forests manage over 3.9 million acres of land in the Cascades. Much has been heavily logged. Eleven areas within these forests, however, have been afforded stringent protections as federal wilderness areas. Several hikes in this guide are in the Alpine Lakes Wilderness and the Norse Peak Wilderness.

Other public lands you'll encounter on the hikes in this book are Washington State parks, managed primarily for recreation and preservation; Washington State Department of Natural Resources lands, managed primarily for timber harvesting, with pockets of natural area preserves; and county parks, which are often like state parks but on a regional level.

It's important that you know who manages the land you'll be hiking on, for each agency has its own fees and rules. Confusing? Yes, but it's our land and we should understand how it's managed for us. And remember that we have a say in how our lands are managed, too, and can let the agencies know whether we like what they're doing or not.

Hinman to the north, the Stuart Range to the far northeast—even views southeast to the Kittitas Valley and farmland and, of course, Mount Rainier to the southwest. Take your time here; it is a special place.

80 Howson Creek

RATING/ DIFFICULTY	ROUNDTRIP	ELEV GAIN/ HIGH POINT	SEASON
***/4	5 miles	2400 feet/ 4400 feet	June–Oct

Map: Green Trails Kachess Lake No. 208; **Contact:** Okanogan–Wenatchee National Forest, Cle Elum Ranger District; **Notes:** NW Forest Pass required; **GPS:** N 47 21.162, W 121 06.238

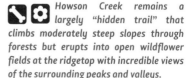 *Howson Creek remains a largely "hidden trail" that climbs moderately steep slopes through forests but erupts into open wildflower fields at the ridgetop with incredible views of the surrounding peaks and valleys.*

GETTING THERE

From Seattle drive east on I-90 to take exit 80 (signed "Roslyn/Salmon la Sac"). Head north on Bullfrog Road and at the roundabout junction with State Route 903, go left into Roslyn on SR 903 and continue through town and up the valley. At mile 13 (from the roundabout), reach the Cle Elum River Campground on your left. Pass the entrance to the campground, and in about 100 yards look for a dirt track on the right, where you can pull down off the road and drive back 50 feet to park in a small circle area under the trees.

ON THE TRAIL

The unsigned trail leaves the parking area by way of an old rugged roadbed. It climbs gradually at first but steepens at times to give you a good workout early on in the hike. The route crosses Howson Creek at 0.8 mile, and the crossing can be dicey early in the year when snowmelt swells the creek to a torrent, but by mid-July most years the crossing can be done while keeping your feet dry by way of well-spaced rocks. Still, caution should be exercised at all times, as the rocks and logs can be slippery when wet.

The trail angles steeply up the far creek bank—you might have to move to your right a bit (during our research outing the trail out of the creekbed was partially hidden by brush and downed logs).

At nearly 1 mile into the hike the trail opens onto the first views from a sloping field of rock-strewn wildflowers. From these slopes, look west to see the long line of Kachess Ridge and the summit of Red Mountain across the valley.

For the next 1.5 miles, you'll climb toward the ridgetop at 4400 feet elevation, skirting the flank of a huge talus slope along the way. Keep an eye—and ear—out for pikas here. These little "rock rabbits" are incredibly cute and emit a sharp little "*Eeee!*" call when staying in touch with one another. The trail does ramble another mile or so to intersect the Sasse Mountain Trail, but the open talus slopes viewpoint here

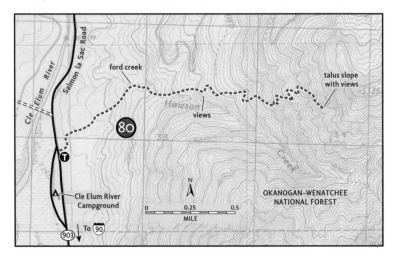

The Howson Creek Trail offers grand open views west and north toward peaks such as Red Mountain.

below the ridgetop at 2.5 miles provides a perfect place to park your butt on the talus and enjoy massive views of Lake Cle Elum, Kachess Ridge, and Mount Rainier while enjoying lunch with the pikas.

81 Hex Mountain

RATING/ DIFFICULTY	ROUNDTRIP	ELEV GAIN/ HIGH POINT	SEASON
***/4	6 miles	1400 feet/ 4990 feet	July–Oct

Map: Green Trails Kachess Lake No. 208; **Contact:** Okanogan–Wenatchee National Forest, Cle Elum Ranger District; **Notes:** NW

Forest Pass required; **GPS:** N 47 26.808, W 121 02.576

🌼 ⬅ Start hiking through an old logged area still dotted here and there with massive old-growth trees (left as bird habitat?). This old selective cut today stands as a wildflower bonanza, with arrowleaf balsamroot providing the first color of spring, followed quickly by lupine, paintbrush, and other colorful blooms. Western tanagers flit through the trees, and hummingbirds thrive among the flowers. Farther up the route, the trail enters the trees and pops out on a serpentine rock ridge leading to the Hex Mountain summit just off the Sasse Ridge Trail. Be aware that this is motorcycle country, so don't be surprised if you encounter some noisy company on summer weekends.

GETTING THERE

From Seattle drive east on I-90 to take exit 80 (signed "Roslyn/Salmon la Sac"). Head north on Bullfrog Road and at the round-about junction with State Route 903, go left into Roslyn on SR 903 and continue through town and up the valley. At mile 7.4 (from the roundabout), turn right onto Forest Road 4305. Proceed up FR 4305 for 0.5 mile and then stay left to remain on FR 4305. At 2.3 miles turn left onto a side road signed "Sasse Mountain Trail" (FR 4305-118). Continue 1 mile farther (3.3 miles total from SR 903) to the end of the road and the trailhead.

ON THE TRAIL

With the first step on the trail, you'll be climbing. The ascent begins gently and almost immediately puts you into a landscape covered with wildflowers. Over the first 1.4 miles, the route alternates between open logged areas ("wildflower meadows") and stands of young but diverse forests. Occasionally, massive old ponderosa pines shade the forest glades.

At 1.4 miles, cross an old logging road and start a more serious climb through a clear-cut—on hot summer days, this section can be a scorcher. In just under a mile find an unmarked trail junction. The left-hand trail

leads directly to the summit of Hex in a steep but view-rich climb to the summit at 3 miles. Take plenty of time to catch your breath and soak in the views from here, peering down to Cle Elum Lake below and Mount Rainier in the distance.

Note: If you want a longer but easier summit hike, continue straight at the junction

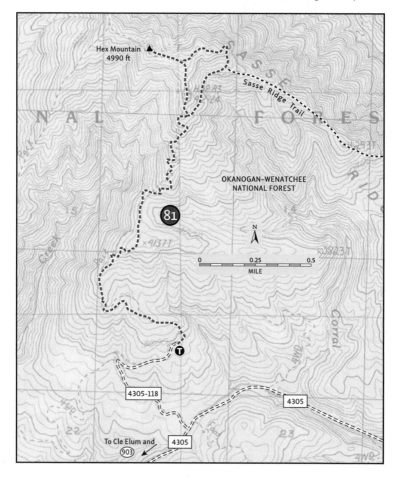

The summit approach to Hex Mountain. Views and wildflowers!

at 2.3 miles and, a half mile farther on, turn left onto the Sasse Ridge Trail. This leads you another 0.6 mile in a gentler ascent to the summit.

82 Boulder Creek–Gallagher Head Lake

RATING/ DIFFICULTY	ROUNDTRIP	ELEV GAIN/ HIGH POINT	SEASON
****/4	9 miles	2100 feet/ 5606 feet	July–Oct

Maps: Green Trails Kachess Lake No. 208 and Mount Stuart No. 209; **Contact:** Okanogan–Wenatchee National Forest, Cle

Elum Ranger District; **Notes:** NW Forest Pass required; **GPS:** N 47 18.134, W 121 03.720

⚙ 🔧 🐾 *The Boulder Creek basin has largely been ignored by the Washington hiking community, and that's a shame! This route offers incredible wildflower viewing and a rich immersion into the natural world of the Cascade's dry-side ecosystem. You'll encounter birds and beasts, flowers and trees that exemplify the beauty of the eastern Washington montane.*

GETTING THERE
From Seattle drive east on I-90 to take exit 80 (signed "Roslyn/Salmon la Sac"). Head north on Bullfrog Road and at the roundabout junction with State Route 903, go left into Roslyn on SR 903 and continue through town and up the valley. At mile 16.5 (from the roundabout) you'll reach Salmon la Sac Campground. Stay right on FR 4330 and in 1.6 miles pass the Davis Peak trailhead. Continue on and 5.1 miles past Salmon la Sac, turn right onto Forest Road 138. Drive 0.4 mile up FR 138 to a Y junction. If you don't want to risk driving on rough road beyond this point, turn around, park clear of the road near here, and walk the 0.5-mile rough road to the trailhead. If you want to risk it, stay right at the Y and drive the rough half mile to the end of the road and the true trailhead, which has very limited parking for only a few cars.

ON THE TRAIL
The trail starts on an easy hillside traverse that leads into the Boulder Creek valley. The trail runs under the heavy canopy of a lush second-growth pine forest, keeping you well shaded as you climb toward the lake at the head of the valley.

At 1.4 miles the trail crosses Big Boulder Creek, which, despite the lack of a bridge or fixed footlog, is a relatively easy crossing. Once across the small creek, the trail continues upvalley through forest, now more sun-dappled and open than it is lower down. Near the 2-mile mark, the trail enters the first wildflower meadows, presenting sun-filled clearings filled with shooting stars and columbine early in the season.

Around 2.1 miles out, the trail crosses the creek once more. This crossing proved easy in early August, but an early July outing—when snowmelt was at its peak—proved more

Meadows of shooting star wildflowers around Gallagher Head Lake

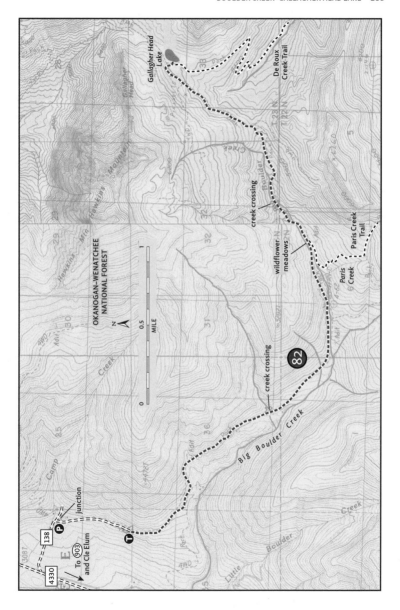

difficult. Use caution when the waters are swollen with snowmelt. The trail to Gallagher Head Lake meets the Paris Creek Trail on the right at 2.4 miles. Stay left on the Big Boulder Creek Trail to continue on to the lake.

In the next mile, cross Big Boulder Creek twice more—at 3.2 and 3.4 miles—then the trail begins to angle eastward away from the Boulder Creek basin to a low saddle at 4 miles. Here the trail accesses an old road. Stay left to trek up to Gallagher Head Lake, and at 4.4 miles Trail 1392 merges onto the old road you are walking on from the right (this is the De Roux Creek Trail). Stay straight on the road another 0.1 mile and arrive by the lakeshore meadows full of shooting stars and paintbrush in midsummer. Hawkins Mountain rises to the northwest, and massive Esmeralda Peaks are reflected in the lake view to the east.

83 Coal Mines Trail

RATING/ DIFFICULTY	ROUNDTRIP	ELEV GAIN/ HIGH POINT	SEASON
***/1	6.5 miles	200 feet/ 2200 feet	Year-round

Map: Green Trails Cle Elum No. 241; **Contact:** Okanogan–Wenatchee National Forest, Cle Elum Ranger District; **Notes:** NW Forest Pass required; **GPS:** N 47 18.134, W 121 03.720

Though not a wilderness trail, this route offers an unmatched exploration of the region's wild history, and it rambles through some beautiful natural terrain while providing that history lesson. The Northern Pacific Railway originally used this route to move railcars full of coal from Roslyn and Roland down to

Cle Elum and Ellensburg, and on to Yakima and beyond. Numerous coal mines littered the valley between Cle Elum and Ronald, with the last closing just a few decades ago in 1967. Much of the valley still sits above old mine shafts. Keep that in mind as you hike, and you'll find yourself making sure your footfalls are light and easy!

GETTING THERE
From Seattle drive east on I-90 to take exit 84. The exit ramp merges onto 1st Street in Cle Elum, dropping into town past Safeway and McDonald's on the right. At the bottom of the hill, at the first light past McDonald's, turn left onto Stratford Street. Continue north on Stratford across West 2nd Street to find the trailhead on the left. Parking is along the street, with ample parking on Stratford between West 1st and West 2nd streets alongside Flag Pole Park.

ON THE TRAIL
The trail starts from the corner of 2nd Street and Stratford, ambling northwest through a quiet Cle Elum neighborhood before entering a woodland setting full of cottonwoods, alders, and maples, then ponderosa pines and firs. The generally flat trail rambles westward for a mile to Crystal Creek, passing numerous interpretive signs that call attention to long-abandoned mines such as Mine #7, Happy Hollow, and Mine #5. Indeed, some of these mines were surrounded by small community settlements, including Ducktown and the aforementioned Happy Hollow.

At around 1.3 miles, the route passes Coal Washer—an old facility that used Crystal Creek waters to flush sediment and impurities from the rich coal ore before it was shipped for market. Here you can

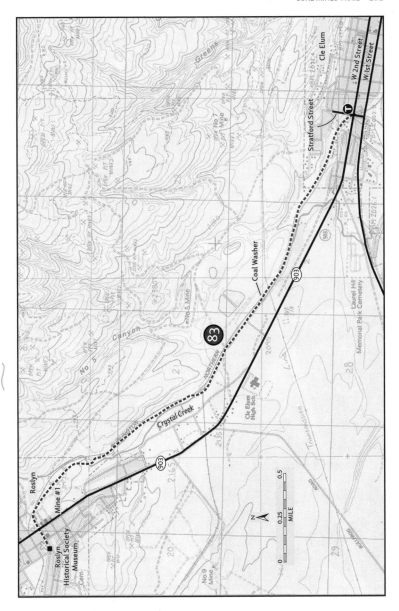

Greens

Cle Elum

W 2nd Street

W 1st Street

Stratford Street

Cle Elum

No 7 Mine

Coal Washer

903

No 5 Mine

83

Canyon

NORTHERN

No 5 Mine

Crystal Creek

Cle Elum
High Sch.

Laurel Hill

Memorial Park Cemetery

Transmission

903

Roslyn

Mine #1

903

Roslyn
Historical Society
Museum

Cem.

No 9
Mine

N

0   0.25   0.5
MILE

also see some of the old mine tailings—non-coal-bearing rocks removed from the mines to expose the valuable coal. The tailings were stacked high to get them out of the way as quickly as possible, and these man-made hills still stand today.

As you stroll past the 2-mile mark, look for the signs noting the railroad spur to Mines #9 and #10. Though these mine shafts are sealed, visitors can see where the mine openings stood, welcoming sturdy miners into the bowels of the earth.

Roll on another mile to reach Mine #1 and some rundown mine buildings on the edge of Roslyn. The trail continues into the heart of Roslyn and beyond, but at a bit past 3 miles you'll find yourself behind

the Roslyn Historical Society Museum. If it is open, take the time to wander through the artifacts in this small museum before heading back down through history to your awaiting car.

84 North Fork Taneum Creek

RATING/ DIFFICULTY	ROUNDTRIP	ELEV GAIN/ HIGH POINT	SEASON
***/2	8 miles	300 feet/ 3300 feet	May–Nov

Maps: Green Trails Cle Elum No. 241 and Easton No. 240; **Contact:** Okanogan–Wenatchee National Forest, Cle Elum Ranger District; **Notes:** NW Forest Pass required; **GPS:** N 47 06.927, W 120 57.199

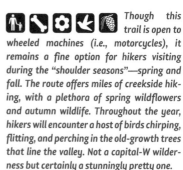 *Though this trail is open to wheeled machines (i.e., motorcycles), it remains a fine option for hikers visiting during the "shoulder seasons"—spring and fall. The route offers miles of creekside hiking, with a plethora of spring wildflowers and autumn wildlife. Throughout the year, hikers will encounter a host of birds chirping, flitting, and perching in the old-growth trees that line the valley. Not a capital-W wilderness but certainly a stunningly pretty one.*

GETTING THERE
From Seattle drive east on I-90 to exit 93 (Elk Heights Road), and after exiting turn left to cross over the freeway. Continue 0.3 mile then turn right onto Thorp Prairie Road. At 3.8 miles from the freeway off-ramp, turn right onto East Taneum Road, recross I-90, and in another 0.2 mile (4 miles total) turn

Remains along the Coal Mines Trail

right onto West Taneum Road. Drive 7.1 miles on West Taneum, passing the Ice Water Campground at 6.1 miles. The road name changes to Forest Road 33 just beyond the campground, and after another 2.8 miles (12.9 total miles) veer right at the Y junction to stay on FR 33. Drive 1.4 miles farther before turning right off the paved road onto FR 33-133. A final 1.1 miles up the gravel FR 33-133 leads to the well-signed trailhead at a sharp switchback in the road. Parking is available alongside the road here.

ON THE TRAIL

The trail immediately enters old-growth and old second-growth forest as it angles gently toward the creek. For the first three-quarters of a mile, the trail contours along the hill, staying relatively flat as it explores the forest. At 0.7 mile, it slides along a vast mud-filled bottomland area that's full of skunk cabbage and yellow violets—time it right in the spring, and this marsh is awash in yellow blooms from the two plants.

Pushing on up the valley the trail enters forest that is home to a strong, stable population of barred owls and woodpeckers. Keep an eye out for the owls and an ear out for the hammering of the woodpeckers. We found a nesting pair of barreds around the 1.5-mile mark in a tree high above the creek.

At 1.8 miles out, the trail opens up to provide excellent views down the creek valley, and those views continue up to the 2.2-mile mark, where you'll find sprawling meadows of flowers, butterflies, and anthills—with easy creek access as well. But don't stop here. Push on to the 2.6-mile mark to find a broad gravel bar in the creek that makes a wonderful picnic spot for lunch or just a snack break or rest.

The trail passes a horse ford at about 3.9 miles and a sturdy bridge for hikers at 4

View up North Fork Taneum Creek from the bridge crossing

miles. This is a great location to grab a snack, and then turn around and head back down.

85 Taneum Ridge–Fishhook Flats Loop

RATING/ DIFFICULTY	LOOP	ELEV GAIN/ HIGH POINT	SEASON
***/3	14 miles	1400 feet/ 4200 feet	June–Oct

Maps: Green Trails Cle Elum No. 241 and Easton No. 240; **Contact:** Okanogan–Wenatchee National Forest, Cle Elum Ranger

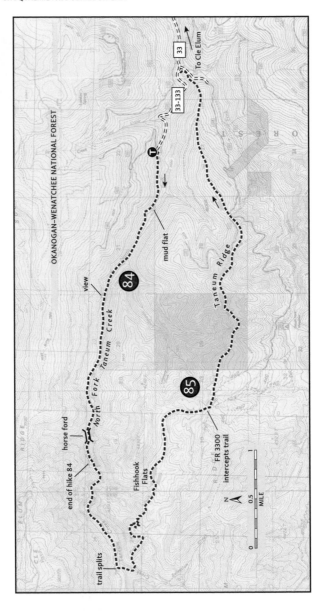

District; **Notes:** NW Forest Pass required;
GPS: N 47 06.927, W 120 57.199

*Too often hikers forget the wild,
remote country south of Interstate 90 in the Cle Elum area—perhaps
because this is unprotected forest land, open
to motorized recreation. But that's no excuse
to miss out on the rugged beauty of this
region. Majestic pine forests fill the valleys
of the Taneum basin, and vast herds of
Rocky Mountain elk (wapiti) roam far and
wide through the region. This trail explores
some of that picturesque country, taking
you into the heart of the wapiti rangelands.*

GETTING THERE

From Seattle drive east on I-90 to exit 93
(Elk Heights Road) and after exiting, turn
left to cross over the freeway. Continue 0.3
mile then turn right onto Thorp Prairie Road.
At 3.8 miles from the freeway off-ramp, turn
right onto East Taneum Road, recross I-90,
and in another 0.2 mile (4 miles total) turn
right onto West Taneum Road. Drive 7.1
miles on West Taneum, passing the Ice Water
Campground at 6.1 miles. The road name
changes to Forest Road 33 just beyond the
campground, and in another 2.8 miles (12.9
total miles) veer right at the Y junction to
stay on FR 33. Drive 1.4 miles farther before
turning right off the paved road onto Forest
Road 33-133. A final 1.1 miles up the gravel
FR 33-133 leads to the well-signed trailhead
at a sharp switchback in the road. Parking is
available alongside the road here.

ON THE TRAIL

Start this hike on the North Fork Taneum
Creek route (Hike 84), but once you hit that
bridge at 4 miles, keep trekking up the valley.
You may encounter motorcycles here, but

*A hiker pauses near a massive old-growth
ponderosa pine tree in the Taneum Creek
valley below Taneum Ridge*

it's more likely you'll see nothing more than
a bicycle—and, if you are lucky, some elk or
big mule deer.

The trail splits at 5.5 miles, with the
left fork leading you to Fishhook Flats.
Take that left and, for the next mile the
trail climbs steeply, ascending the flank of
Taneum Ridge. The pitch of the trail lessens
after that, and for 2 miles the trail rambles
through open meadows leading to the
broad fields known as Fishhook Flats.

At 8.5 miles, the trail intercepts a road—Forest Road 3300—which you'll need to follow to the east. But after just a hundred yards or so, find the trail on the left. It leads you back onto Taneum Ridge and Trail 1363. From here, it's a relatively easy and highly enjoyable 3-mile hike back across the ridge to the starting point. There are lots of ups and downs, and while the ridge is mostly forested (don't expect wide-open views at this low elevation), there are a handful of really pretty areas with great views of Cle Elum Ridge and the Stuart Range. The last mile is a fast downhill back to the Y junction in the road. Walk back up the road to your car.

86 Lost and Manastash Lakes

RATING/ DIFFICULTY	ROUNDTRIP	ELEV GAIN/ HIGH POINT	SEASON
****/3	7 miles	700 feet/ 5100 feet	June–Oct

Maps: Green Trails Cle Elum No. 241 and Easton No. 240; **Contact:** Okanogan–Wenatchee National Forest, Cle Elum Ranger District; **Notes:** NW Forest Pass required; **GPS:** N 47 01.536, W 120 56.328

This wonderful trek starts in an open pine, larch, and fir forest before entering mature dense forests. As you hike, you'll pass open rocky slopes bursting with color from June through early August, and a lovely Lost Lake, then hike over a hump to reach Manastash Lake.

GETTING THERE

From Seattle drive east on I-90 to exit 101 (Thorp) and after exiting, turn right. Continue to Cove Road and turn right, driving south on Cove Road to its junction with Manastash Road. Turn right onto Manastash Road and drive 7.5 miles to the end of the pavement and the start of Forest Road 31. At 16.8 miles

Manastash Lake

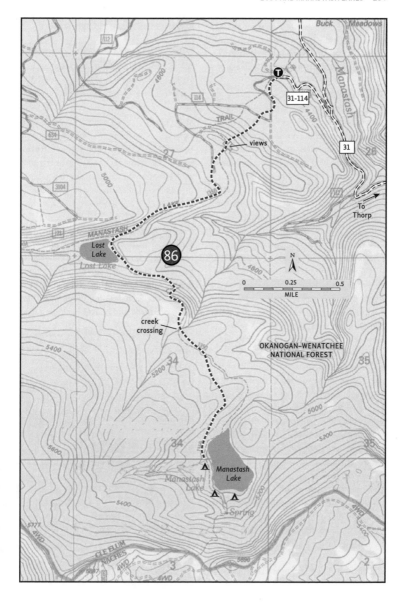

from Cove Road, turn left onto FR 31-114, and follow it up to the official Manastash Lake/Lost Lake trailhead. In a short 0.4 mile, this road ends at the trailhead parking area.

ON THE TRAIL

From the parking area, start climbing on the well-marked trail. The path climbs a spectacular sidehill meadow filled with wildflowers—balsamroot starts the color show in May, and a variety of wildflower species keep the color going throughout the spring and summer. At nearly 0.7 mile the route offers views down the Manastash Creek drainage toward the Kittitas Valley and across to Table Mountain to the north.

At the 0.8-mile mark, at an unmarked trail junction, stay to the left on the main trail to Lost Lake, which you'll reach at 1.6 miles. This pretty lake is frequented by common mergansers and ospreys, proving there are trout in the lake, and the forests around the lake are alive with hairy and downy woodpeckers. A trail leads along the north side for access farther down the lake.

To continue on your trek, head left at the camp areas when you reach the lake. Skirt the lakeshore for a short distance, then start back into the dense forest on the way to Manastash Lake. The forest starts as mostly silver fir and some pines but slowly changes to western larch and even some western red cedar in the wettest areas.

The trail crosses a small creek at 2.6 miles, then drops to the shores of Manastash Lake at 3.5 miles. Backpackers will find many fine campsites along the western shore. Autumn visitors will find the western larch in full golden display (especially early October).

The Kachess Ridge Trail passing through one of many lush meadows above the French Cabin Creek drainage

87 French Cabin Creek

RATING/ DIFFICULTY	ROUNDTRIP	ELEV GAIN/ HIGH POINT	SEASON
****/3	7 miles	1400 feet/ 5500 feet	June–Oct

Map: Green Trails Kachess Lake No. 208; **Contact:** Okanogan–Wenatchee National Forest, Cle Elum Ranger District; **Notes:** NW Forest Pass required. High-clearance vehicle recommended for last 0.5 mile to true trailhead, but can park and walk; **GPS:** N 47 19.971, W 121 10.816

A moderate hike leads through open pine forests, across sprawling fields of flowers, to glorious views of surrounding alpine peaks. Lupine, shooting stars, and bear grass—the French Cabin Creek basin has them all. Birds and beasts, including deer

and elk, love the meadows and open forests for the dense insect population and nutrient-rich forage. Fortunately, the lack of standing water means that most of the bugs are creepy crawlers rather than buzzing skeeters, which leaves you free to enjoy the grand views and lush flora and fauna without pesky biters and bloodsuckers.

GETTING THERE

From Seattle drive east on I-90 to take exit 80 (signed "Roslyn/Salmon la Sac"). Head north on Bullfrog Road. At the roundabout junction with State Route 903, go left through Roslyn on SR 903 and continue about 13 miles. Just past the upper end of Cle Elum Lake, turn left onto French Cabin Road (Forest Road 4308). Drive 6.5 miles up FR 4308 to a small dirt road, FR 4308-132 (marked with a sign for French Cabin Creek Trail). Turn right onto this road and drive 0.5 mile to the road's end. FR 4308-132 is narrow and rough. Those driving low-clearance passenger cars should park at the bottom of the road and walk the 0.5 mile to the trailhead.

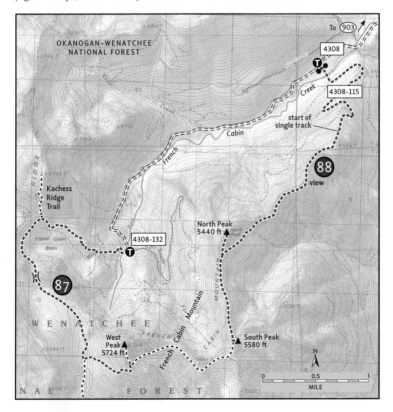

ON THE TRAIL

The trail starts with a steady climb up a steep, badly eroded trail through the forest. For nearly 1 mile the route stays under the overhanging branches, providing relief from the sun but no views and little local scenery to enjoy (occasional forest glades do provide glimpses of tiny forest flowers, such as Columbia lewisia, scarlet gilia, and glacier lilies).

At 1 mile the trail breaks out into a clearing with views up to the spires of French Cabin Mountain. In another 0.25 mile the scattered clumps of trees and meadows give way to a small section of clear-cut as the trail hooks out into a section of private timberland.

Just inside the clear-cut, the trail intersects the Kachess Ridge Trail. Stay left and descend briefly before climbing once more to reach a high pass (elev. 5000 feet) separating the forest and meadows of French Cabin Creek's basin from the sprawling meadows of Silver Creek basin. Stop and enjoy the views of the flower fields before you drop steeply into Silver Creek's meadows. Then for more than 1.5 miles you'll climb gently as you wander through grass and knee-high wildflowers in the sun-drenched meadows below French Cabin Mountain.

At 3.5 miles from the trailhead you'll find another trail junction. Heading left here leads you up to the flank of West Peak for great views of the Kachess Ridge and French Cabin peaks. Turn around and head back the way you came before the trail starts to descend toward the other side.

Distant views of Mount Stuart from Kachess Ridge near French Cabin Mountain

88 French Cabin Mountain

RATING/ DIFFICULTY	ROUNDTRIP	ELEV GAIN/ HIGH POINT	SEASON
****/5	10 miles	1750 feet/ 5580 feet	July–Oct

Map: Green Trails Kachess Lake No. 208; **Contact:** Okanogan–Wenatchee National Forest, Cle Elum Ranger District; **Notes:** NW Forest Pass required; **GPS:** N 47 21.041, W 121 8.185

You'll climb in a long, steady push over the course of this 5-mile trail—no switchbacks and few turns, just a straight out-and-back to the South Peak of French Cabin Mountain—dropping briefly and then climbing steeply

again to skirt just below the lower North Peak on the way. Near the southern summit the trail pierces sprawling wildflower meadows, with expansive views in all directions. Down near the start of the trail you'll enjoy the cooling shade of pine forests. This is a lonesome path, with few visitors and no water, so make sure you pack everything you need.

GETTING THERE

From Seattle drive east on I-90 to take exit 80 (signed "Roslyn/Salmon la Sac"). Head north on Bullfrog Road. At the roundabout junction with State Route 903, go left through Roslyn on SR 903 and continue about 13 miles. Just past the upper end of Cle Elum Lake, turn left onto French Cabin Road (Forest Road 4308). Drive 3.8 miles up FR 4308 to a junction with FR 4308-115 on the left. Turn here and park near the gate that blocks vehicle access onto FR 4308-115. Don't block the gate when parking.

ON THE TRAIL

Start up the gated road (FR 4308-115), climbing 1.9 miles to its end and the start of the single-track trail. Continue climbing steeply another 1.2 miles, pushing upward to a 5000-foot knoll, before dropping briefly and then climbing steeply onto the meadow-crowned top of North Peak at around 4 miles. You'll have to scramble off-trail a few hundred yards to attain the true 5440-foot summit.

Another mile or so of rolling up and down along the ridge leads to South Peak (elev. 5580 feet). The trail continues past this

The Cascade crest regions of Chikamin Peak and Lemah Mountain rise sharply to the west of Pete Lake.

meadow-covered summit to a junction with the French Cabin Creek Trail (Hike 87). Stop at the top, though, for the best views: south to Mount Rainier, north to Thorp Mountain, east to Cle Elum Lake and the Sasse Mountain/Hex Mountain ridgeline, and west to West Peak and the long line of Kachess Ridge.

89 Pete Lake

RATING/ DIFFICULTY	ROUNDTRIP	ELEV GAIN/ HIGH POINT	SEASON
***/3	9 miles	400 feet/ 3200 feet	June–Oct

Map: Green Trails Kachess Lake No. 208; **Contact:** Okanogan–Wenatchee National Forest, Cle Elum Ranger District; **Notes:** NW Forest Pass required; **GPS:** N 47 26.097, W 121 11.127

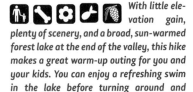 *With little elevation gain, plenty of scenery, and a broad, sun-warmed forest lake at the end of the valley, this hike makes a great warm-up outing for you and your kids. You can enjoy a refreshing swim in the lake before turning around and returning along the gentle forest trail.*

GETTING THERE

From Seattle drive east on I-90 to take exit 80 (signed "Roslyn/Salmon la Sac"). Head north on Bullfrog Road. At the roundabout junction with State Route 903, go left through Roslyn on SR 903 and continue about 15 miles, passing the upper end of Cle Elum Lake. Turn left (west) onto Forest Road 46 and drive 5 miles

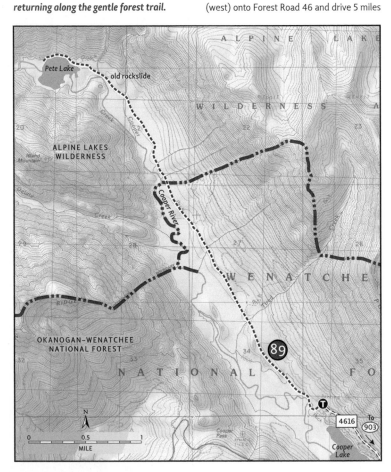

to Cooper Lake. Turn right onto Forest Road 4616, crossing Cooper River, and continue 1 mile past the upper loops of the campground to the trailhead at the end of the road near the upper end of the lake.

ON THE TRAIL

This trail is essentially a continuation of the Cooper River Trail (Hike 90), as it follows the broad Cooper River valley upstream from Cooper Lake to its headwaters at Pete Lake. The trail begins in deep forest, with close views of the river during the early stretch. Watch for activity in the deeper pools, as beavers are making every effort to turn the river into a series of interconnected ponds.

The valley is blanketed with thick old-growth forest and the occasional river meadow, but there are few distant views. The lack of vistas, though, means you can focus on close-in scenery. Lush foliage and forest wildflowers line the trail. All that vegetation means good feeding for wildlife. Rabbits, weasels, fishers, and martens scurry around the bushes. Black-tailed deer roam in great numbers through the area, and bobcats, coyotes, and cougars prowl around the lairs of those vegetarian beasts.

As the trail nears the lake, around the 3-mile mark, it passes an old, massive rockslide. The slide covers the south side of the valley. The trail skirts the worst of the rubble but provides good views of the pile of rock and displaced earth.

Pete Lake fills a broad basin near the upper end of the valley. The eastern shore of the lake offers good views of Summit Chief Mountain to the north and the surrounding ridges. The lake boasts a healthy population of rainbow trout—you might be lucky enough to pull a pan-sized fish out of the lake for a lunchtime protein burst.

90 Cooper River

RATING/ DIFFICULTY	ROUNDTRIP	ELEV GAIN/ HIGH POINT	SEASON
***/2	6 miles	500 feet/ 2800 feet	May–Oct

Map: Green Trails Kachess Lake No. 208;
Contact: Okanogan–Wenatchee National

Cooper River

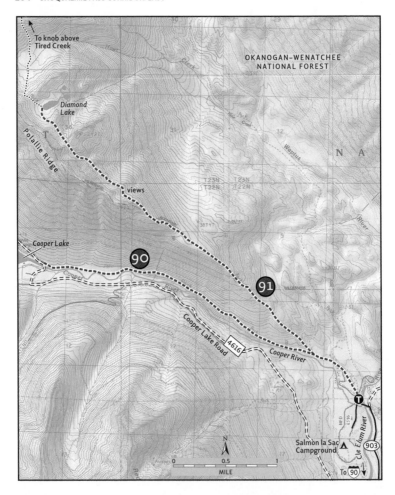

Forest, Cle Elum Ranger District; **Notes:** NW Forest Pass required; **GPS:** N 47 24.264, W 121 5.947

 This riverside trail offers no expansive views and doesn't explore any wildflower meadows or high alpine country. But it does track alongside a beautiful mountain river that sports a healthy population of hungry trout. It also provides ample opportunity to practice your bird-watching, as a number of avian species thrive here, including the river-loving water ouzel and

the fish-loving kingfisher. The trip can be done as a one-way hike by shuttling vehicles or by hitching a ride back down the road from Cooper Lake.

GETTING THERE

From Seattle drive east on I-90 to take exit 80 (signed "Roslyn/Salmon la Sac"). Head north on Bullfrog Road. At the roundabout junction with State Route 903, go left through Roslyn on SR 903 and continue about 16 miles, passing the upper end of Cle Elum Lake, to Salmon la Sac. At the Y in the road near the Salmon la Sac Campground, take the left branch toward the campground. Cross the Cle Elum River bridge and turn right, away from the campground, and reach the trailhead parking area in another 0.5 mile.

ON THE TRAIL

The trail follows the pretty Cooper River valley upstream to Cooper Lake. The trail stays on the north side of the river, and at times the valley narrows enough for you to hear (and possibly see) traffic on the road that runs on the other side of the valley. Ignore that interruption as you explore the dense old-growth forest around you.

The trail splits 0.7 mile from the trailhead. To the right is a path that climbs steeply up Polallie Ridge (Hike 91). Continue to the left instead, staying close to the river. If you're an angler keep an eye out for likely fishing holes. Take your time—the trail is gentle enough for you to adopt a mile-eating pace between fishing sessions. History buffs should pay attention to the trees about 10 feet above trail height. Look for brown or cream-colored oval ceramic rings about 4 inches in diameter. The rings are insulating holders for the old bare wire that serves

as telephone line linking the multitude of fire lookout stations with the forest service ranger stations in the valley. Many of the insulators still hang from the trees, and frequently tangles of wire dangle from them.

About 2 miles from the trailhead the valley broadens a bit and the river begins to meander side to side across the gentle valley floor. You'll find some small patches of berries here, and occasional clumps of wildflowers along the riverbanks.

At 3 miles you'll encounter Cooper Lake Road (FR 4616), which crosses Cooper River just below the lake outlet. Turn around here, or cross the road bridge to access the road leading back down to Salmon la Sac.

91 Polallie Ridge

RATING/ DIFFICULTY	ROUNDTRIP	ELEV GAIN/ HIGH POINT	SEASON
****/5	8 miles	3000 feet/ 5300 feet	June–Oct

Map: Green Trails Kachess Lake No. 208; **Contact:** Okanogan–Wenatchee National Forest, Cle Elum Ranger District; **Notes:** NW Forest Pass required; **GPS:** N 47 24.264, W 121 5.947

Pack sunscreen, your wildflower guide, binoculars for bird-watching, and water—plenty of water! This trail climbs ceaselessly along an open ridge, providing some of the greatest panoramic views to be found in the eastern Cascades. This is also a bird-rich region, thanks to the plethora of wildflowers and their associated insect populations, and a popular grazing route for deer and even herds of mountain goats. This all adds up to a wonderful wilderness experience. All you have to do to enjoy it is plod upward, endlessly, on a sun-baked trail without a bit of water in sight.

GETTING THERE

From Seattle drive east on I-90 to take exit 80 (signed "Roslyn/Salmon la Sac"). Head north on Bullfrog Road. At the roundabout junction with State Route 903, go left through Roslyn on SR 903 and continue about 16 miles, passing the upper end of Cle Elum Lake, to Salmon la Sac. At the Y in the road near the Salmon la Sac Campground, take the left branch toward the campground. Cross the Cle Elum River bridge and turn right, away from the campground, and reach the trailhead parking area in another 0.5 mile.

ON THE TRAIL

The trail begins with a long climb up the eastern side of Polallie Ridge, ascending exposed switchbacks that weave through rock gardens. Pause frequently to enjoy the views across the Cle Elum Valley to Jolly and Sasse mountains. In 3 miles the trail finally tapers to a more moderate pitch at around 5000 feet elevation. But the respite from the climbing is short-lived.

A few hundred yards of easy ridgetop hiking is followed by a roll down to 4800 feet elevation, then a climb up to 5300 feet. Soon, it's down to 4900 feet, then up to 5200. The saving graces are the occasional views from the top and scattered along the way, with a jewel of a lake—Diamond Lake—nestled in a broad meadow about 4 miles up the trail.

EXTENDING YOUR TRIP

If you haven't worked enough, press on up the ridge. You can add another 2.5 miles of climbing to get to a 5422-foot knob above Tired Creek. Remains of the former lookout site dot the open meadow here with spectacular views of Mount Hinman and Mount Daniel to the north.

Mount Daniel seen from the former lookout site on the western end of Polallie Ridge

Views west toward the Cascade crest from Davis Peak

92 Davis Peak

RATING/ DIFFICULTY	ROUNDTRIP	ELEV GAIN/ HIGH POINT	SEASON
*****/5	11 miles	3900 feet/ 6426 feet	June–Oct

Map: Green Trails Kachess Lake No. 208;
Contact: Okanogan–Wenatchee National
Forest, Cle Elum Ranger District; **Notes:** NW
Forest Pass required; **GPS:** N 47 24.913, W
121 04.860

Personal trainers charge hundreds of dollars for this kind of extreme exercise. The opportunity to sweat buckets goes for a premium in places like Los Angeles and New York. Yet you get to subject yourself to this brutal experience for free. What's more, while you exhaust yourself on this long, hot hike up a ruthlessly steep trail, you also earn great rewards: views that can't even be imagined by people chained to their treadmills. From Davis Peak you'll soak in sweeping views that include all of the splendid Alpine Lakes Wilderness and beyond.

GETTING THERE

From Seattle drive east on I-90 to take exit
80 (signed "Roslyn/Salmon la Sac"). Head
north on Bullfrog Road. At the roundabout
junction with State Route 903, go left
through Roslyn on SR 903 and continue

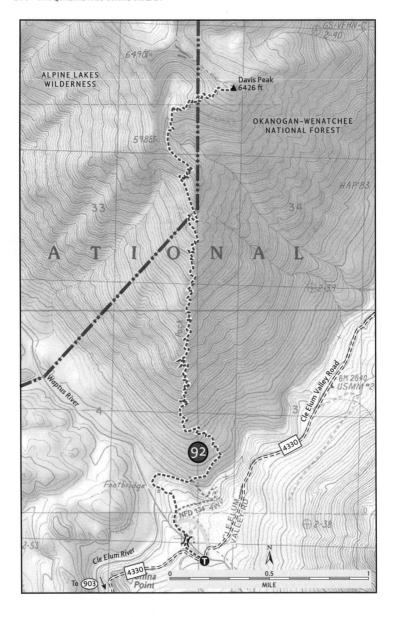

ALPINE LAKES
WILDERNESS

6490

Davis Peak
▲6426 ft

OKANOGAN–WENATCHEE
NATIONAL FOREST

5988

GS·VFHN·C
2·40

HAP'83

33

34

2·39

A T I O N A L

Waptus River

4

3

Cle Elum Valley Road

BM 2640
USMM #2

92

4330

Footbridge

NFD 134·4WO

2·55

CLE ELUM VALLEY RD

2·38

0

Cle Elum River

4330

To 903

enina
Point

T

N

0   0.5
MILE

about 16 miles, passing the upper end of Cle Elum Lake, to Salmon la Sac. Go right at the Y to stay on the main road (rather than entering the campground), and in 1.6 miles look for the Paris Creek/Davis Peak trailhead parking area on the right.

ON THE TRAIL

From the parking area, hike across the road and follow the dirt road less than a quarter mile to a bridge over the Cle Elum River. Continue along the trail for another 0.25 mile or so to where the path widens onto an old logging road for the next mile. By the end of this mile, the trail has turned vertical, entering a seemingly endless series of switchbacks. The trail bounces you back and forth so much you'll feel like a pinball—especially on the fast descent.

About 2.5 miles from the trailhead, you'll break out of the thinning forest cover, with the remainder of the climb—all 3 miles of it—under the full glare of the sun. Make sure your sunscreen is waterproof, or you'll sweat it off in no time. The sun-drenched, clear-cut "wildflower meadows" are a curse on hot summer days, but even then they are also a blessing, since with every plodding step upward you'll find ever-better views.

By the time you reach the crown of Davis Peak at 5.5 miles, you'll have earned the stellar views that ring you. Your panoramic vision stretches 360 degrees, sweeping in the vast expanse of the Alpine Lakes Wilderness in all its glory. Mount Rainier also pokes up on the southern horizon. It's all stunning, and it's all yours—you earned it, so sit back and enjoy it!

A female blue grouse pauses in a tree, waiting for the commotion to pass on by.

93 Jolly Mountain

RATING/ DIFFICULTY	ROUNDTRIP	ELEV GAIN/ HIGH POINT	SEASON
***/5	12 miles	4000 feet/ 6440 feet	July–Oct

Map: Green Trails Kachess Lake No. 208; **Contact:** Okanogan–Wenatchee National Forest, Cle Elum Ranger District; **Notes:** NW Forest Pass required; **GPS:** N 47 24.264, W 121 5.947

You'll feel jolly on top, but you'll jolly well earn it. As you climb the trail you'll be questioning the value of the views from the top—are they worth the thigh-burning, lung-popping workout of the ascent? But once you reach the top, you'll forget the sweat and tears of the trail as you soak in the mind-numbing, eye-pleasing panorama encircling you.

GETTING THERE

From Seattle drive east on I-90 to take exit 80 (signed "Roslyn/Salmon la Sac"). Head north on Bullfrog Road. At the roundabout junction with State Route 903, go left through Roslyn on SR 903 and continue about 16 miles, passing the upper end of Cle Elum Lake, to Salmon la Sac. Look for the trailhead on the right, between Cayuse Horse Camp and the picnic area.

ON THE TRAIL

From the trailhead, find the trail behind the horse barn at the Forest Service workshop. The trail crosses Salmon la Sac Creek and starts upward immediately. The trail zigs and zags for a steep 3.2 miles through forest, with occasional views into the Cle Elum Valley, to reach the first trail junction.

Stay right and climb the southern face of the valley's headwall. In another mile turn left at another trail junction, and climb even more steeply for another 0.5 mile to reach a third junction. This time, take the left fork and continue a long traverse around the north flank of Jolly Mountain.

The views now increase in frequency and magnificence. A half mile of traversing leads to the last trail junction at 6000 feet. On this north face of the mountain lingering snowfields are likely from this point on—the slippery snow may persist into August. Be careful crossing these slick patches of winter remembrances.

From the last trail junction at 6000 feet, turn right and climb a long, moderate mile to the summit of Jolly Mountain. The last 6 miles brought you up more than 4000 vertical feet. Congratulate yourself on a great achievement. Then look out from your lofty perch. On a clear day, enjoy views of everything within 100 miles as your fatigue

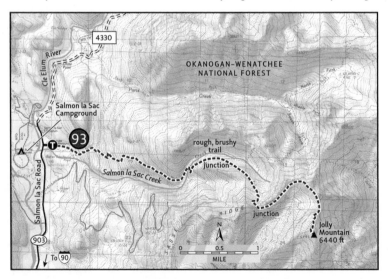

falls away and the jolliness of the summit takes over.

94 Paddy-Go-Easy Pass

RATING/ DIFFICULTY	ROUNDTRIP	ELEV GAIN/ HIGH POINT	SEASON
***/4	7 miles	2700 feet/ 6100 feet	July–Oct

Map: Green Trails Stevens Pass No. 176; **Contact:** Okanogan–Wenatchee National Forest, Cle Elum Ranger District; **Notes:** NW Forest Pass required; **GPS:** N 47 31.974, W 121 04.955

Starting in valley-bottom meadows, you'll enjoy open country start to finish. Oh, you'll dip into stands of trees now and again, but for the most part you'll be surrounded by wildflowers, alpine grasses, and low bushes. That low-growing vegetation means there's nothing but the distant mountains to prevent your views from stretching to the far horizon. And as you climb, the views get longer and longer. By the time you reach the pass you'll be peering out over the expanse of the Cle Elum River valley and, on the other side of the ridge, to the Wenatchee Mountains, within the Alpine Lakes Wilderness.

GETTING THERE

From Seattle drive east on I-90 to take exit 80 (signed "Roslyn/Salmon la Sac"). Head north on Bullfrog Road. At the roundabout junction with State Route 903, go left through Roslyn on SR 903 and continue about 16 miles, passing the upper end of Cle Elum Lake, to Salmon la Sac. Go right at

A hiker descends the trail from Paddy-Go-Easy Pass with views down the Cle Elum River valley.

the Y to stay on the main road (rather than entering the campground), and continue up Cle Elum Valley Road (Forest Road 4330) another 9.5 scenic miles through beautiful meadows. Cross the concrete-lined vehicle ford at Scatter Creek. Continue on to the Fish Lake Ranger Station, and about a half mile farther find the Paddy-Go-Easy trailhead parking area in the meadows on the right.

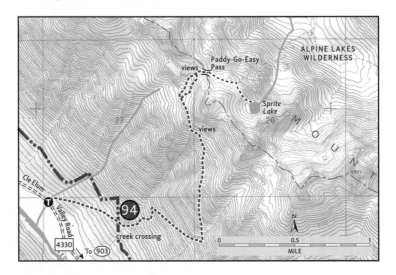

ON THE TRAIL

The trail leaves the roadside meadows and heads into a stand of forest right off the bat. About a half mile up the trail, you'll cross a small creek and then start climbing with vigor. Within the next 0.5 mile the trail turns even steeper, leaving the last big section of forest just over 1 mile from the trailhead. Now you enter steep hillside meadows. The views, too, open up here. Look across the Cle Elum Valley to see Cathedral Rock (Hike 95) towering over the opposite valley wall.

Enjoy those views—they get progressively better—for the next mile. At 2.5 miles the trail splits. Both paths go to the pass. Take either, then come back on the other. For what it's worth, the left fork is a more direct route—I prefer it on the downhill return. So, go right to swing out past an old hard-rock mine (gold? silver? not much of either was ever found here) and a small creek. The trails merge for the final 0.25 mile to the pass.

Paddy-Go-Easy Pass (elev. 6100 feet) is nestled below the 400-foot red-rock cliffs of an unnamed peak.

EXTENDING YOUR TRIP

Press on another 0.6 mile and you'll drop into the Sprite Lake basin. You'll find fabulous campsites around the lake.

95 Cathedral Rock

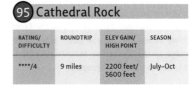

RATING/ DIFFICULTY	ROUNDTRIP	ELEV GAIN/ HIGH POINT	SEASON
****/4	9 miles	2200 feet/ 5600 feet	July–Oct

Map: Green Trails Stevens Pass No. 176; **Contact:** Okanogan–Wenatchee National Forest, Cle Elum Ranger District; **Notes:** NW Forest Pass required; **GPS:** N 47 32.699, W 121 32.699

 *Meadows, river, and lakes. Smooth trails, gentle*

Magnificent Cathedral Rock, near Cathedral Pass, is a landmark along the central Cascade portion of the Pacific Crest Trail in Washington.

climbs, and a lot of grassy pastures in which to rest and relax. This route offers a taste of some of the finest meadows, prettiest lakes, and craggiest mountains in the Alpine Lakes Wilderness, all in a moderate hike along a picturesque ridge.

GETTING THERE

From Seattle drive east on I-90 to take exit 80 (signed "Roslyn/Salmon la Sac"). Head north on Bullfrog Road. At the roundabout junction with State Route 903, go left through Roslyn on SR 903 and continue about 16 miles, passing the upper end of Cle Elum Lake, to Salmon la Sac. Go right at the Y to stay on the main road (rather than entering the campground), and continue up Cle Elum Valley Road (Forest

Road 4330) to near the end of the road. Just before entering the Tucquala Meadow Campground, turn left into a wide trailhead parking lot.

ON THE TRAIL

From the parking area, hike down a short dirt road to the Cle Elum River, and find the trailhead at a bridge over the river. At 2.5 miles the trail passes Squaw Lake. This is a popular camping destination for families with small children or for folks who want to escape the noise and crowds without working excessively hard—the hiking distance isn't too great, and the shallow lake is perfect for wading or swimming.

Moving past the lake, the trail follows the ridge north, alternating through grassy

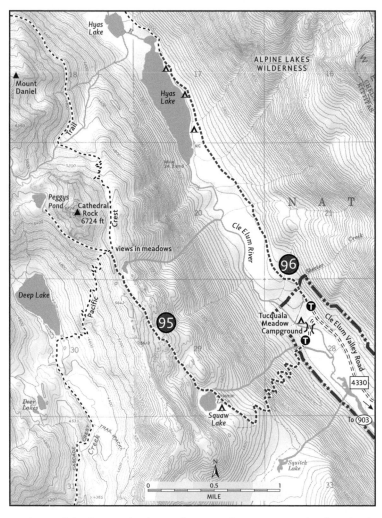

meadows and thin forest, with a few small tarns dotting the meadows along the way. At 4.5 miles the trail ends at a junction with the Pacific Crest Trail (PCT).

At this point you're directly under the towering spire of Cathedral Rock. Look closely and you might see some Spiderman wannabes scaling its rocky walls—Cathedral

Meadows and wetlands surrounding the Hyas Lake region

is quite popular with rock climbers. Find a place in the meadows for a leisurely lunch in the shadow of this monolith.

EXTENDING YOUR TRIP

At the junction with the PCT, hikers have three options to extend their adventures. Turn left and hike south, descending to Deep Lake—a beautiful blue-water lake fed by waterfalls off the south flank of Mount Daniel. Or you can turn right and follow the PCT north along the flank of Mount Daniel toward Deception Pass offering stunning views east across the valley toward Granite Mountain. Finally, you can cross the PCT and follow a faint climbers track to the northwest, skirting the steep southwest face of Daniel to a picturesque little cirque holding a small alpine pool known as Peggys Pond in just shy of a mile more hiking.

96 Hyas Lake

RATING/ DIFFICULTY	ROUNDTRIP	ELEV GAIN/ HIGH POINT	SEASON
**/1	4 miles	100 feet/ 3500 feet	July–Oct

Map: Green Trails Stevens Pass No. 176; **Contact:** Okanogan–Wenatchee National Forest, Cle Elum Ranger District; **Notes:** NW Forest Pass required; **GPS:** N 47 32.714, W 121 05.906

🚶🐾♿ *A flat hike through old forests leads to a wide expanse of water. Hyas Lake is actually a pair of pools in the middle of the Cle Elum River. The lower pool is a broad but shallow lake that sprawls nearly all the way across the valley floor and stretches more than a mile from one end to the other. The upper pool is a smaller, even shallower lake. In reality, it's the same lake, but the waters have been divided by a hearty growth of marsh grasses—as the grasses grew, they trapped more and more sediment, until finally a small band of muddy ground stretched across the upper end of the long Hyas Lake, leaving the smaller fragment just a few dozen yards above the lower lake. Plan to venture at least as far as the middle of the lower lake—and the best rest stops are at the upper end of the lake.*

GETTING THERE

From Seattle drive east on I-90 to take exit 80 (signed "Roslyn/Salmon la Sac"). Head north on Bullfrog Road. At the roundabout junction with State Route 903, go left through Roslyn on SR 903 and continue about 16 miles, passing the upper end of Cle Elum Lake, to Salmon la Sac. Go right at the Y to stay on the main road (rather than entering the campground), and continue up Cle Elum Valley Road (Forest Road 4330) another 12 miles to the end of the road. The trailhead parking area is just past the Tucquala Meadow Campground.

ON THE TRAIL

Heading up the Cle Elum River Trail you'll wander along for a flat mile as the trail weaves through the trees, well back from the river. As you hike, listen for the twitter of birds—the songs of small flittering birds will be your first indication that you're nearly to the lake.

The lower section of Hyas Lake is a broad grassland. About 1.1 miles from the trailhead, you'll finally see the open waters of the lake. For the next mile, the trail gradually trends toward the lakeshore. Note that the trail is so flat and generally well maintained that we've encountered eager anglers carrying sizable rowboats up this pathway to fish for resident rainbow trout in the shallow waters of the lake.

The best places to stop are about 2 miles from the trailhead. You'll find campsites that serve perfectly as picnic sites, too. Wade out into the refreshingly cool water, and look up on the towering peaks of Mount Daniel and Cathedral Rock (Hike 95) before heading for home.

Opposite: A hiker near Mount Lillian surveys the views.

teanaway and blewett country

Sunshine, wildflowers, wild animals, and remote trails. That's the Teanaway country in a nutshell. The long, scenic Middle Fork and North Fork Teanaway River valleys provide access to some of the most wonderful and unique hiking opportunities in Washington. The trails climb long ridges through open forests and meadowlands populated with mule deer, elk, and mountain goats. Black bear are common here, too, in part because of the abundance of purple gold (fat, juicy huckleberries!). And birds of all shapes, sizes, and colors call the Teanaway home, making these trails a paradise for bird-watchers. Then there are the flowers. Pick a trail, any trail, in the Teanaway country, and you have a great chance of seeing a wide assortment of wildflowers in bloom. Lupine, columbine, shooting stars, tiger lilies, paintbrush, penstemon, buckwheat, aster, daisies . . . the list goes on and on. In short, regardless of what you want from your wildland trail, you'll find it here.

97 Red Top Lookout and Agate Beds

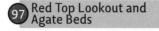

RATING/ DIFFICULTY	ROUNDTRIP	ELEV GAIN/ HIGH POINT	SEASON
****/2	3 miles	400 feet/ 5361 feet	July–Nov

Maps: Green Trails Mount Stuart No. 209 and Liberty No. 210; **Contact:** Okanogan–Wenatchee National Forest, Cle Elum Ranger District; **Notes:** NW Forest Pass required; **GPS:** N 47 17.802, W 120 45.567

There are several routes leading hikers to the summit of Red Top, but we prefer ours because it climbs easily, making it enjoyable for families and kids, and

Stunning views across the Teanaway toward the Stuart Mountain Range from Red Top Mountain

because the relatively easy ascent leaves hikers with plenty of energy for additional exploration of the nearby agate beds. Although the old manned system of mountaintop fire spotters was abandoned long ago in favor of satellite imagery, Red Top's lookout tower still stands. And north of the summit, hikers will find more history lessons—in human greed. Semiprecious agates and thunder eggs (rocks with crystalline structures inside) litter this region, and rock hunters have picked over the exposed rocks and dug scores of holes—some just a couple of feet deep, others 6 to 8 feet deep and 10 to 20 feet

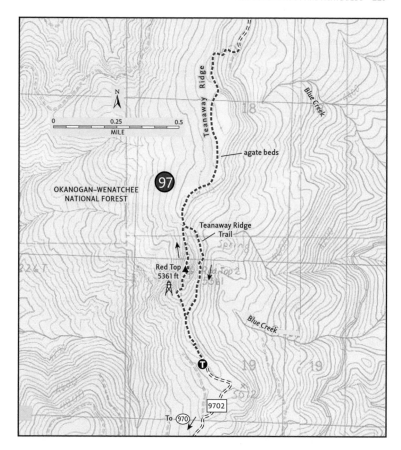

around—in search of buried treasure. The *Teanaway Ridge Trail rambles north from Red Top mountain through this "mine" zone, offering plenty of opportunities to see the diggings.*

GETTING THERE

From Seattle drive east on I-90 to exit 85 (East Cle Elum). Cross over the freeway overpass and turn right (northbound) on State Route 970. Drive 17 miles on SR 970 before turning left onto Forest Road 9738 just past the Mineral Springs Campground. Continue 2.6 miles before turning left onto FR 9702, signed "Red Top Mtn: 5." Stay on FR 9702 for 3.9 miles to a junction, with the road straight ahead signed "Red Top: 1." Stay straight and in 0.4 mile turn right onto the road signed "Red Top Parking Area." Another half mile leads to the parking lot and trailhead.

ON THE TRAIL

The trail starts away from the trailhead and angles quickly up the ridgeline, arriving at the summit of Red Top in just a half mile. Enjoy the panoramic views from here—it seems you can almost touch Mount Stuart on clear days. Then continue north and drop down a steep, somewhat exposed path through the talus and jumbled rocks to an intersection with the Teanaway Ridge Trail around 0.7 mile. Turn left and stride out along the nearly level trail as it jumps from open meadows to forest glades and back again.

Agate "miners" have pitted both meadow and forest here with their holes. Let the kids pick through the rocks around the area— they may get lucky and turn up an Ellensburg Blue (agate) or even a thunder egg.

At about 1.5 miles, the trail nears another access road above Blue Creek. Turn back here and, on the return, you can bypass the summit by sticking to the Teanaway Ridge Trail as it rolls under the east face of Red Top to get you back to the trailhead.

98 Middle Fork Teanaway

RATING/ DIFFICULTY	ROUNDTRIP	ELEV GAIN/ HIGH POINT	SEASON
***/2	7 miles	300 feet/ 3000 feet	May–Nov

Map: Green Trails Mount Stuart No. 209; **Contact:** Okanogan–Wenatchee National Forest, Cle Elum Ranger District; **Notes:** NW Forest Pass required; **GPS:** N 47 17.868, W 120 57.744

 *Mountain rivers are magical, crystal-clear ribbons that inundate your senses. They can be cool massages for your feet. They offer delicate music for your eyes, sparkling flashes in the alpine*

Middle Fork Teanaway River

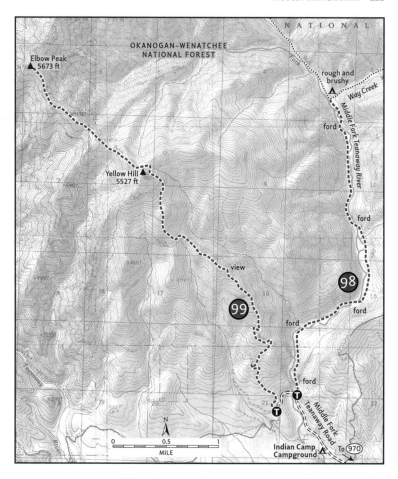

sunlight. When properly treated, they offer needed refreshment for thirsty hikers. The Middle Fork Teanaway River offers all of this and more as it tumbles through a gorgeous mountain valley, home and habitat to a variety of birds, beasts, and, yes, bugs. This riverside trail passes through rich valley meadows, grand old forests, and

comfortable campsites for those who can't resist the chance to stay longer than a single day.

GETTING THERE

From Seattle drive east on I-90 to exit 85 (East Cle Elum). Cross over the freeway overpass and turn right (northbound) on State Route

970. Cross the Teanaway River bridge, and in another mile turn left onto Teanaway Road. At 7.3 miles up the Teanaway Road, turn left onto West Fork Teanaway Road and drive 0.7 mile to the Teanaway Campground. Turn right onto Middle Fork Teanaway Road. Continue 4.5 miles to the Indian Camp Campground. Continue 0.5 mile farther to the trailhead on the right, found near a sharp left turn in the road.

ON THE TRAIL

The Middle Fork Teanaway Trail (No. 1393) climbs gradually along the pretty river for an easy and fast hike if that's what you want. But I recommend enjoying it as an easy and slow hike. Bring the kids and stroll up the trail, letting the youngsters explore as you walk.

The trail leaves the trailhead with a fording of the river. Proceed upstream for 0.25 mile to the point where the river valley narrows into a steep-walled canyon. At this point the trail runs on a bench above the river, but within the next 0.5 mile the trail slides closer to the river and occasionally gets too close—the tread disappears periodically in small washouts.

Unfortunately, the trail receives only occasional maintenance, so the tread may be rough—or missing—in places. Fortunately, the gentle slope of the land makes scrambling through these rough sections fairly easy.

As you near the 1-mile mark the trail crosses the river once more via a shallow ford. You'll cross the river again in about another 0.25 mile, then go back across yet again at just past 2 miles. Between fords, the trail alternates between cool forests and sun-streaked forest clearings. Look for wildlife—both ground-based critters such as deer and airborne beasts such as nuthatches

A hiker roams up a bootpath for the views near the summit of Yellow Hill.

and gray jays—in the margin areas where the forests open onto the clearings.

At 3 miles from the trailhead you'll come to yet another ford. About a half mile past this last crossing, you'll find a side stream—Way Creek—tumbling down to join the Middle Fork. In addition to the creek junction, you'll also find a trail junction. Continue a few dozen yards past the trail junction to find a broad campsite near the river. Stop here for lunch before turning back to complete your 7-mile hike.

EXTENDING YOUR TRIP

If you still have energy and a need for more wildlands, press on up the river trail. It continues another 3.5 miles. But beyond Way Creek the trail gets brushier and even rougher than what you've experienced so far.

99 Elbow Peak

RATING/ DIFFICULTY	ROUNDTRIP	ELEV GAIN/ HIGH POINT	SEASON
****/4	10 miles	2800 feet/ 5673 feet	June–Nov

Maps: Green Trails Kachess Lake No. 208 and Mount Stuart No. 209; **Contact:** Okanogan–Wenatchee National Forest, Cle Elum Ranger District; **Notes:** NW Forest Pass required. Trail open to motorcycles; **GPS:** N 47 17.719, W 120 57.898

The Teanaway country is home to an assortment of birds and animals, as well as some truly magnificent wild country. It's not protected as wilderness, so you might hear or see motorcycles along the trails, but the grandeur of the country is worth that risk—fortunately, when you encounter

motorcycles they disappear quickly from sight, even if the exhaust fumes and ringing in your ears linger for a time. This trail, though open to motors, offers hikers a rewarding excursion up a beautiful mountain in one of the most stunning parts of the Cascades, and Elbow Peak provides grand views and glorious wildflower-viewing opportunities.

GETTING THERE

From Seattle drive east on I-90 to exit 85 (East Cle Elum). Cross over the freeway overpass and turn right (northbound) on State Route 970. Cross the Teanaway River bridge, and in another mile turn left onto Teanaway Road. At 7.3 miles up Teanaway Road, turn left onto West Fork Teanaway Road and drive 0.7 mile to the Teanaway Campground. Turn right onto Middle Fork Teanaway Road. Continue 4.5 miles to the Indian Camp Campground. Continue 0.7 mile farther to the trailhead on the right, found just past the Middle Fork Teanaway trailhead (Hike 98).

ON THE TRAIL

The trail starts on a road, but one that has been decommissioned so you won't have to worry about traffic. After you have hiked 1.4 miles on the road, the trail climbs right, steeply up the face of the ridge, ignoring the need for switchbacks on its straight-up run. At 2 miles you'll crest a bench on the long ridge climb where you'll find the first fine views. Look out over the Middle Fork Teanaway country as you catch your breath.

Once you're breathing freely again, push on up the trail as it moderates its pitch. You'll climb more gently along a traverse of the flank of Yellow Hill at around 2.5 miles out. In another mile you'll push up the steep final

UNDERSTANDING ELK

Elk. Such a small, simple word for such a massive, majestic beast. I much prefer the Shawnee Indian name *wapiti*, meaning "white rump." But a name is just a name, and, wapiti or elk, these animals earn the respect and appreciation of anyone fortunate enough to see them in the wild.

But not all elk are created equal. Indeed, Washington boasts two distinct species of elk. Roosevelt elk, named for Theodore Roosevelt, are found on the Olympic Peninsula (hence their nickname, Olympic elk). In the Cascades—and points east—Rocky Mountain elk reign supreme.

Rocky Mountain elk are somewhat smaller than their Roosevelt cousins (a big Roosevelt bull may weigh more than a half ton), but they generally sport broader, heavier antler sets. A large part of this antler difference stems from the different habitats of each subspecies. Roosevelt elk tend to be in the foliage-rich rain forests of the Olympic Peninsula, so broad, heavy antlers become more problematic. Rocky Mountain elk thrive in the drier, more open forests of the Cascades, but they also move out over the plains of the eastern Cascade foothills and even out onto the desert steppes of the Columbia River basin. Indeed, Rocky Mountain elk once existed in vast herds on the Great Plains, alongside the mighty American bison.

Elk of both types feed by browsing on a variety of vegetation, from grasses to berries to evergreen needles. The most impressive time to experience elk is autumn, when the herds are in rut—in other words, mating season. Like most ungulates, the elk males (bulls) fight among themselves to establish dominance and decide which bull gets to mate with the female elk (cows).

As part of the ritual, the bulls challenge each other by issuing ringing calls. Known as bugling, these calls can be an eerie trumpet tone that sends chills down the spine. Listening to the undulating high-pitched calls as twilight falls over a forest glade will make even the most unimaginative hiker think that they're lost in the forest primeval.

The best bets for experiencing wapiti in the Snoqualmie region are along the trails in Teanaway country and in the Chinook Pass area.

pitch to the eastern slope below the summit of Yellow Hill (elev. 5527 feet). If going up to the summit area of Yellow Hill is an objective, a bootpath on your left will likely be visible for great views south as you head up.

This summit scramble provides your first clear views of Mount Rainier to the south. Elbow Peak towers upvalley, nearly in your grasp. If you want a short hike, stop at Yellow Hill. Mile-hungry hikers,

though, should pause just long enough to snap a picture or two—the views are very photogenic—before dipping back down to the ridge to start up the long slope toward Elbow Peak.

Over the next 1.5 miles you'll swing around Yellow Hill and roll up and down along the ridgeline up the southeast face of Elbow. Every step brings great views. Jolly Mountain looms just past Elbow Peak. Mount

Stuart stands as an impressive sentinel to the northeast. And, of course, mighty Mount Rainier rises to the south.

The last 0.5 mile of hiking requires a scramble through the rocks atop Elbow. Finally, at 5 miles, the faint trail crosses the summit. From the top of Elbow Peak (elev. 5673 feet), enjoy outstanding views over all of Teanaway country and beyond into the Alpine Lakes Wilderness.

100 Koppen Mountain

RATING/ DIFFICULTY	ROUNDTRIP	ELEV GAIN/ HIGH POINT	SEASON
****/4	7 miles	2300 feet/ 6031 feet	July–Nov

Map: Green Trails Mount Stuart No. 209; **Contact:** Okanogan–Wenatchee National Forest, Cle Elum Ranger District; **Notes:** NW

Forest Pass required; **GPS:** N 47 23.326, W 120 52.339

The Koppen Mountain Trail offers incredible views of the Stuart Range and the jagged peaks of Teanaway country. Such views are found on many other trails in this area, but what those other routes don't have is the quiet and solitude found at Koppen. Enjoy this largely forgotten trail and you'll be able to selfishly soak in those views without having to share.

GETTING THERE

From Seattle drive east on I-90 to exit 85 (East Cle Elum). Cross over the freeway overpass and turn right (northbound) on State Route 970. Cross the Teanaway River bridge, and in another mile turn left onto Teanaway Road. Drive north on Teanaway

A hiker enjoying the rocky summit of Koppen Mountain

Road, veering right as it becomes first North Fork Teanaway Road and then unpaved Forest Road 9737 at 29 Pines Campground. Drive 4 miles to Beverly Campground and then continue on to FR 9737-120. Turn left and follow it to the abandoned De Roux Campground and the trailhead.

ON THE TRAIL

Start up the trail as it parallels De Roux Creek heading west. After nearly 1.6 miles of forest hiking, the trail forks. Go left to leave De Roux

Creek and start a steep climb out of the valley (the right fork goes to Hike 101, De Roux Creek–Gallagher Head Lake). You'll soon be sweating as you ascend switchbacks for just over a half mile to a 5040-foot pass on the shoulder of Koppen Mountain. You'll find fine views here, but don't stop now—the scenery and the views get better as you go higher.

At the pass the trail splits. Follow the wide boot-beaten path to the left as it climbs the north shoulder of Koppen Mountain. This trail was actually built before World War II,

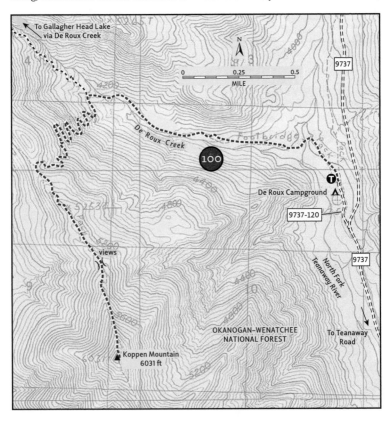

when Koppen was home to a fire lookout station. Since the trail was built for fire spotters rather than recreationists, it tends to be steep and straight—these men truly believed that the fastest way from point A to point B was a straight line, even if that line ran vertically! Fortunately, the slope isn't too steep, and the trail is enjoyable.

The path rolls upward through grassy meadows to the open summit of Koppen Mountain (elev. 6031 feet), about 3.5 miles from the trailhead. Drop your pack and lie down in the cool grass. Look skyward to watch the resident raptors soar on the afternoon thermals. Look to the northeast to gawk at towering Mount Stuart beyond Iron Peak. Look northwest to Hawkins Mountain and the Esmeralda Peaks. Look down to the long valley of the North Fork

Teanaway River. Look out, or you might become so lost in the spectacular scenery that you'll lose track of time and end up spending the night!

EXTENDING YOUR TRIP
From the top of Koppen Mountain, you may choose to add mileage to your day by continuing south along the long, view-rich ridge that separates the North Fork and the Middle Fork Teanaway River valleys.

101 De Roux Creek–Gallagher Head Lake

RATING/ DIFFICULTY	ROUNDTRIP	ELEV GAIN/ HIGH POINT	SEASON
***/3	8 miles	1900 feet/ 5600 feet	May–Nov

Map: Green Trails Mount Stuart No. 209; **Contact:** Okanogan–Wenatchee National Forest, Cle Elum Ranger District; **Notes:** NW Forest Pass required; **GPS:** N 47 20.535, W 120 55.506

 The shores of Gallagher Head Lake offer a panoramic background dominated by Hawkins Mountain and the Esmeralda Peaks. The vast meadows around the lake are awash in color much of the summer as scores of wildflower species push up into bloom at various times and seasons.

GETTING THERE
From Seattle drive east on I-90 to exit 85 (East Cle Elum). Cross over the freeway

De Roux Creek surrounded by lush meadows of shooting stars along the upper portion of the trail leading toward Gallagher Head Lake

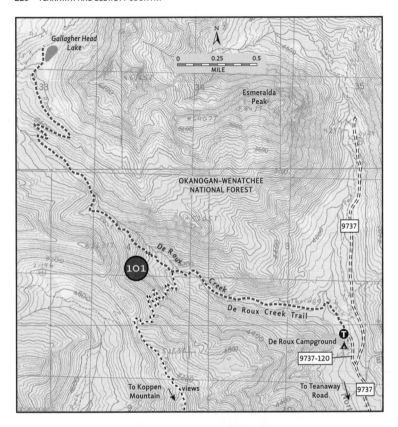

overpass and turn right (northbound) on State Route 970. Cross the Teanaway River bridge, and in another mile turn left onto Teanaway Road. Drive north on Teanaway Road, veering right as it becomes first North Fork Teanaway Road and then unpaved Forest Road 9737 at 29 Pines Campground. Drive 4 miles to Beverly Campground and then continue on to FR 9737-120. Turn left and follow it to the abandoned De Roux Campground and the trailhead.

ON THE TRAIL

Follow the De Roux Creek Trail west and, at about 1 mile out, stay right to continue along De Roux Creek. For the first 1.6 miles the trail climbs upward somewhat as it meanders through open forest generously sprinkled with broad clearings and wildflower meadows. The trail stays near De Roux Creek along this stretch, crossing the shallow waters just past that first trail junction (about 1.1 miles).

At the 1.6-mile mark, the trail splits. Bear right and continue climbing, more steeply

Premier views up the North Fork Teanaway valley toward the Stuart Range from Medra Pass

now, through the broad meadows of upper De Roux Creek basin. Toward the head of the basin, the trail turns steeper, but the rocky hillside meadows around you are blanketed with dozens of wildflower species—every color imaginable, it seems—to help keep your heart light as you gain more than 1000 feet in slightly over a mile to reach another trail junction at 5600 feet, 4 miles from the start.

The right fork of this trail junction leads to Gallagher Head Lake in just a few hundred yards. This lake is a beautiful jewel well worth visiting. There is a faint jeep track leading to the lake from the north, so expect to see some off-road vehicle damage along the shoreline, however.

After a visit to Gallagher Head Lake, return the way you came.

102 Johnson Creek–Medra Pass

RATING/ DIFFICULTY	ROUNDTRIP	ELEV GAIN/ HIGH POINT	SEASON
****/3	8 miles	2200 feet/ 5420 feet	July–Nov

Map: Green Trails Mount Stuart No. 209; **Contact:** Okanogan–Wenatchee National Forest, Cle Elum Ranger District; **Notes:**

NW Forest Pass required; **GPS:** N 47 22.872, W 120 53.144

![hiker and binoculars icons] *Hike to a fun little-visited part of Teanaway country. Views of the entire North Fork Teanaway valley await you from the top of Medra Pass along this route. Then there's Mount Stuart: the massive monolithic rock towers over the northern horizon. Overhead, Cooper's hawks commonly soar, and underfoot, carpets of wildflowers surround the trail. This is truly a glorious wilderness trail, even if it's not officially recognized as wilderness.*

GETTING THERE

From Seattle drive east on I-90 to exit 85 (East Cle Elum). Cross over the freeway overpass and turn right (northbound) on State Route 970. Cross the Teanaway River bridge, and in another mile turn left onto Teanaway Road. Drive north on Teanaway Road, veering right as it becomes first North Fork Teanaway Road and then unpaved Forest Road 9737 at 29 Pines Campground, 13 miles from SR 970.

Continue 4.7 miles up the dirt FR 9737, and just past the Beverly Campground turn into the Johnson Creek trailhead parking area on the right. The signed trailhead is on the other side of the road.

ON THE TRAIL

This route is exceptional! The first 0.7 mile of the trail is in constant earshot and mostly in sight of beautiful Johnson Creek on a mostly flat trail that moves you quickly to the first trail junction. At 0.9 mile, turn right at the trail junction to remain on the Johnson Creek Trail and start the hike up alongside pleasant Johnson Creek. Colorful carpets of queen's cup, trillium, yellow violets, marsh marigolds, vanilla leaf, and other wildflowers line the creek banks for the next mile and a half.

At 1.4 miles, the trail fords Johnson Creek—this is an easy crossing come summer but can be difficult during the high water of snowmelt season in early spring. You'll find another ford at 2.3 miles, and just a quarter mile past that, the hike gets serious.

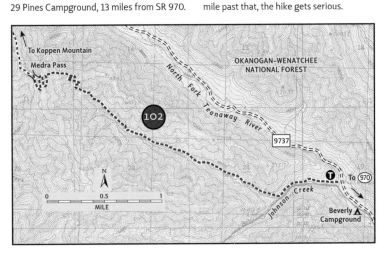

The trail turns away from the creek and climbs steeply now, ascending through the typical stunning Teanaway ecosystem of open rocky slopes covered in alpine wildflowers: scarlet gilia, Columbia lewisia, bitterroot, and other wonderful dry rocky soil specimens.

The first grand views open up at 3.4 miles, with picturesque vistas across the North Fork Teanaway valley and up into Esmeralda basin.

Medra Pass is reached at 4 miles, with even better views opening up here. Mount Stuart can finally be seen to the northeast. This makes a fine turnaround place for an outstanding day on the trail.

EXTENDING YOUR TRIP
Energetic hikers can push on another 1.6 miles beyond the pass to climb to the summit of 6031-foot Koppen Mountain, but the trail can be faint and hard to follow at times. Use caution.

103 Way Creek Trail–Middle Fork Teanaway

RATING/ DIFFICULTY	ROUNDTRIP	ELEV GAIN/ HIGH POINT	SEASON
***/2	4.4 miles	1000 feet/ 3600 feet	May–Nov

Map: Green Trails Mount Stuart No. 209; **Contact:** Okanogan–Wenatchee National Forest, Cle Elum Ranger District; **Notes:** NW Forest Pass required; **GPS:** N 47 20.535, W 120 55.506

Teanaway country is home to an assortment of birds and animals, as well as some truly magnificent wild country. It's not protected as wilderness, so

The Middle Fork Teanaway River cutting past cliffs in a small gorge just upstream from the Way Creek Trail

you might see, or more likely hear, motorcycles along the trails, but the grandeur of the country is worth that risk—fortunately, when you encounter motorcycles, they disappear quickly from sight, even if the exhaust fumes and ringing in your ears linger for a time.

GETTING THERE
From Seattle drive east on I-90 to exit 85 (East Cle Elum). Cross over the freeway overpass and turn right (northbound) on State Route 970. Cross the Teanaway River

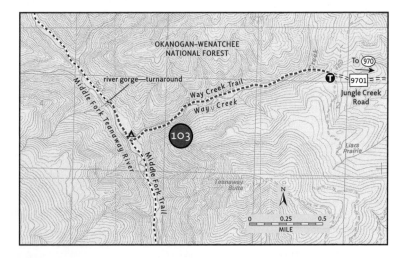

bridge, and in another mile turn left onto Teanaway Road. Drive north on Teanaway Road, veering right as it becomes first North Fork Teanaway Road and then unpaved Forest Road 9737 at 29 Pines Campground, 13 miles from SR 970. Turn left at the Y junction just past the campground, driving now on Jungle Creek Road (FR 9701). Continue up this rough road for 4.2 miles to the trailhead and parking area at the road's end. Note: Hikers driving low-clearance vehicles should park just 2.7 miles up this road at a wide spot and walk the last 1.5 miles of deeply rutted road.

ON THE TRAIL

The route descends Way Creek Trail from the trailhead, dropping through pine forest that gives way to deciduous groves along the creek itself. About a third of a mile out, the trail crosses the creek via an easy rock-hop ford. From here, the route follows the north side of the creek downvalley toward the Middle Fork Teanaway valley.

The open canopy of the forest allows ample sunshine to brighten the valley floor, which brings out great swathes of wildflowers, making this a lovely gentle trail for late spring and early summer. Periodic views downvalley show the gorgelike cut of the Middle Fork Teanaway valley ahead.

At 1.5 miles, the trail angles up the slope away from the creek for a short way before dropping back to the creekside and then intercepts the Middle Fork Teanaway Trail at 1.8 miles. A nice forested campsite sits near the mouth of Way Creek as it empties into the Middle Fork. The surrounding forest includes a lot of maple and cottonwood, allowing sunlight to filter through their open branches.

Turn right onto the Middle Fork Trail to continue into some broader wildflower meadows and to access the rushing waters of that river. At 2.2 miles, the trail seems to sprout right from the rock wall of the river gorge, with the river running just below the trail tread (in high water, the trail could be water-covered, so use caution during snowmelt).

Beyond the gorge, the trail cuts into dense forest, so make this your turnaround location.

104 Bear Creek

RATING/ DIFFICULTY	ROUNDTRIP	ELEV GAIN/ HIGH POINT	SEASON
***/1	3.5 miles	500 feet/ 3550 feet	May–Nov

Maps: Green Trails Liberty No. 210 and Mount Stuart No. 209; **Contact:** Okanogan–Wenatchee National Forest, Cle Elum Ranger District; **Notes:** NW Forest Pass required; **GPS:** N 47 22.120, W 120 47.077

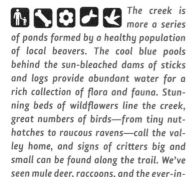 *The creek is more a series of ponds formed by a healthy population of local beavers. The cool blue pools behind the sun-bleached dams of sticks and logs provide abundant water for a rich collection of flora and fauna. Stunning beds of wildflowers line the creek, great numbers of birds—from tiny nuthatches to raucous ravens—call the valley home, and signs of critters big and small can be found along the trail. We've seen mule deer, raccoons, and the ever-industrious beavers, and found tracks of bears, bobcats, and tiny deer mice.*

GETTING THERE

From Seattle drive east on I-90 to exit 85 (East Cle Elum). Cross over the freeway overpass and turn right (northbound) on State Route 970. Cross the Teanaway River bridge, and in another mile turn left onto Teanaway Road. Drive north on Teanaway Road, veering right as it becomes first North Fork Teanaway Road and then unpaved Forest

Spectacular up-close looks at the logging operation of the local beaver community along the Bear Creek Trail

Road 9737 at 29 Pines Campground. Drive about 0.8 mile, and at the first road junction after crossing the bridge over Stafford Creek, turn right onto FR 9703, signed "Stafford Creek," and drive 3.5 miles to the road's end.

ON THE TRAIL

Leave the trailhead and begin the gentle climb up the Bear Creek Trail (the trail to the right at the trailhead—the route to the left climbs Miller Creek valley). The trail follows the lovely little creek and pierces a remarkably peaceful forest of pine and fir. This dry forest is open and airy, hosting an array of forest wildflowers, including trillium, glacier lily, vanilla leaf, paintbrush, and phlox.

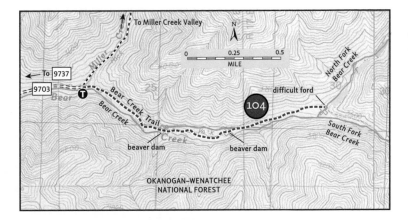

At 0.6 mile, the creek spreads into a wide pond behind a large beaver dam. Nature's engineers thrive in this valley, and an even larger dam and more expansive dam pond is found at 1.1 miles. If you have a fishing rod at hand, try angling for the small resident trout in these pools.

The creek forks at about 1.75 miles, and the trail crosses the rushing waters of the North Fork Bear Creek. The banks are not very steep, but the creek is wide, the water fast, and the ford difficult and treacherous much of the year except in late summer. Turn back here; even if you get across the creek, the trail on the other side is brushy and difficult to follow on its 2-mile climb to the Teanaway Ridge Trail.

Map: Green Trails Mount Stuart No. 209; **Contact:** Okanogan–Wenatchee National Forest, Cle Elum Ranger District; **Notes:** NW Forest Pass required; **GPS:** N 47 22.120, W 120 47.077

N N N *This route covers some of the best of the Teanaway country, offering high ridgetop views, cool forest groves, acres of wildflowers, and some thigh-burning climbs to make you feel like you really earned all that natural splendor.*

GETTING THERE

From Seattle drive east on I-90 to exit 85 (East Cle Elum). Cross over the freeway overpass and turn right (northbound) on State Route 970. Cross the Teanaway River bridge, and in another mile turn left onto Teanaway Road. Drive north on Teanaway Road, veering right as it becomes first North Fork Teanaway Road and then unpaved Forest Road 9737 at 29 Pines Campground. Drive about 0.8 mile, and at

105 Standup Creek to Stafford Creek Overlook

RATING/ DIFFICULTY	ROUNDTRIP	ELEV GAIN/ HIGH POINT	SEASON
****/4	7 miles	2950 feet/ 6150 feet	July–Oct

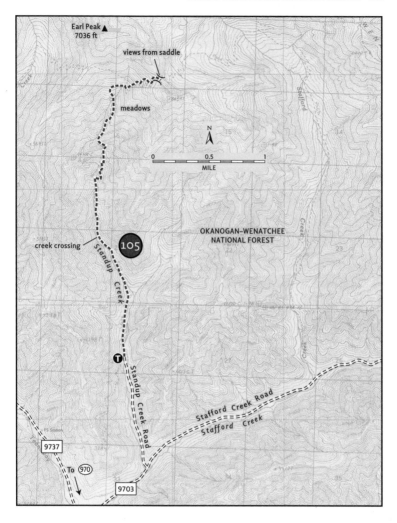

the first road junction after crossing the bridge over Stafford Creek, turn right onto FR 9703 signed "Stafford Creek" and drive about a mile to Standup Creek Road on the left. Turn here and drive the rough road 0.75 mile to the road-end trailhead, or park and hike this rough road.

Bunchberry in bloom

ON THE TRAIL

The Standup Creek Trail starts climbing immediately as it moves upward alongside the creek. The trail passes through pretty, fragrant pine forest. At about 1.4 miles, the trail crosses the creek and climbs the eastern valley wall, skirting away from the waterway to climb toward the creek's upper basin.

At 2.2 miles, the climb gets more serious as the trail weaves through a series of switchbacks, ascending upward through steeply sloped meadows. For the next mile, you'll stroll past so many flowers you'll feel like you're in a painting—or a perfume factory. Watch for hummingbirds here as the energetic little things swarm the flower fields in great numbers.

The Standup Creek Trail pushes upward around the flank of Earl Peak to the pass at the top of the basin forming the headwaters of Standup Creek, at 3.5 miles (6150 feet elevation). From here you can look back down the valley you just climbed and see east into the deeper and wider cut of Stafford Creek valley. Overhead (to the north) looms Earl Peak. Turn around here.

106 Esmeralda Basin

RATING/ DIFFICULTY	ROUNDTRIP	ELEV GAIN/ HIGH POINT	SEASON
****/3	7 miles	1750 feet/ 5960 feet	July–Oct

Map: Green Trails Mount Stuart No. 209; **Contact:** Okanogan–Wenatchee National Forest, Cle Elum Ranger District; **Notes:** NW Forest Pass required; **GPS:** N 47 26.203, W 120 56.230

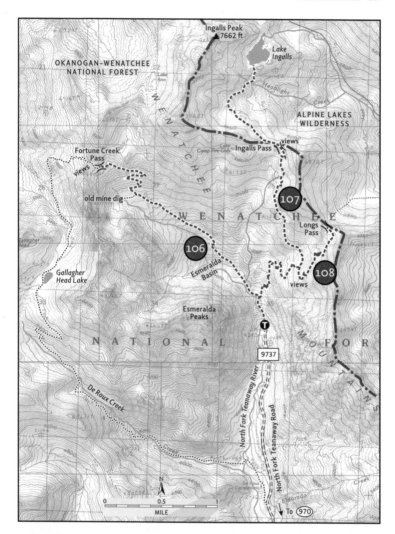

Sometimes we need to readjust our perspectives to fully enjoy our outdoor experiences. Hiking in the Pacific Northwest typically means traveling through some of the most scenic mountains in the world. The high, jagged crest of the Cascades—punctuated by the glistening cones of the great *volcanoes—dominates the views. The attraction of those majestic scenic vistas, though, can prevent us from appreciating the scenery closer at hand—or foot. In the Esmeralda Basin you'll find your eyes straying not to the distant views but to the local wonders along the trail: an array of flower species, flittering birds, and even a dead forest sheared off 6 to 10 feet above the ground by a powerful avalanche.*

GETTING THERE

From Seattle drive east on I-90 to exit 85 (East Cle Elum). Cross over the freeway overpass and turn right (northbound) on State Route 970. Cross the Teanaway River bridge, and in another mile turn left onto Teanaway Road. Drive north on Teanaway Road, veering right as it becomes first North Fork Teanaway Road and then unpaved Forest Road 9737 at 29 Pines Campground. Continue to the road's end.

ON THE TRAIL

Start on a three-in-one trail along an old miners road for 0.25 mile to a trail junction. Go left, while hikers seeking higher paths go right to Longs Pass (Hike 108) or Lake Ingalls (Hike 107).

The trail climbs gradually through forest and clearings for 1 mile, frequently within sight and sound of the gentle stream that is the North Fork Teanaway River. You'll pass through a broad field of shooting stars— gorgeous purple-and-white flowers that typically bloom in mid-July.

Over the next mile the trail climbs, skirting an avalanche slope, and passes more meadows. As you climb through that avalanche slope, take a look at the trees. Many of the stumps are 6 to 10 feet tall—the depth of the consolidated snowpack when the big slide occurred. That dense snowpack stayed in place, protecting the lower parts of the trees, while the snow above slid, sheering off the tops.

A hiker roams across the open serpentine lands near Fortune Creek Pass above Esmeralda Basin.

The trail reaches a junction of sorts near 2 miles, where the old miners track veers away to the left while the main trail continues up and to the right to reach the valley headwall. Here, you'll start a serious climb to the 5960-foot Fortune Creek Pass at 3.5 miles from the trailhead. Sweet views of the surrounding mountains await you, but even as you soak them in, your eyes will be drawn downward to the brilliant wildflowers at your feet.

EXTENDING YOUR TRIP

To make a long (15-mile) loop, continue down the far side of the pass to a junction with a rough road. Turn left and hike the road/trail to Gallagher Head Lake, and just beyond it turn left onto the De Roux Creek Trail. Descend the De Roux Creek valley about 4 miles to North Fork Teanaway Road (Forest Road 9737). You'll have to walk the road nearly 2 miles upstream to your car at the road's end.

107 Lake Ingalls

RATING/ DIFFICULTY	ROUNDTRIP	ELEV GAIN/ HIGH POINT	SEASON
*****/5	9 miles	2600 feet/ 6500 feet	July–Oct

Map: Green Trails Mount Stuart No. 209; **Contact:** Okanogan–Wenatchee National Forest, Cle Elum Ranger District; **Notes:** NW Forest Pass required; **GPS:** N 47 26.203, W 120 56.230

⚙ ✦ *Sometimes you just want to get high—physically, not psychedelically—and the Lake Ingalls Trail, in the Alpine Lakes Wilderness, lets you do that while still exploring some of the grandest*

wildflower displays in the Cascades. You'll climb, descend, and climb again, crossing through no less than three distinct ecosystem types, each with its own species of wildflowers to entice and enchant you.

GETTING THERE

From Seattle drive east on I-90 to exit 85 (East Cle Elum). Cross over the freeway overpass and turn right (northbound) on State Route 970. Cross the Teanaway River bridge, and in another mile turn left onto Teanaway Road. Drive north on Teanaway Road, veering right as it becomes first North Fork Teanaway Road and then unpaved Forest Road 9737 at 29 Pines Campground. Continue to the road's end.

ON THE TRAIL

Start out on the old miners road leading up the Teanaway Valley. Within the first 0.25 mile the wide roadbed fades to a true trail. It also splits, the path to the left heading to Esmeralda Basin and Fortune Creek Pass (Hike 106).

Go right to start your climb out of the Teanaway Valley. You'll be hiking through the first flora stratum you'll encounter on this hike, with huckleberry bushes, a few lilies, and other lesser-known flowers, such as pipsissewa and wintergreen.

At 2 miles go left at another trail junction (right leads to Longs Pass). The trail angles upward, climbing steadily and at times steeply. As you near Ingalls Pass the trail meanders through a rock-strewn meadowland. Along the long, slow climb to the pass you'll enter a drier ecosystem full of alpine firs. Bitterroot, Columbia lewisia, white paintbrush, penstemon, and spreading stonecrop (a pretty little succulent plant) grow in profusion.

The final 0.3 mile switchbacks up to Ingalls Pass, about 3 miles from the trailhead. Here you'll enjoy spectacular views of Mount Stuart and Ingalls Peak across the Ingalls Creek valley in front of you, and the Esmeralda Peaks across the Teanaway River valley behind you.

The trail now descends briefly before contouring around the upper flank of Headlight Basin. As you crest the pass and descend into the rocky basin, you'll enter rich heather meadows filled with bistort, paintbrush, and—in one spring-fed ravine—a 10-acre spread of shooting stars. This lush valley sports many fine campsites alongside small tarns and creeks in the open heather and flower fields. Of course, an abundance of rich foliage and plenty of water means that birds and animals frequent this basin. Move silently and watch carefully for the best chances to see deer, mountain goats, marmots, coyotes, and countless bird species. To make the visual feast over-the-top amazing, this entire basin is landmined with alpine larch trees. Time your visit for early October and you (as well as many other hikers) are in for a special treat!

After gawking, pop your eyes back into your head and push on—the next mile swings around the upper edge of the basin, crossing a few creeks and weaving around some nice ponds. As you leave the flowers you'll traverse a broad granite slope and climb up and over a tangle of granite slabs and boulders before dropping to rock-rimmed Lake Ingalls. Views are hard to come by here—rock hard, that is.

Swing out to the left as you reach the lake and drop down to rest on the long rock slabs that taper down into the water. From here, look across the mirror-finish lake to the magnificent face of mighty Mount Stuart to the east, while the craggy top of Ingalls Peak towers directly over the lake on the west.

Mount Stuart dominates the view east from the Lake Ingalls basin.

108 Longs Pass

RATING/ DIFFICULTY	ROUNDTRIP	ELEV GAIN/ HIGH POINT	SEASON
*****/4	5 miles	2100 feet/ 6250 feet	July–Oct

Map: Green Trails Mount Stuart No. 209; **Contact:** Okanogan–Wenatchee National Forest, Cle Elum Ranger District; **Notes:** NW Forest Pass required; **GPS:** N 47 26.203, W 120 56.230

If you want the best possible views with the shortest hiking distance, this trail is for you. Few 5-mile hikes offer the quality of views you'll find here. You'll cross steeply sloped alpine meadows, explore cool pine forests, climb through granite rock gardens laced with heather and huckleberries, and stare in awe at the jagged skyline created by the massive hulk of Mount Stuart. All in all, this is one of my favorite hikes in one of my favorite parts of the Cascades—the magical Teanaway country.

GETTING THERE
From Seattle drive east on I-90 to exit 85 (East Cle Elum). Cross over the freeway overpass and turn right (northbound) on State Route 970. Cross the Teanaway River bridge, and in another mile turn left onto Teanaway Road. Drive north on Teanaway Road, veering right as it becomes first North Fork Teanaway Road and then unpaved Forest Road 9737 at 29 Pines Campground. Continue to the road's end.

ON THE TRAIL
As with the Lake Ingalls Trail (Hike 107), the trail starts out on an old miners road

In your face . . . Mount Stuart, seen from Longs Pass in all its glory

marked Esmeralda Basin (I've always wondered: was Esmeralda a young sweetheart of one of the old miners?). A short distance from the trailhead, the wide roadbed fades to a true trail. It splits at 0.25 mile, with one path departing to the left into the lovely wildflower meadows of Esmeralda Basin and Fortune Creek Pass.

For Longs Pass go right. The path winds upward more steeply now, slicing through thinning forests to the 2-mile mark, where the route forks once more. To the left is a steep ascent to Ingalls Pass and beyond to

Lake Ingalls (Hike 107). Once more, go right. But first take a long drink of water and strip off any extra clothing you might be wearing—you will be sweating very soon.

The Longs Pass Trail leaves the junction and rolls upward in a brutal series of switchbacks through old rock-lined meadows. As you're working hard you'll also be baked by the sun beating down on you and reflecting up at you. Fortunately, the climb is just 0.5-mile long, though it gains about 600 feet in that distance.

At Longs Pass (elev. 6250 feet) stop and catch your breath before lifting your eyes to the views before you. Mount Stuart looms large in front of you—a massive granite slab reaching into the sky just across the Ingalls Creek valley, which sprawls beneath you on the far side of the pass.

109 Bean Creek Basin

RATING/ DIFFICULTY	ROUNDTRIP	ELEV GAIN/ HIGH POINT	SEASON
****/3	5 miles	2000 feet/ 5300 feet	June–Oct

Map: Green Trails Mount Stuart No. 209; **Contact:** Okanogan–Wenatchee National Forest, Cle Elum Ranger District; **Notes:** NW Forest Pass required; **GPS:** N 47 23.326, W 120 52.339

Mount Stuart dominates the eastern half of the Alpine Lakes Wilderness, towering so high above its surrounding peaks that it can be seen from trails throughout the region.

Upper Bean Creek basin, land of open forest and wildflowers

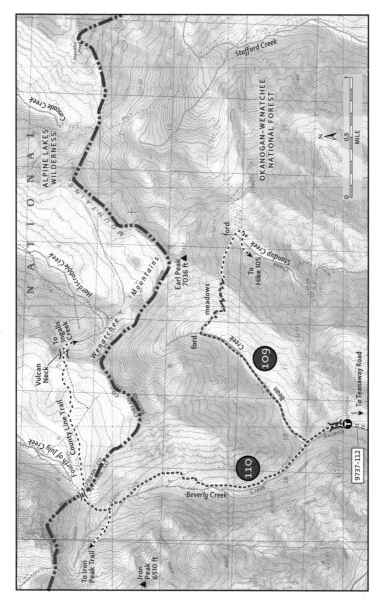

Stafford Creek

Cascade Creek

ALPINE LAKES
WILDERNESS

NATIONAL

OKANOGAN–WENATCHEE
NATIONAL FOREST

N

0   0.5
MILE

Hardscrabble Creek

Standup Creek

ford

To Hike 105

Earl Peak
7036 ft

M
o
u
n
t
a
i
n
s

W
e
n
a
t
c
h
e
e

To
Ingalls
Creek

Vulcan
Neck

County Line Trail

meadows

ford

Bean Creek

109

To Teanaway Road

Fourth of July Creek

Beverly

110

Beverly Creek

Creek

9737-112

To Iron
Peak Trail

Iron
Peak
6510 ft

Bean Creek is one of those trails affording views of the spectacular rock slabs of Stuart. But there's more to this trail than mountain views. Indeed, there are splendid views of Iron Peak, Earl Peak, and other summits in the Stuart Range. But it's the little things that make Bean Creek special. A plethora of blooming plants—wildflowers of all varieties—grace the valley. And an army of wild critters calls the basin home, from mule deer to deer mice, from gray jays to pileated woodpeckers.

GETTING THERE

From Seattle drive east on I-90 to exit 85 (East Cle Elum). Cross over the freeway overpass and turn right (northbound) on State Route 970. Cross the Teanaway River bridge, and in another mile turn left onto Teanaway Road. Drive north on Teanaway Road, veering right as it becomes first North Fork Teanaway Road and then unpaved Forest Road 9737 at 29 Pines Campground. Continue north for just under 4 miles before turning right (east) onto FR 9737-112, signed for Beverly Creek. Drive 1.4 miles to the road's end and trailhead.

ON THE TRAIL

Cross Beverly Creek on the stout bridge near the trailhead and climb creekside on an old, overgrown roadbed. At 0.5 mile turn right at the first trail junction and start up Bean Creek valley. The trail drives upward through the tight valley, lined lightly with trees and carpeted with bear grass, buckwheat, and other blooming plants under the waving branches of the pines and firs.

Many of the trees that used to dot the hillsides can be seen rotting in piles at the bottom of the steep valley—dropped by a violent avalanche some years before. The trail continues a steep climb for nearly a

mile, crossing the creek to access more cool forest and small forest meadows higher up the valley. The creek can be fast and tough to wade early in the year when melting snows swell the flow.

At 2 miles the trail leaves a stand of forest and erupts onto a broad swath of green, speckled with reds, blues, purples, yellows, and whites—that is, a vast grassy meadow filled with the odoriferous heads of blooming wildflowers.

At this point the trail forks. Stay left on the fainter trail to climb into the flower fields of Bean Creek basin. The trail leads to a wonderful camp along the creek, and then angles up into a garden of color, dotted with alpine firs and stunted pines. As you ascend the 0.5 mile from this last trail junction, you'll find the meadows growing larger and the stands of trees growing smaller, until finally the meadow wins out and takes over all of the basin before you. Here, at around 5300 feet, you'll be standing amid flowers that stretch across scores of acres.

Above the meadows tower the jagged tops of Earl Peak, Mount Stuart, and Iron Peak. Break out lunch, then enjoy a nap in the sun before heading for home.

110 Beverly Creek–Fourth of July Creek Overlook

RATING/ DIFFICULTY	ROUNDTRIP	ELEV GAIN/ HIGH POINT	SEASON
****/3	7 miles	1900 feet/ 5560 feet	June–Oct

Map: Green Trails Mount Stuart No. 209; **Contact:** Okanogan–Wenatchee National Forest, Cle Elum Ranger District; **Notes:** NW Forest Pass required; **GPS:** N 47 23.326, W 120 52.339

Scrambling along open ridge-tops draped in grass and wild-flowers, hikers here easily lose the trail as it fades under the rich plant life and disappears between jumbles of rock. Further complicating things, the glorious views from the ridge prevent hikers from devoting their full attention to the trail—there's just too much beauty and natural splendor to enjoy. Great meadows stretch out all around, and on every horizon stand picture-perfect mountain ranges, with the hulking presence of Mount Stuart to the north dominating all other views.

GETTING THERE

From Seattle drive east on I-90 to exit 85 (East Cle Elum). Cross over the freeway overpass and turn right (northbound) on State Route 970. Cross the Teanaway River bridge, and in another mile turn left onto Teanaway Road. Drive north on Teanaway Road, veering right as it becomes first North Fork Teanaway Road and then unpaved Forest Road 9737 at 29 Pines Campground. Continue north for just under 4 miles before turning right (east) onto FR 9737-112, signed for Beverly Creek. Drive 1.4 miles to the road's end and trailhead.

ON THE TRAIL

Start up the wide trail as it follows Beverly Creek upstream and, in a half mile, stay left at the trail junction to continue along this creek. For a mile the trail continues up the valley through sun-dappled forests with a lot of wildflowers—and in the autumn, ripe huckleberries!—gracing the forest floor. At 1.5 miles, the trail climbs a steep series of switchbacks

Columbia lewisia—a superstar showcase of a wildflower—is seen throughout the Teanaway region.

on sun-blasted slopes above the creek before starting a long traverse at 2 miles.

The trail continues to climb gradually as it traverses the upper Beverly Creek basin, and at about 2.5 miles, it turns upward once more for the final steep climb to the 5560-foot pass separating Beverly Creek basin from Fourth of July Creek basin.

This pass, 3.5 miles from the start, sits on the spine of the Wenatchee Mountains, below the craggy rock summit of Iron Peak. One look at the reddish hue of the mountain explains the name—the iron-rich rocks have oxidized (rusted) to a russet orange. Mount Stuart, Argonaut Peak, and most of the rest of the Stuart Range fill the northern view. For extended mileage go right (east) at the

pass on the County Line Trail and experience faint tread in a rocky ridgeline hike, with a rock mass of Vulcan Neck standing out as a highlight about an additional mile east from the pass.

111 Navaho Pass

RATING/ DIFFICULTY	ROUNDTRIP	ELEV GAIN/ HIGH POINT	SEASON
*****/3	11 miles	3000 feet/ 6000 feet	July–Oct

Map: Green Trails Mount Stuart No. 209; **Contact:** Okanogan–Wenatchee National Forest, Cle Elum Ranger District; **Notes:** NW Forest Pass required; **GPS:** N 47 21.983, W 120 48.160

This route covers some of the best of the Teanaway country, offering high alpine splendor and lush riparian habitats. Visit early for acres of wildflowers, or late for autumn colors—the vine maples are brilliant red, the cottonwoods and alders bright yellow, and the few scattered larches are glowing spires of gold. Beyond the trees, you'll gawk at vast walls of granite towering on all sides. Deer graze the valley bottoms, while mountain goats prance on the ridgetops. Overhead, turkey

Broad open views north from near Navaho Pass reveal much of the Stuart Range.

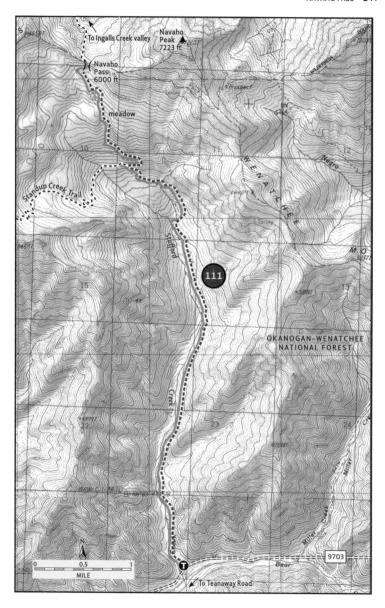

vultures, eagles, and hawks soar on the mountain thermals. What more could any hiker want?

GETTING THERE

From Seattle drive east on I-90 to exit 85 (East Cle Elum). Cross over the freeway overpass and turn right (northbound) on State Route 970. Cross the Teanaway River bridge, and in another mile turn left onto Teanaway Road. Drive north on Teanaway Road, veering right as it becomes first North Fork Teanaway Road and then unpaved Forest Road 9737 at 29 Pines Campground. At the first road junction after crossing the bridge over Stafford Creek, turn right onto FR 9703 (signed "Stafford Creek") and drive 2.5 miles to the Stafford Creek trailhead, found just after you cross Stafford Creek.

ON THE TRAIL

The Stafford Creek Trail climbs alongside the stream, passing through pretty, fragrant pine forest. Ponderosa pines down low are followed by whitebark pines and a few lodgepole pines. Intermingling with the pines are spruces, hemlocks, a few larches, and even a smattering of massive old Douglas-firs. Clark's nutcrackers seem to thrive in the stands of pines, eating the seeds as they pass through these high-elevation trees. Throughout the evergreen forests you'll also find a few deciduous species, including some stands of cottonwood, the random aspen or two, and a few alders.

The trail sticks to the east side of the creek—floodwaters once devoured parts of the trail, but volunteer trail crews working with Forest Service professionals restored or replaced the flood-damaged sections.

The trail climbs moderately for 4 miles, where it merges with the Standup Creek Trail. Go right at the junction as the trail turns steeper. Trudge for more than 1 mile up switchbacks that climb the headwall of the Stafford Creek valley. The thigh-burning climb is made tolerable, and indeed enjoyable, by the vast expanse of wildflowers spread before and around you. The whole upper basin is blanketed in wildflower meadows—somewhat swampy meadows, as the shallow bench serves as a catch basin for snowmelt runoff, creating this uniquely rich environment for water-loving wildflowers at 5600 feet elevation.

A half mile past these meadows, the trail crests Navaho Pass (elev. 6000 feet). Trails lead off in multiple directions from the pass, running east around Navaho Peak, west toward Earl Peak and Beverly Creek, and straight north down into the Ingalls Creek valley. The pass, though, is the perfect end of your hike. Hiking east on the County Line Trail from the pass for just a few minutes offers one of the best views from this area. From here you'll enjoy a northern skyline dominated by Mount Stuart and the granite wall of the Stuart Range. To the south, look out over the long valley of the North Fork Teanaway to Mount Rainier and Mount Adams far in the distance.

112 Miller Peak

RATING/ DIFFICULTY	ROUNDTRIP	ELEV GAIN/ HIGH POINT	SEASON
****/3	8 miles	3200 feet/ 6400 feet	July–Oct

Maps: Green Trails Mount Stuart No. 209 and Liberty No. 210; **Contact:** Okanogan–Wenatchee National Forest, Cle Elum Ranger

The final approach trail to the summit of Miller Peak

District; **Notes:** NW Forest Pass required. Trail open to motorcycles; **GPS:** N 47 22.112, W 120 47.146

There's something special about the Teanaway country. Fragrant pine forests. Sprawling wildflower fields. Grand views. Wildlife of all kinds and sizes. Miller Peak has all this and more. The long climb along an exposed, sunbaked ridge provides unmatched views, reaching south to Mount Adams and north over the ragged teeth of the Stuart Range. That open ridge also offers up the risks of sunburn and heat exhaustion, so pack plenty of sunscreen and carry more water than you think you might need. Also, be prepared to encounter motorcycles along this trail. Though their use is sporadic and chances are you won't see the dirt bikers, their presence is felt even when they aren't around—the motorcycles gouge deep ruts into the trail tread and grind the soil into dust.

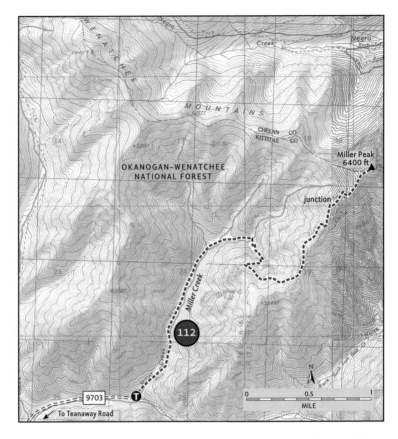

GETTING THERE

From Seattle drive east on I-90 to exit 85 (East Cle Elum). Cross over the freeway overpass and turn right (northbound) on State Route 970. Cross the Teanaway River bridge, and in another mile turn left onto Teanaway Road. Drive 13 miles to 29 Pines Campground, where the pavement ends. Veer right, and continue about 1 mile. At the first road junction after crossing the bridge over Stafford Creek, turn right onto Forest Road 9703 (signed "Stafford Creek") and drive 4 miles to the road's end.

ON THE TRAIL

As you leave the trailhead, go left up the Miller Creek Trail (to the right is the Bear Creek Trail). You'll climb at a moderate rate for nearly 2 miles, crossing the creek a couple of times in the first mile. The trail was built to multiuse standards, meaning it's open to hikers, mountain bikers, and motorcyclists.

Since those wheeled users need gentle grades, the climb is easy on hikers' legs.

At 2 miles the trail climbs out of the creek basin, ascending easy switchbacks up the valley wall for 0.5 mile to the crest of the ridge that runs north to the top of Miller Peak. The trail runs up this ridge, climbing through forest and meadow for the next mile to a trail junction just below the summit of Miller Peak.

Go straight, through the junction, and follow a faint path 0.5 mile to the 6400-foot summit of Miller and expansive views. To the west is the Teanaway Range, and north of that, the mighty Stuart Range, dominated by the hulk of Mount Stuart. Around your feet, locoweed and bitterroot grow throughout the rough scree slopes, and pikas cheep and chirp all around you.

HOW TO HELP THIS TRAIL

Motorcycles tend to chew up trail tread, turning compact—and thus stable—dirt into dust. That dust is highly susceptible to erosion from both wind and rain, leading to deep ruts and mud holes in the trail. After your visit, write to the land manager and mention any damage you encountered that was caused by motorcycles. Provide photos if possible, and send a copy of your letter to the good folks at the Washington Trails Association, the leading volunteer trail-maintenance organization in the state.

113 Teanaway Ridge

RATING/ DIFFICULTY	ROUNDTRIP	ELEV GAIN/ HIGH POINT	SEASON
***/3	6 miles	1900 feet/ 5489 feet	July–Oct

Huge old-growth ponderosa pines along the Iron Bear Trail leading to Teanaway Ridge

Map: Green Trails Liberty No. 210; **Contact:** Okanogan–Wenatchee National Forest, Cle Elum Ranger District; **Notes:** NW Forest Pass required. Rough road for final 0.5 mile to trailhead. Trail open to motorcycles; **GPS:** N 47 21.258, W 120 43.101

Because of this route's high trailhead, much of your elevation gain is done before you start walking, meaning you can enjoy a high ridge route with relatively modest effort. The trail rambles along the ridge, rolling up and down, with wildflowers underfoot and views stretching for hundreds of miles—as far south as Mount Rainier and as far north as Mount Stuart. The big rock of Diamond Head stands to

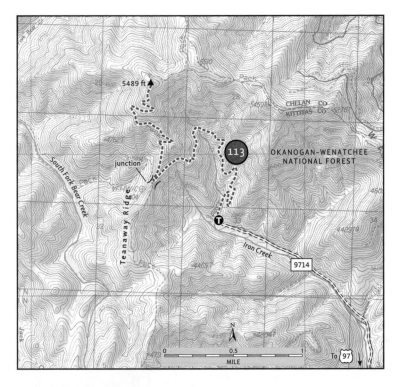

the east. This trail is open to motorcycle use, so visit midweek to minimize the chance of running into these noisy beasts.

GETTING THERE

From Seattle drive east on I-90 to exit 85 (East Cle Elum). Cross over the freeway overpass and turn right (northbound) on State Route 970. Turn left (north) on US Highway 97 and drive 2.5 miles beyond Mineral Springs Resort to Iron Creek Road (Forest Road 9714). Turn left (west) and follow Iron Creek Road for 3.6 miles to the road's end and trailhead. The road's final 0.5 mile is very rough. If you fear for your car's

undercarriage, park lower and hike the last leg of the road.

ON THE TRAIL

The trail climbs steeply away from the trailhead, switchbacking up through rocky wildflower gardens. The path weaves upward for 1 mile, gaining 800 feet to reach a trail junction at the pass separating Iron Creek and Bear Creek valleys. One trail drops to the west into Bear Creek valley, another turns left (south) onto the southern arm of the Teanaway Ridge, and the trail you want goes right (north) to climb along the ridge to the north.

You'll continue to climb, now working along the rocky crest of the Teanaway Ridge. For the next 2 miles you'll roll upward. At times you'll run straight up the ridge spine. Occasionally you'll follow switchbacks as they weave up steep sections. Between climbs the trail traverses the edge of the ridge, crossing spectacular wildflower fields and climbing through an old forest-fire area with silver skeletons of fire-killed trees. Views abound, but as grand as the scenery and the panoramas are, the best are found at the end of the hike.

At 3 miles from the trailhead the trail crosses the summit of an unnamed knob, the high point of the ridgeline (elev. 5489 feet). From here, 360-degree views greet you. To the east, Tronsen Ridge (Hike 114) stretches across the horizon. To the northwest, ever-present Mount Stuart looms large. And the mighty snow cone of Mount Rainier punctuates the southern sky.

HOW TO HELP THIS TRAIL

Motorcycles tend to chew up trail tread, turning compact—and thus stable—dirt into dust. That dust is highly susceptible to erosion from both wind and rain, leading to deep ruts and mud holes in the trail. After your visit, write to the land manager and mention any damage you encountered that was caused by motorcycles. Provide photos if possible, and send a copy of your letter to the good folks at the Washington Trails Association, the leading volunteer trail-maintenance organization in the state.

114 Tronsen Ridge

RATING/ DIFFICULTY	ROUNDTRIP	ELEV GAIN/ HIGH POINT	SEASON
****/2	8 miles	1000 feet/ 5800 feet	June–Oct

Map: Green Trails Wenatchee No. 211S; **Contact:** Okanogan–Wenatchee National Forest, Cle Elum Ranger District; **Notes:** NW Forest Pass required. High-clearance vehicle required to access northern trailhead; **GPS:** Southern trailhead: N 47 19.361, W 120 31.590. Northern trailhead: N 47 23.052, W 120 34.488

Start high, stay high, and enjoy the endless bounty of the wild country between the Cascade crest and the dry, open deserts of eastern Washington. Tronsen Ridge provides a little of both worlds. Long, dry ridges topped with open meadows and wildflower fields resemble the desert gardens of the Yakima Plateau, but dense stands of fir and ponderosa pine offer up the flavor of the mountains. The glorious meadows and forests atop the long ridge are wonderful playgrounds for wildlands enthusiasts. At various points, Tronsen Ridge grants peekaboo views out to Mount Adams, Mount Rainier, Mount Stuart, and countless other lesser peaks nestled in the eastern Cascades.

GETTING THERE

From Seattle drive east on I-90 to exit 85 (East Cle Elum). Cross over the freeway overpass and turn right (northbound) on State Route 970. Turn left (north) on US Highway 97, drive to Blewett Pass, and turn right (southeast) onto Forest Road 9716. In 3.7 miles turn left onto FR 9712 and continue 5 miles to Haney Meadow and the Ken Wilcox Horse Camp. Drive another mile past the camp and, after crossing Naneum Creek, find the southern trailhead in the Upper Naneum Meadow at a sharp right-hand switchback in the road.

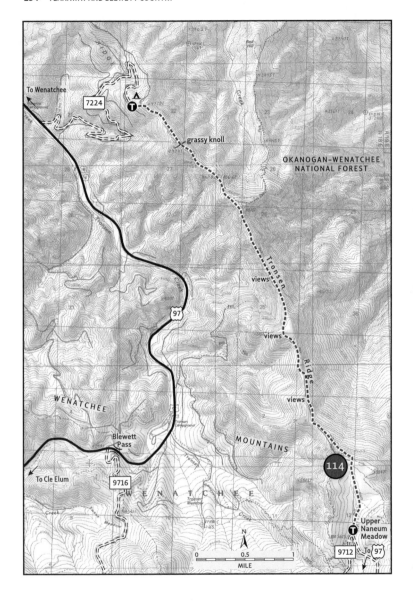

Hikers with high-clearance vehicles can also access the northern trailhead: continue north on US 97 for 5 miles past Blewett Pass, turn right onto Five Mile Road (FR 7224), and drive 3.5 miles to an undeveloped campsite and trailhead.

ON THE TRAIL

The trail heads north through Upper Naneum Meadow, climbing gradually (a mere 100 feet) in the first 0.5 mile before sloping downward for a slow, soft descent along the ridge for the next 4 miles. The high point of the ridge, a grassy knob 0.5 mile into the hike, provides unmatched views of the eastern Wenatchee Mountains area and beyond.

After leaving this knob, the trail heads into a roller coaster ride to the north, climbing short peaks and ridge knolls, then dropping into low saddles. The net elevation change over the next 4 miles is a loss of 1000 feet.

Many of the ridge's high points are grassy bumps full of wildflowers, while the low saddles often are thinly timbered. Be on the lookout for the stunningly beautiful Tweedy's lewisia in areas along the ridge. It is perhaps the most beautiful wildflower (and rather rare) in all of Washington State! Look for wildlife all along the ridge, but especially in the transition zones between forest and meadows.

Open ridgeline hiking at its best along Tronsen Ridge

A hiker soaks in the views from above the massive landslide area on the eastern side of Mount Lillian.

EXTENDING YOUR TRIP
For additional adventures, with map and compass in hand (and good navigation skills) you can explore off-trail onto rocky promontories with awesome views of Mount Stuart, Mount Rainier, and the Wenatchee Mountains.

115 Mount Lillian

RATING/ DIFFICULTY	ROUNDTRIP	ELEV GAIN/ HIGH POINT	SEASON
****/2	3 miles	600 feet/ 6150 feet	June–Oct

Map: Green Trails Wenatchee No. 211S; **Contact:** Okanogan–Wenatchee National Forest, Cle Elum Ranger District; **Notes:** NW Forest Pass required; **GPS:** N 47 19.361, W 120 31.590

As you explore this route near Diamond Head, you'll quickly realize that you are a long way from Waikiki, but you won't care. For Northwest hikers, this route that climbs to grand views from amid fields of wildflowers is a much closer approximation to paradise than that crowded sand beach in the

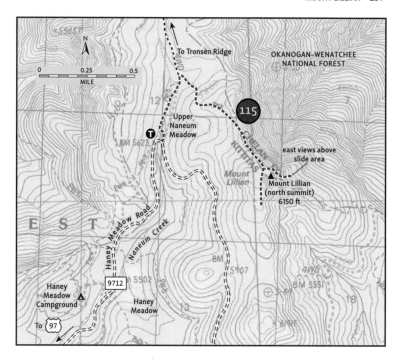

South Pacific. Mount Lillian, on the south ridge of Diamond Head, provides grandiose views of the peaks of the Wenatchee Range as well as of the granite summits of the Teanaway.

GETTING THERE

From Seattle drive east on I-90 to exit 85 (East Cle Elum). Cross over the freeway overpass and turn right (northbound) on State Route 970. Turn left (north) on US Highway 97, and drive to Blewett Pass and turn right (southeast) onto Forest Road 9716. In 3.7 miles turn left onto FR 9712 and continue 5 miles to Haney Meadow and the Ken Wilcox Horse Camp. Drive another mile past the

camp and, after crossing Naneum Creek, find the trailhead in the Upper Naneum Meadow at a sharp right-hand switchback in the road.

ON THE TRAIL

From the parking area, head north along the old road-turned-trail as it rolls through the lush vegetation of the Upper Naneum Meadow. The route starts climbing gradually (a mere 100 feet) in the first 0.5 mile before reaching a junction with the Tronsen Ridge Trail. Turn right here to turn your back on the long expanse of Tronsen and look up on the summit of Lillian. The trail continues to climb gradually around the eastern flank of Mount Lillian.

The route cuts through stands of lodgepole pines, interspersed with towering orange-barked ponderosas, when not surrounded by wildflower meadows. Just shy of the 1-mile mark, the trail turns steeper as it starts the final run up the north face of Lillian. Here, the slope is open meadow, thickly covered in balsamroots in the late spring. The summit ridge is reached at 1.3 miles and the best views are found a littler farther south (and below the true summit) at about 1.5 miles. From there you can look west across to Mount Stuart and the Teanaway country peaks. The eastern side of the ridge here is also wide open due to an ancient landslide that is stunning to look down upon. But the wide-open view east reveals unobstructed views into the Columbia basin.

Opposite: The north end of the Yakima River canyon opens into the Kittitas Valley from the Rattlesnake Dance Ridge Trail.

ellensburg basin

The desert country east of the Cascades offers wonderful hiking opportunities for nature lovers. The high deserts of eastern Washington are unique, with an amazing array of plant and animal species thriving in the dry climate of the upper Columbia basin. But the wildlife and wildflowers aren't the only sources of beauty and majesty in Washington's desert. This country is some of the most rugged and remote in the state. Deep coulees—carved by ice age–era floods—cut across the desert, and jagged rimrock bluffs line the river canyons in this stark landscape.

What's more, the desert country east of the Cascades offers snow-weary hikers an escape during the long winter months. When snow clogs the trails and basins of the Cascades and the Olympics, the desert routes remain open and largely snow-free. Some higher-elevation desert routes might receive a dusting of snow, but rather than hamper travel, that light snow cover enhances the beauty of this remarkable country. An inch or two of snow coating the sagebrush and black basalt rock of a deep coulee creates a glorious portrait in black and white through which you can hike. Most routes, though, remain snow-free year-round. That's not to say they escape the cold bite of winter—indeed, the desert is often colder than the mountains—but the lack of precipitation that defines a desert means that snow is as scarce as rain.

116 John Wayne Trail

RATING/ DIFFICULTY	ROUNDTRIP	ELEV GAIN/ HIGH POINT	SEASON
***/1	6+ miles	200 feet/ 1700 feet	Year-round

Map: Department of Natural Resources Yakima; **Contact:** Washington State Parks;

Notes: Washington Discover Pass required; **GPS:** N 47 03.559, W 120 40.403

This may be one of the best sections of the John Wayne Pioneer Trail, which runs through the center of the long, linear Iron Horse State Park (hundreds of miles long, but just a few dozen yards wide in many areas). You'll pass through rustic farmland, alongside a wild stretch of the upper Yakima River, and possibly see ospreys, eagles, vultures, elk, otters, beavers, and mule deer, not to mention countless bovines!

GETTING THERE
From Seattle drive east on I-90 to exit 101. At the end of the off-ramp, turn left over the freeway and, just past the side-road access to the Thorp fruit market, turn left onto Thorp Depot Road (signed as an Iron Horse State Park/John Wayne Trail trailhead). Continue 0.3 mile to a large well-signed trailhead.

ON THE TRAIL
Start west on the John Wayne Trail as it crosses rustic farmlands, passing through cattle pastures and between large fields of wheat and hay, and past some small orchards. At 1.2 miles, the old railroad route crosses a broad irrigation canal as it edges ever closer to the Yakima River.

At 1.75 miles, the route crosses Taneum Road. Though it's possible to join the trail off this road, there is no safe parking nearby, so stick to the official trailhead you used. A rancher near here usually has expecting cows in the pastures adjacent to the trail during the spring, so it's likely you'll see tiny, incredibly cute calves if you hit the trail during calving season. We witnessed

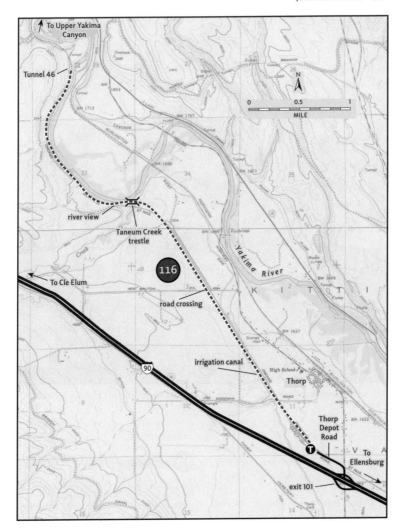

no fewer than two dozen of the fuzzy-faced babies during our research trek.

The trail crosses the Taneum Creek trestle at 2.9 miles and the trail now brings you close enough to the Yakima River to see the mouth of the Taneum as it empties into the Yakima. Keep an eye on the river and you might see some anglers. The amateurs (fly

The Yakima River seen from the John Wayne Trail, near to where Taneum Creek merges into it

fishermen) tend to float down the river in boats, casting long lines with skinny sticks. The professionals (otters) tend to play in the currents along the shores, frequently diving underwater to snatch dinner where they can.

In less than a quarter mile, the trail enters the lower end of the Upper Yakima Canyon—a beautiful gorge cut through chalk bluffs and basalt rimrock. Turn around here, or keep walking. The views remain largely unchanged from here up to Tunnel 46 at 4.6 miles, which was open at time of publication—but you should research this before your hike.

117 Westburg Trail

RATING/ DIFFICULTY	LOOP	ELEV GAIN/ HIGH POINT	SEASON
***/2	4 miles	1800 feet/ 3560 feet	Apr–July

Map: Department of Natural Resources Yakima; **Contact:** Washington Department of Fish and Wildlife; **Notes:** Washington

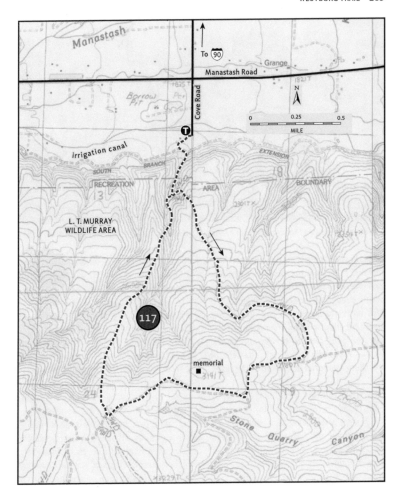

Discover Pass required; **GPS:** N 47 03.559, W 120 40.403

Ray Westburg was a popular Ellensburg wrestling coach who died at the young age of forty-seven in 1997. This trail was built and dedicated to him, with a memorial placed at the high point on the ridge. The route isn't heavily used by hikers, but it is popular with birds—birds on the ground and in the air. You can expect to find grouse scurrying through the brush and Lewis's woodpeckers pounding on the

The memorial site on Manastash Ridge overlooks amazing views north across the Kittitas Valley.

trees. In the air, look for a mix of northern flickers, bluebirds, meadowlarks, and the ever-present red-tailed hawks. And if birds aren't enough of an aerial display, this is also butterfly heaven in the late spring. Deer and elk also roam the region, and no one can find fault with the spectacular views—especially from the site of the Westburg Memorial at the top of the ridge.

GETTING THERE

From Seattle drive east on I-90 to exit 101 (Thorp) and after exiting, turn right. Continue to Cove Road and turn right, driving south on Cove Road to its junction with Manastash Road. Continue straight, crossing Manastash Road, and in another hundred yards or so, find the large parking area along the right-hand side of the soon-to-dead-end road.

ON THE TRAIL

The trail starts on an old jeep track that first crosses an irrigation canal on a set of railroad timbers, and then heads up a steep gully. Note that this stretch of the trail is

prime snake terrain, so be cautious. At about 0.3 mile the trail splits, with both paths leading to the same junction about a mile farther up the route, so you can actually turn this into a small loop. We went left. From the split, the trail (both of them) climbs steeply. Indeed, in the 1.5 miles from the split to the memorial site, the trail gains almost 1800 feet in elevation, all without benefit of switchbacks.

But as the trail climbs, the scenery just gets better. Birds keep you company along the entire trek, but there are also amazing flower displays all around. Areas of the open slope were blue with brodacia. Elsewhere, lupine, balsamroot, phlox, paintbrush, yellow aster-like beauties, and microsensis painted the terrain. And oh! the bitterroot—when the bitterroot is in bloom, any exposed rocky soil area flushes pink.

The memorial site (which can be seen from all along the trail) offers stunning views of the Kittitas Valley as well as the sweep of the Cascade Range, with Mount Stuart capping the mountain scene.

118 Observation Road– Manastash Ridge

RATING/ DIFFICULTY	ROUNDTRIP	ELEV GAIN/ HIGH POINT	SEASON
****/2	10 miles	900 feet/ 3930 feet	Mar–May

Map: Department of Natural Resources Yakima; **Contact:** Washington Department of Fish and Wildlife; **Notes:** Washington Discover Pass required; **GPS:** N 46 54.291, W 120 44.548

Flowers galore and views unmatched. Wildlife abounding on the hills around you

and in the air above you. What more could anyone want on a spring outing? The hike uses a gated road to lead up to the Manastash Ridge Observatory, operated by the University of Washington. As you'd except at a location where an expensive observatory station is placed, the views are remarkable. The entire length of Umtanum Ridge stretches out before you, and all around desert wildflowers—from bitterroot blooms to balsamroot flowers—abound. Deer and elk thrive on the rich vegetation and mild winter conditions here, and you'll frequently find elk calves following their nursing mothers in these meadows. And be on the lookout for a thriving wild turkey population.

The hike up Observation Road on Manastash Ridge features frequent views of vast, open sageland looking toward Umtanum Ridge.

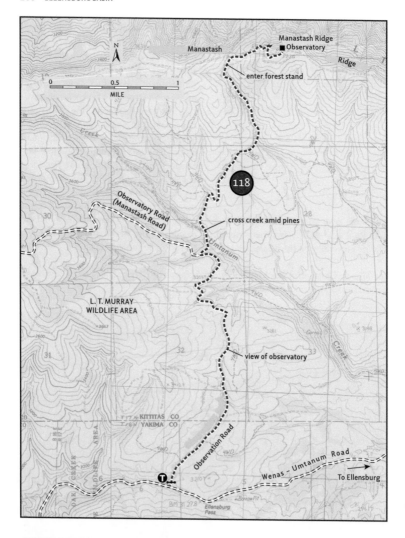

GETTING THERE

From Seattle, drive east on I-90 to exit 109 in Ellensburg. At the end of the exit ramp, turn right to drive under the freeway, and at 0.7 mile turn left at Wenas–Umtanum Road at the traffic light. Stay on this road, which turns to gravel at 5.3 miles, and at 15.7 miles from the freeway exit the road starts descending and you'll find a road to the right. This is Observation Road, the road you will hike, gated until May 1 each year. Park here.

ON THE TRAIL

From the road gate, hike up the closed road as it winds up the slope. You'll travel 2.4 miles through open stands of pine forest and sagebrush steppe to a junction with the main Observatory Road (Manastash Road). Deer and elk are most commonly seen here.

At the road junction, turn right and climb west and then north on Manastash Ridge. You'll now be in fully open slopes surrounded by desert flowers and sagebrush—and increasingly impressive views. To the southeast the full length of Umtanum Ridge seems to be in view leading eastward. Numerous species of buckwheat, sage violets, and big-headed clover fill the sagebrush territory. Listen to the constant singing of the western meadowlarks, and spot mountain bluebirds pausing at the tips of the huge sagebrush plants.

At 4.6 miles you'll top out on the ridge. Turn right and continue another quarter mile to the observatory. Wander around the building and appreciate the incredible views enjoyed by the folks who work here. Of course, they need to be looking upward at night, so maybe you are the more fortunate one!

119 Rattlesnake Dance Ridge Trail

RATING/ DIFFICULTY	ROUNDTRIP	ELEV GAIN/ HIGH POINT	SEASON
****/2	2.2 miles	1200 feet/ 2600 feet	Apr–July

Map: Department of Natural Resources Yakima; **Contact:** US Bureau of Land Management (BLM), Spokane Office; **Notes:** BLM day use (available onsite) or

The most amazing views of the Yakima River canyon to be found, seen from near the high point up the Rattlesnake Dance Ridge Trail

America the Beautiful Pass required; **GPS:** N 46 53.875, W 120 30.238

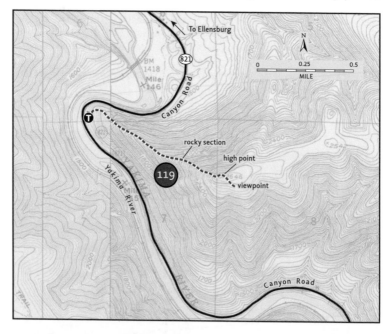 *This remarkable route packs an incredible experience in a short distance. The route offers the most spectacular view of the Yakima Canyon twisting its way south from here. Just use caution and keep one eye (and an ear) on the ground in front of you so you don't end up doing the snake-avoidance jig that gave the ridge its name. That said, the trail does get frequent use by humans, so the snakes tend to keep a low profile and avoid the heavily traveled trail—still, be cautious especially if you are hiking with dogs. By mid-April most years, the desert flowers are showing their colors.*

GETTING THERE

From Seattle drive east on I-90 to exit 109 (signed "Ellensburg/Canyon Road"), and at the end of the ramp, turn left onto Canyon Road/State Route 821. Drive south on Canyon Road/SR 821 and just as you get to where the canyon cliffs loom large around you, near the 6.2-mile mark from I-90, the road bends sharply to the left. Park in the large open parking area on the left (inside of the road curve). The trail starts at the point of the ridge in the middle of this parking area.

ON THE TRAIL

The trail climbs from step one and doesn't let up until it reaches the top of the ridge. In fact, the first switchback comes mere yards after leaving the trailhead. Though you have good views along the entire route—you are hiking on a sagebrush-and-desert-grass ridge after all—at 0.7 mile, you'll have attained enough elevation gain to be able to look north back into the Ellensburg basin and south into the canyon. From here on up, you should exercise extra caution as the trail winds steeply through rough, rocky terrain—and the basalt rocks of this area are sharp and jagged. Also, be careful where you put your hands on a hot day (that is, don't reach onto rocks and ledges you can't see over if you don't want a snake surprise).

At 1 mile, the trail reaches a cross at the high point of this part of the ridge where you'll enjoy great views toward the Kittitas Valley and west down into the depths of the Yakima Canyon. But don't just stop here. Roam freely downslope a bit to the south for an even better view at the 1.15-mile mark. This location offers the best view of the winding Yakima River as it rolls through the canyon.

120 Umtanum Creek Canyon

RATING/ DIFFICULTY	ROUNDTRIP	ELEV GAIN/ HIGH POINT	SEASON
****/1	6+ miles	600 feet/ 2200 feet	Oct–May

Map: Department of Natural Resources Yakima; **Contact:** US Bureau of Land Management (BLM), Spokane Office; **Notes:** BLM day use (available onsite) or America the Beautiful Pass required; **GPS:** N 46 51.309, W 120 28.956

Starting with a spring stride over a bouncy suspension bridge above the trout-rich waters of the Yakima River, this trail meanders up an ever-narrowing canyon. But it also seems to be a path to the past, as the trail leaves the highway and the car-camping anglers behind and

A hike up Umtanum Creek canyon starts off with a wonderful crossing of the Yakima River via suspension bridge.

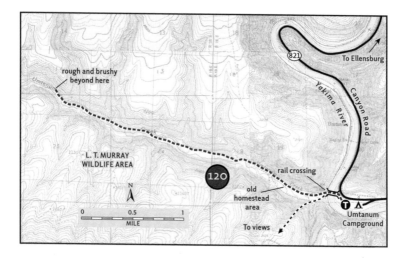

rolls up a rugged desert canyon. Along the route, you'll step into the past as the trail cuts through an old homestead (complete with overgrown, brambly apple orchard) and into pristine desert wildlife habitat. The year-round waters of Umtanum Creek draw a vast collection of critters to this canyon, including a thriving population of beavers. We've even encountered badgers in the canyon.

GETTING THERE

From Seattle drive east on I-90 to exit 110. After exiting, continue east on I-82 about 3.5 miles to exit 3 (Thrall Road). At the stop sign, turn right on State Route 821. Turn left at the next stop sign to continue southeast along State Route 821 into Yakima Canyon (signed Yakima Canyon), and continue about 8 miles to the Umtanum Recreation Area (between mileposts 16 and 17) and the large gravel parking lot on the right (west) side of the road.

ON THE TRAIL

The trail leaves the park area by way of a long steel suspension bridge over the Yakima River. At the far end of the bridge the trail crosses under the Burlington Northern Santa Fe Railway tracks and immediately enters the wildlife refuge. Shortly after you head up the main trail, you'll see a side trail leading left. This leads up the southern walls of the canyon onto more of Umtanum Ridge. Stay straight for the canyon.

The trail meanders through a broad sagebrush flat for a half mile or so before crossing an old fence line (a few rotten posts and a low mound of dirt are about all that remains of the fence). You'll see the remnants of an old cabin—mostly just its rock foundation—and a scraggly grove of apple trees around this old homestead site.

That's the last real imprint of humans in this wild canyon. Various species of sage provide texture and fragrance to the canyon floor, while the canyon walls tower overhead.

LOW-IMPACT RECREATION

In days gone by, wilderness travelers did as they pleased when hiking through the backcountry. If a trail got muddy or wet, a new one was created parallel to the first. If folks wanted a warm drink with lunch, they'd start a campfire. And campers would cut young, fragrant pine boughs to create soft bedding.

As more and more people took to the hills, those actions began to leave large, noticeable scars on the land. Today, with millions of hikers flocking to the backcountry, these kinds of intrusive practices would leave the wilderness blighted for decades to come. To ensure that we don't destroy the essence of the wild country we all enjoy visiting, hikers today are encouraged to employ the Leave No Trace (LNT) principles.

In short, these principles and practices are built around the idea that human visitors to the backcountry should "leave only footprints, take only pictures." In fact, done right, even the footprints will be minimized.

Hikers who encounter mud holes in the middle of trails should suck it up and stride through the puddle rather than stomp down the vegetation around the edge of the mud. Each passing hiker skirts wider and wider around the ever-growing mud hole until the trail is wide enough to drive a truck in, and the vegetation is stomped into oblivion. If you've planned ahead, you're likely wearing hiking boots appropriate for your trail experience, and in Washington that generally means that they are waterproof. So stepping in mud does you no harm and helps prevent trail erosion.

Likewise, hikers should resist creating new trails. This doesn't mean that you should never step off-trail. By all means, hikers should explore off-trail if they are comfortable doing so. But when you step off the established trail, you should do it in a place that won't leave a permanent scar and won't affect nesting birds, wildlife, or fragile plants, and once off-trail, you need to move well away from the trail. There's no reason to explore off-trail if you're only going to be 20 feet away from that established path. Likewise, cutting across a switchback turn yields you nothing (maybe shaving a couple of seconds off your travel time), but it does lasting damage to the trail and the environment around the trail. Cutting switchbacks leads to loss of vegetation and establishment of "cut trails" that channel rainwater and snowmelt. This leads to erosion of the hillside and trail tread.

A willingness on the part of all hikers to practice a little patience and to put up with a little discomfort (such as getting a touch muddy) will help keep our trails open and enjoyable for everyone.

Visit in winter and you might find a dusting of snow (or possibly even a few inches of the fluff). A thin blanket of snow is actually a benefit to hikers as it serves as a tapestry on which the comings and goings of the local population is recorded. If you find snow, you'll also find tracks left by deer, bighorns, coyotes, small mammals, and game birds. The creek is the only water source for miles around, and it's easy to see the pathways of animals that come down from the canyon rim to get water.

The trail crosses the creek at about a mile. The crossing is typically an easy rock hop, though at times you'll be forced to find a shallow spot between beaver ponds—or carefully cross on a beaver dam. There is extensive beaver activity on this small desert creek. Some dams (made primarily from the local aspen, cottonwoods, and alder) stand 6 or 8 feet tall, creating ponds that stretch several dozen yards upstream. Frequently, the dams are built back-to-back with a new one standing at the upper edge of the lower dam's pond.

About 2 miles up the trail, the trail skirts around a stand of low alder. On several visits to the area, we've encountered a portion of the resident herd of bighorn sheep (usually numbering fifty or sixty animals) either bedded down in this area or vacating their beds.

The alder grove apparently provides good shelter for them on cold winter nights.

The trail continues upcanyon, but past the 3-mile mark, it becomes narrow and largely overgrown. Rather than push on through the brush, turn around here and return through the rich canyon—as much as you saw on the way in, there is still plenty to see on the way back down.

121 Umtanum Ridge

RATING/ DIFFICULTY	ROUNDTRIP	ELEV GAIN/ HIGH POINT	SEASON
***/2	4+ miles	800 feet/ 2200 feet	Oct–May

Map: Department of Natural Resources Yakima; **Contact:** US Bureau of Land Management (BLM), Spokane Office; **Notes:** BLM day use (available onsite) or America

Long views extending up Umtanum Creek canyon can be seen from most anywhere on either side of the canyon

the Beautiful Pass required; **GPS:** N 46 51.309, W 120 28.956

![sheep/flower/boot icons]Bighorn sheep roam the canyon walls and browse the grass-rich slopes between sections of rimrock. Deer bound throughout the area. Coyotes hunt the heavy populations of rabbits, red-diggers (large ground squirrels), and upland birds (quail, pheasant, chukar, grouse, Hungarian partridge, and more). Rattlesnakes are frequently seen in the summer (another reason to visit in winter months!) as they congregate to take advantage of the mice, voles, and ground squirrels that thrive in the creek-fed grasses and tree stands. And all around, underfoot and on the canyon walls, desert wildflowers color the canyon.

GETTING THERE

From Seattle drive east on I-90 to exit 110. After exiting, continue east on I-82 about 3.5 miles to exit 3 (Thrall Road). At the stop sign, turn right on State Route 821. Turn left at the next stop sign to continue southeast along State Route 821 into Yakima Canyon (signed Yakima Canyon) and continue about 8 miles to the Umtanum Recreation Area (between mileposts 16 and 17) and the large gravel parking lot on the right (west) side of the road.

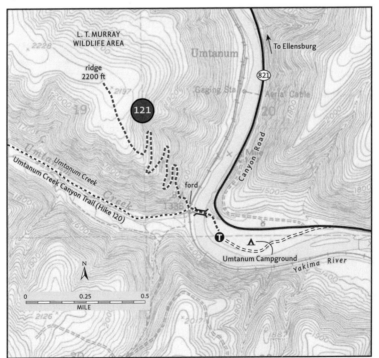

ON THE TRAIL

Cross the steel-span suspension bridge and pass under the railway tracks on the far side of the bridge. Then, as the main trail runs into the sagebrush-lined mouth of Umtanum Canyon, turn right and wade across Umtanum Creek, following a fainter but well-trod path to the right. This trail angles upward along the face of the northern wall of Umtanum Canyon.

The trail grows fainter as it climbs and frequently—especially in spring when the desert flora thrives and spreads—disappears. At this point, simply pick your path, sticking to bare soil and rock when possible, to continue upward at an angle. After gaining almost 500 feet, switchback and continue upward to the ridge crest.

After a mile or so, you'll be able to turn and follow the ridge as it continues to climb to the

Umtanum Creek Falls in late winter

west, leaving the Yakima behind and instead following high above the Umtanum Creek valley. Your trail at this point is mostly game tracks and the route of least resistance, so if you lack the confidence to explore without a well-marked trail, stop here and simply enjoy the views. You'll be able to look out over the twists and turns of the Yakima Canyon, and down to Baldy Butte (tallest point to the south, along the east side of the Yakima River). Keep an eye on the slopes around you and you might see the resident herd of bighorn sheep—they frequently reside in this area. Hike as far up the sloping ridgeline as you'd like, but generally the best views and terrain come in the first 2 miles of the trek.

122 Umtanum Creek Falls

RATING/ DIFFICULTY	ROUNDTRIP	ELEV GAIN/ HIGH POINT	SEASON
***/2	6+ miles	700 feet/ 2000 feet	Oct–May

Map: Department of Natural Resources Yakima; **Contact:** Washington Department of Fish and Wildlife; **Notes:** Washington Discover Pass required; **GPS:** N 46 53.954, W 120 38.575

A diversity of landscape and ecosystems are found along this canyon trek. Starting high and hiking downhill, the route begins in open Douglas-fir forest and ends in sagebrush-and-scrub-grass desert canyons. Elk roam the upper woods while bighorn sheep prowl the steep canyon walls around the pounding waterfall. Visit in early spring to enjoy the best wildlife viewing (beasts of all sizes stick to this canyon while the snows still fill the high country). Spring

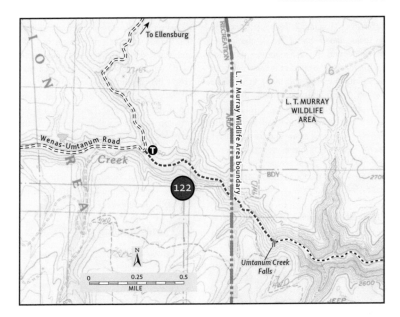

also means that the waterfall is running full with snowmelt water.

GETTING THERE

From Seattle, drive east on I-90 to exit 109 in Ellensburg. At the end of the exit ramp, turn right to drive under the freeway, and at 0.7 mile turn left at Wenas–Umtanum Road at the traffic light. Stay on this road, which turns to gravel at 5.3 miles, for a total of 11 miles from the freeway exit. At 11 miles, find a small signed parking area on the left at a sharp turn in the road.

ON THE TRAIL

The first half mile of the Umtanum Creek Falls Trail rolls between sections of private property—the "No Trespassing" signs that sometimes dot this initial stage refer to the barbwire-protected lands to the side of the trail. Hikers are free to use the trail corridor without fear of trespassing.

At 0.5 mile, the trail enters the state-owned L. T. Murray Wildlife Area lands. For the next half mile, you'll pass through the transition zone between the lowland forest and the high desert. At times, the canyon narrows and the north wall looms higher. With more shade and less scorching sun in the summer, trees thrive. Douglas fir tower high on the shaded slopes, while the canyon floor sports a dense forest of pine and fir. But as you near the 1-mile mark, the canyon walls mellow, opening the entire canyon to the full glare of sun, day in and day out. The result is dramatic—gone are the towering firs and pines, and instead the canyon is filled with fragrant sagebrush groves interspersed with stands of pine.

At just over 1 mile, the stunning punch bowl surrounding the Umtanum Falls opens before you. The creek falls about 40 feet into an oval-shaped basalt bowl—throughout the winter and spring, ice plasters the black rock alongside the falls as the water cascades down into the bowl and then out a narrow canyon. If you wish to scramble around to the opposite side of the basalt bowl for views of the falls in winter and early spring, use extreme caution if snow and ice still linger. In this water-rich basin, ponderosa pines provide shade in the sun-soaked valley.

Hikers may continue down the creek valley for several miles along the "official"

The shrub-steppe lands of the L. T. Murray Wildlife Area are prime wildflower grounds. Bitterroot is one of the most spectacular.

trail, though we recommend exploring. Rock hop across the creek well above the falls and you'll find an easily-scrambled slope to the top of the south wall of the canyon. Follow the canyon rim to view amazing rock formations—myriad volcanic basalt forms that boggle the mind. Later in spring, the ridgetop also sports the first color of the local wildflower show. Buckwheat and balsamroot are especially abundant.

For a good day outing, follow the south canyon rim until it is broken by a broad side canyon—at about 3 miles—before turning back and heading home.

123 Joe Watt Canyon

RATING/ DIFFICULTY	ROUNDTRIP	ELEV GAIN/ HIGH POINT	SEASON
***/3	6+ miles	1000 feet/ 3100 feet	May–Sept

Map: Department of Natural Resources Yakima; **Contact:** Washington Department of Fish and Wildlife; **Notes:** Washington Discover Pass required; **GPS:** N 47 04.267, W 120 44.117

The Joe Watt Canyon area of the L. T. Murray Wildlife Area sprawls over the northeastern corner, encompassing both open sagebrush desert and dry pine forest environments, and wonderful blends of the two. As is often the case when hiking in the desert, the best walking route is actually an old road, with optional side trips comprising off-trail rambles whenever you'd like. More than 25 miles of rough dirt roads ramble through this area, with occasional mountain bikes and horses sharing them with hikers. The potential route options

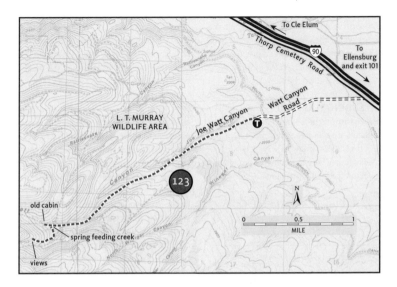

GETTING THERE

From Seattle, drive east on I-90 to exit 101 (Thorp), and at the end of the exit ramp, turn right and drive 0.5 mile to Thorp Cemetery Road. Turn right onto Thorp Cemetery Road and continue 3 miles before turning left onto Watt Canyon Road. In 1 mile, the pavement ends and you'll find a well-signed trailhead parking area for the L. T. Murray Wildlife Area.

ON THE TRAIL

The large trailhead parking area doubles as a rustic campground, so don't be surprised if there are campers here taking advantage of the multitude of trails to explore. We suggest you start your exploration with a trek up the area's namesake canyon, heading west from the trailhead along the old road piercing the heart of Joe Watt Canyon.

This road/trail climbs moderately up the canyon, occasionally dipping alongside the small creek that runs through it (fed by a spring near the head of the canyon). The canyon is home to herds of elk, and at times even bighorn sheep can be seen in the area. As you hike, especially from late spring through late summer, keep an eye (and ear) to the ground to make sure you don't startle a rattlesnake, though it's far more likely you'll be startled by the eruption of a quail or even grouse launching itself from the grass right at your feet.

At about 2.6 miles, the road passes the skeletal structure of an ancient log cabin. This old settlers home is nestled alongside the small creek in a grassy wildflower pasture. This makes a fine turnaround point, but it's worth a quarter-mile scramble up the slopes above the cabin to get a better view of the canyon, the homestead property, and the surrounding countryside before working your way back down the canyon.

EXTENDING YOUR TRIP
Pick up the map brochure (if available) at the trailhead area, or better yet, make sure you have the USGS map and a GPS receiver before heading out. There are numerous roads and unlimited cross-country options here.

124 Robinson Canyon

RATING/ DIFFICULTY	ROUNDTRIP	ELEV GAIN/ HIGH POINT	SEASON
****/3	10+ miles	2200 feet/ 3200 feet	May–Sept

Map: Department of Natural Resources Yakima; **Contact:** Washington Department of Fish and Wildlife; **Notes:** Washington Discover Pass required; **GPS:** N 47 04.267, W 120 44.117

This is a gem of a hike, which provides you easy access to the best of the best of the rich L. T. Murray Wildlife Area. This is prime elk country, and a major wintering and calving ground for the great wapiti (as elk are known to Native Americans). That fact led to the seasonal closure that keeps vehicles well away from the area, but after mid-April, when the closure order is lifted, you can still expect to find herds of the big beasts—especially groupings of elk cows with the young calves. But there's more here

Views up Robinson Canyon from atop the north canyon wall

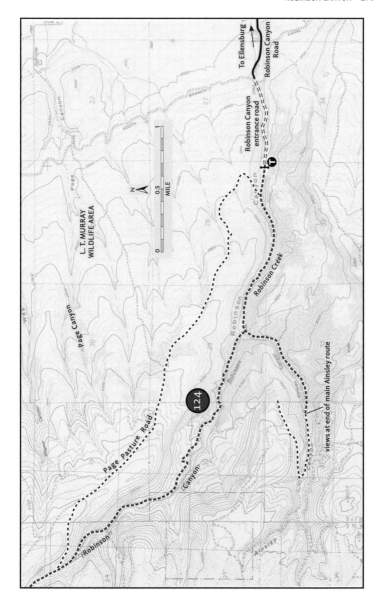

To Ellensburg

Robinson Canyon Road

Robinson Canyon entrance road

SOUTH BRANCH

Canyon

22

27

34

L.T. MURRAY WILDLIFE AREA

Page

N

1

0.5

MILE

0

Page Canyon

Web Canyon

20

28

Robinson Creek

Robinson Canyon

Robinson

124

Page Pasture Road

Robinson Canyon

views at end of main Ainsley route

Ainsley Canyon

than elk. Mule deer (some nearly as big as elk!) also take advantage of the rich browse to get through the long winter months. The entire area is a diverse conglomeration of ecosystems—thick forests stand on the north slopes, while south-facing slopes boast barren basalt cliffs and sage. Aspen trees and cottonwoods grace the creek basins, and wildflowers fill all of the lands in between. Note: Be aware that this area and the access road to hike up into it are typically closed November 1 through April 15 each year to protect wintering elk herds.

GETTING THERE

From Seattle, drive east on I-90 to exit 101 (Thorp). At the end of the exit ramp, turn right and drive about 0.75 mile before turning right on Killmoor Road (found where the main road veers to the left). Drive Killmoor Road 2.5 miles to reach Robinson Canyon Road. Turn right on Robinson Canyon Road (pavement gives way to gravel in a half mile), and drive 1.5 miles to reach the trailhead parking area at the elk fence gate. Park outside the gate and hike in, or drive through and park in the flat area just inside the gate (closing the gate behind you).

ON THE TRAIL

After entering the gate, follow the dirt two-track through the broad meadows, and in about 0.3 mile, you'll find Robinson Creek as it bisects the meadows. All vehicle use of the primitive road ends at the creek crossing; beyond this point, vehicles are prohibited.

Just past Robinson Creek, a sidetrack (Page Pasture Road) climbs out of the canyon. Stay on the main road, really a trail now as the road is washed out and overgrown at first, and about 1 mile from your car, recross Robinson Creek in a nicely wooded area.

In another half mile, reach a second road junction where Ainsley Canyon angles down from the south. Hiking up this road leads to stunning views in just a half mile (2 miles from your car). The gorgeous views look toward Ainsley Canyon's steep basalt cliffs and along the creek far below. The thin forests of this area provide comforting shelter for deer and elk, so keep a close eye on the trees as you trek along and you'll likely see some of the big browsers.

A badger hides by its burrow in the L. T. Murray Wildlife Area.

To extend your hike, return to the main road and continue up Robinson Canyon. At mile 4 (from your car) the road leaves the bank of Robinson Creek and the best scenery is now behind you. Turn around, and with the 1-mile side trip up Ainsley Canyon, you'll have a leg-stretching outing of 10 miles.

125 Whiskey Dick Mountain: Wind Farms

RATING/ DIFFICULTY	ROUNDTRIP	ELEV GAIN/ HIGH POINT	SEASON
***/3	5 miles	1000 feet/ 3873 feet	Apr–Nov

Map: Department of Natural Resources Yakima; **Contact:** Puget Sound Energy; **Notes:** Lands within the Wild Horse Wind and Solar Facility are open to hunting, hiking, bird-watching, horseback riding, and other recreational activities by written permission only. Gates along the Beacon Ridge Road are open April 1 to November 30, from two hours before sunrise to two hours after sunset. To get permission to walk the grounds, complete the online application form, available at http://pse.com/aboutpse /ToursandRecreation/WildHorse/Pages /Wild-Horse-Access.aspx, then pick up your permit at the visitors center (or just fill out the form and pick up the permit at the center). You'll also be required to watch a short (two-minute) safety video concerning walking near the turbines; **GPS:** N 46 59.971, W 120 12.203

This hike offers a lesson in both natural history and future development. The winds that have scoured this area for eons now power homes across the state thanks to massive wind turbines that line the ridges. But even with those modern marvels towering over the landscape, the area retains its wild nature, with hosts of critters thriving in the shadow of those renewable energy towers.

GETTING THERE

From Seattle, drive east on I-90 to exit 115 (Kittitas). Go north over the freeway, and at 1.2 miles turn right at the stop sign. Veer to the left onto County Road 81, and at 1.2 miles from the stop sign (2.4 miles from I-90) turn right onto Vantage Highway. Drive 6.2 miles, then turn left onto Beacon Ridge Road. In 2.1 miles you'll pass the Bluebird trailhead on the left. Continue up the road to the visitors center to get your hiking permit (see note above), then return here to start your hike.

ON THE TRAIL

The trail leaves the wide parking area at Bluebird trailhead and starts climbing north along a steep draw. You'll see turbines on the ridgelines above you at times, but pay special attention to the desert wildflowers at your feet, and watch for birds and beasts in the sagebrush around you. At 0.7 mile, the trail switches back to the west and in a quarter mile crosses the road leading to the visitors center.

Cross the road and continue up onto the ridge crest, then push on north to intercept the road leading from the visitors center to the summit of Whiskey Dick Mountain. For the last couple hundred yards you'll need to hike this road in the shadow of more massive turbines to go back to the visitors center. To continue your hike, head northwest from the visitors center on the road to a gated area and head up the ridge northwest off the road. Follow a fenceline and continue on through more desert wildflowers and increasing

Blooming hedgehog cactus dot the landscape even around the wind turbines of the Whiskey Dick Mountain wind farm.

views throughout the region to attain the summit with its grand views. There, you'll also find a solar panel farm—yet another way to capture nature's energy for human use with minimal impact on our planet.

EXTENDING YOUR TRIP

With the Puget Sound Energy permit in hand, you are free to wander the area at will, provided you stay at least 100 yards away from any turbine or solar installation.

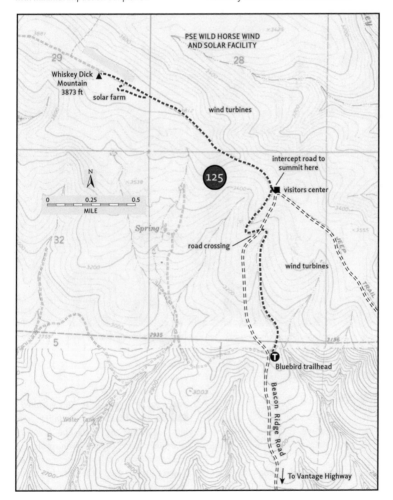

A pair of bighorn sheep tussle in the winter sun within the L. T. Murray Wildlife Area.

126 Whiskey Dick Mountain: Rocky Coulee

RATING/ DIFFICULTY	ROUNDTRIP	ELEV GAIN/ HIGH POINT	SEASON
****/3	8+ miles	1750 feet/ 2261 feet	March–July

Map: Department of Natural Resources Yakima; **Contact:** Washington Department of Fish and Wildlife; **Notes:** Washington

Discover Pass required; **GPS:** N 47 04.267, W 120 44.117

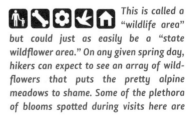 *This is called a "wildlife area" but could just as easily be a "state wildflower area." On any given spring day, hikers can expect to see an array of wildflowers that puts the pretty alpine meadows to shame. Some of the plethora of blooms spotted during visits here are*

thyme-leaved desert parsley, Douglas buckwheat (huge masses of it), thyme-leaved buckwheat, shaggy daisy/shaggy fleabane, linear-leaved daisy (also called line-leaved fleabane), Cusick's sunflower, Hooker's onion, woolly-pod milk vetch, brodacia, silky lupines, rock penstemon, Thompson's paintbrush, thread-leaved phacelia, Hooker's balsamroot, white phlox, Scouler's penstemon, small-flowered penstemon, cushion fleabane, large-flowered collomia, narrow-leaved collomia, bitterroot, hedgehog cactus, and bitter-brush. Bring your wildflower guide to keep track of the plants, but also keep in mind that this is a wildlife area, so expect to see some critters, too.

GETTING THERE

From Seattle, drive east on I-90 to exit 115 (Kittitas). Go north over the freeway, and at 1.2 miles turn right at the stop sign. Veer to the left onto County Road 81, and at 1.2 miles from the stop sign (2.4 miles from I-90) turn right onto Vantage Highway. Drive past the first access to the Quilomene Wildlife Area at 12 miles, and at 13.7 miles turn left onto the rough dirt road accessing the wildlife area. At 0.4 mile on this rough road veer right at the Y, and at 0.6 mile veer right at the second Y. A good place to park is at 1.2 miles from the highway.

ON THE TRAIL

Our recommended route has you bypassing the first access road into the Quilomene Wildlife Area (that first access is just past highway milepost 18). Note: That access is an equally great hike to add to your agenda for other visits, as you hike an old rutted road into the wildlife area that will take you to the crest ridge of Whiskey Dick Mountain and

Desert lupines at your feet, views down Rocky Coulee—this is true shrub-steppe desert hiking at its best on Whiskey Dick Mountain!

opportunities to see blooming hedgehog cactus in mid-May. Our route has you hiking along the long ridge across from Whiskey Dick Mountain before plunging down into Rocky Coulee, and then hiking up the east-ernmost end of Whiskey Dick Mountain to roam the ridgeline along that peak.

The hike along the old road goes fast, as the path is wide, smooth, and relatively level as it contours along the ridge. After a quick couple of miles, the road drops 800 feet

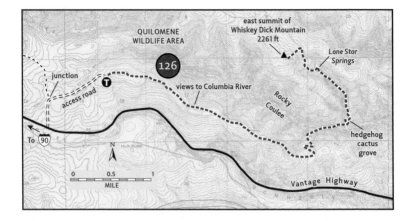

elevation to the bottom of Rocky Coulee. (Note that with high-clearance vehicles, it might be possible to drive this far, but doing so has you driving over some of the most beautiful wildflower fields.) The wildflowers carpet the entire desert floor, from the ridgetop to the coulee bottom. This section of the route is rich in bitterroot, hedgehog cactus, and balsamroot, as well as various species of buckwheat, lupine, and daisies.

Coyotes hunt throughout the coulee country here, and they can often be heard, if not actually seen, in the morning and evening—their yips and howls echo off the coulee walls. After following the coulee basin for a mile or so, the route turns up the side of Whiskey Dick Mountain, where there are more stunning wildflowers, with increasingly clear and stunning views over the rest of the wildlife area. Keep an eye on the sky to catch the raptors soaring, and another eye on the brush to spot mule deer and white-tailed deer.

You'll top out on the low summit of Whiskey Dick a bit over 4 miles from your starting point. This is the place to turn around and enjoy the long, scenic desert stroll back to your car.

Opposite: Sweeping views of Lake George and the grand Noble Knob

enumclaw plateau

State Route 410, leading from Enumclaw to Yakima over Chinook Pass, draws far less traffic than any other mountain pass in the Cascades, yet the trails along this corridor offer as much if not more in the way of hiking. The trails west of the pass include some of the most spectacular views you'll find anywhere in Washington's backcountry—the view of Mount Rainier from the Lake George–Noble Knob route is truly outstanding. The Enumclaw Plateau provides a high bench land between the Puget Sound lowlands and the sharp rise of the Cascades. Bordered by the Green River to the south and the Issaquah Alps foothills to the north, this plateau—though dotted with cities and communities—offers some uniquely beautiful wild country to explore.

127 Pinnacle Peak

RATING/ DIFFICULTY	ROUNDTRIP	ELEV GAIN/ HIGH POINT	SEASON
***/2	2 miles	1000 feet/ 1825 feet	Year-round

The former lookout site on the summit of Pinnacle Peak

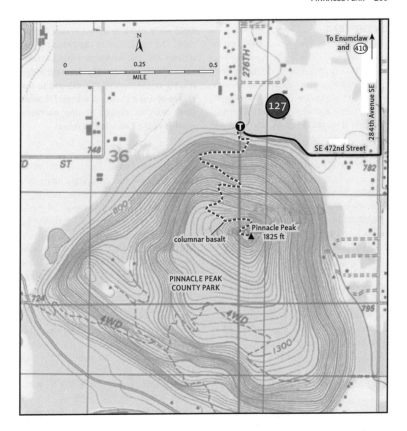

Map: Green Trails Enumclaw No. 237;
Contact: King County Parks and Recreation;
GPS: N 47 10.764, W 121 58.443

The Cal Magnusson Trail leads up this geologic wonder: a near-perfect cinder cone volcano sitting in the middle of the Enumclaw Plateau. The trail, named for one of Washington's most revered mountaineers and the man who helped launch REI's quality-assurance test lab (still one of the best

testing facilities in the outdoor industry today), climbs steeply to the summit of the cone.

GETTING THERE

From Enumclaw, drive east on State Route 410, and at the last traffic light in town, turn right onto 284th Avenue Southeast (signed for King County Fairgrounds). Drive 1.5 miles, then turn right onto Southeast 472nd Street. In 0.5 mile, look for the trailhead parking area on the left.

ON THE TRAIL

The trail gains a tad more than 1000 feet in exactly one mile—that's a good workout by anyone's measure. The trail starts off in forest and stays there most of the way. Though the distant views are limited, this forest itself is pretty and worth the visit. Birdsong resounds through the trees, and we saw several Douglas squirrels and a couple of raccoons during our last recon hike.

Just after the halfway point, some rock formations loom out of the forest, and at 0.8 mile, the route opens onto an old road (converted now to trail). As you near the summit, the last few hundred yards of hiking review some remarkable walls of columnar basalt—black hexagon-shaped columns in the exposed rock faces.

At 1 mile, the trail reaches the summit. A close examination reveals some old concrete footings for a long-lost fire watchtower—the old structure must have stood tall because the trees covering the summit limit views in most directions, though there are some nice clear looks to the southwest.

128 Echo Mountain

RATING/ DIFFICULTY	ROUNDTRIP	ELEV GAIN/ HIGH POINT	SEASON
**/2	3.2 or 4 miles	400 feet/ 880 feet	Year-round

Map: King County Parks and Recreation Spring Lake/Lake Desire map; **Contact:** King County Parks and Recreation; **GPS:** N 47 26.219, W 122 05.647

The moss-topped rock slabs at the summit of Echo Mountain make for a wonderful location for a late-morning trail brunch, or an evening meal while enjoying a cool breeze before dark. The trails, built in the 1990s by volunteers with the Washington Trails Association (WTA), wander the forested ridge leading to the summit of Echo and to the shores of Lake Desire. A wonderful wildland oasis to explore in the northern reaches of the Enumclaw Plateau.

GETTING THERE

From Bellevue, drive south on I-405 to exit 4 and turn east onto State Route 169 toward Maple Valley. In 6 miles, turn right onto 196th Street and continue 1.4 miles before turning right onto West Spring Lake Drive Southeast. Veer right at the Y junction and continue another 0.9 mile to enter Spring Lake/Lake Desire Park. There is limited parking (four to six cars), so get there early.

ON THE TRAIL

As you head out from the parking area, grab one of the printed park maps if available or do as we did and snap a picture of the map on the reader map with your smartphone camera. You can also print a map from the park's website.

Starting the hike, head off to the right on a trail angling upward through the forest. At 0.15 mile, you'll reach an old road. Turn right onto it and start your summit climb. You'll ascend moderately along the old road for 0.3 mile (to the 0.45-mile mark) to a sharp left-hand turn. The WTA-built summit trail—our own Alan Bauer shouldered a sizeable portion of the work himself!—heads straight off the apex of that corner, leading past massive moss-draped big-leaf maple trees surrounded by a lush green carpet of ferns, mosses, trilliums, and other rainforest-friendly native plants.

The trail leading to the top of Echo Mountain winds through a mossy forest of firs and maples.

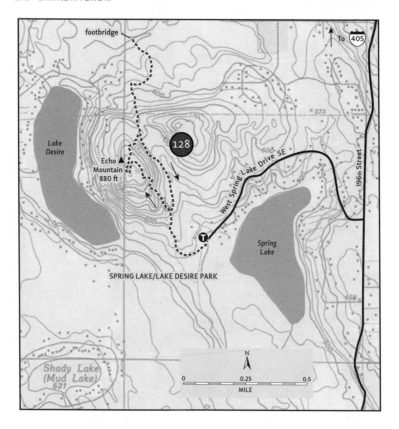

At 0.75 mile, the summit is attained, with open mossy slabs of rock providing cool resting places for happy hiking kids and their families. Just don't get too comfortable. Some of the plants around the rocks are rare and delicate. It's best to rest on the bare rock when possible. The views include wonderful looks south to Mount Rainier across the breadth of the Enumclaw Plateau.

From the summit you can drop down the north side of Echo to find more trails. To close out the 3.2-mile trek, stay left and in about 0.6 mile reach a scenic little footlog bridge over a gurgling brook in an emerald forest. Turn back at the bridge. Or, for a 2-mile outing, go right to loop back to your car.

129 Federation Forest

RATING/ DIFFICULTY	ROUNDTRIP	ELEV GAIN/ HIGH POINT	SEASON
***/2	2–12 miles	200 feet/ 1800 feet	Year-round

Map: Green Trails Greenwater No. 238; Washington State Parks; **Notes:** Washington Discover Pass required; **GPS:** N 47 09.120, W 121 41.367

Nearly 620 acres of pristine old-growth forest alongside the White River, with more than 12 miles of trails looping through the cathedral forest—all preserved as a public parkland thanks to the efforts of the General Federation of Women's Clubs.

Learn more about the club's work at the Catherine Montgomery Interpretive Center at the trailhead area. You can also pick up a map of the park's trails there—it's open April through October. Or just explore this beautiful forest on your own. A number of the routes are marked with interpretive signs, so you'll know when you are standing in awe of a massive Sitka spruce and when it's a huge western hemlock that has your attention. There's even a Hobbit Village to explore!

Hikers admire the many massive old-growth trees in Federation Forest State Park.

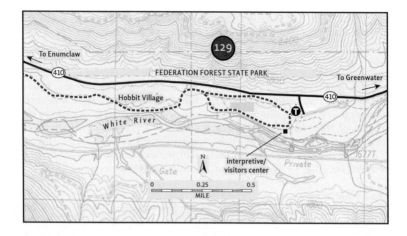

GETTING THERE

From Enumclaw, drive east on State Route 410, and at about 17 miles from the last stoplight in Enumclaw, turn right near milepost 41.

ON THE TRAIL

As lifelong fans of J. R. R. Tolkien's work, we opted to explore the route to Hobbit Village, though there's an impressive network of trails to explore if you want to extend your outing up to 12 or more miles.

To find the hobbits, leave the trailhead and amble west on the core trail leaving the interpretive center. The interpretive signage along this path provides enough detail to teach even the most seasoned Northwest hiker something new and interesting about the local flora and fauna.

As the trail bends westward, you might start seeing evidence of the "halflings" of the area. Visitors have been helping maintain the unofficial Hobbit Village, and at times anonymous hobbit friends will add to the collection, with new doors added to hills, trolls added under rocks, among other

additions. At about a mile out, you'll find the village, with tiny outhouses, little round-doored homes in the hillside, and miniscule fenced gardens. Every visit unveils a different experience of the village, it seems.

Keep hiking to explore more of the forest, including a long loop hike option returning back on the other side of SR 410, or turn back here to savor the experience you've had in Middle Earth. Note: There are many blowdowns to navigate around in wet areas in the far western portion of the state park lands along the river.

130 Kelly Butte

RATING/ DIFFICULTY	ROUNDTRIP	ELEV GAIN/ HIGH POINT	SEASON
****/2	3.6 miles	1000 feet/ 5385 feet	July–Oct

Map: Green Trails Lester No. 239; **Contact:** Mount Baker–Snoqualmie National Forest, Snoqualmie Ranger District, Enumclaw office; **Notes:** NW Forest Pass required.

Rough road for last mile to trailhead; **GPS:** N 47 09.787, W 121 28.453

🚹 🔧 ⚙ 🏠 Kelly Butte provides some of the most spectacular views in the Cascade foothills, with views enjoyed nearly every step of the way to the summit. And the panoramic splendor is just the beginning. Not only does the expanse of the western Cascades sprawl before your eyes, but wildflowers sprawl before your feet along the entire route. Visit in early summer and *you'll find bear grass along the full length of the trail. Come fall, the trail is sweetened with plump huckleberries. At the top of the climb, a recently refurbished fire lookout station provides an incredible lesson in forest history to go with the 360-degree views of the forest itself.*

GETTING THERE

From Enumclaw drive east on State Route 410 (Chinook Pass Highway) to the small town of Greenwater. About 1 mile east of the Greenwater Fire Station (at the eastern

Hikers approaching the wonderful fire lookout at the summit of Kelly Butte

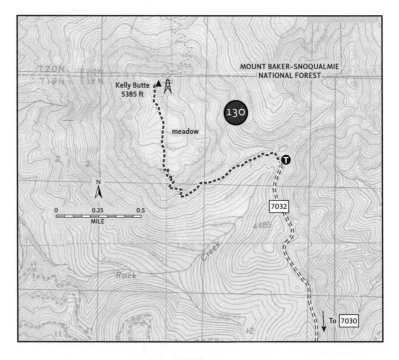

end of the community), turn left (north) onto Greenwater River Road (Forest Road 70). Drive 8.3 miles up FR 70 before turning left onto FR 7030. Continue 4 miles up FR 7030 to reach a T intersection. Turn left onto FR 7032 and continue uphill for 0.6 mile, then veer left at the Y junction. Drive another 0.6 mile, then stay right at the next Y junction. In 1.3 miles from this fork, look for the trailhead and parking area on the left.

ON THE TRAIL

Leave the trailhead and start climbing, gradually at first, along the last portion of the road that leads to the actual trail near the road's end. This portion of road can be driven but is very narrow, overgrown, and rough, and it's

best to park by the trailhead signage. The open ridge provides impressive views from the get-go, so don't hurry this hike.

At 0.7 mile, the route leaves the old roadway track and switchbacks up onto a true single-track trail. From here, the route steepens moderately, but as you pass the 0.9-mile mark you'll realize that the going could be easier as you pass the faint old straight-up path that the old fire watchers used to get to their station.

The path levels out near the 1.3-mile mark as it wanders into longer, more open meadows awash with an array of wildflower blooms from late spring to late summer. And the huckleberries here are a dream. At 1.5 miles, the trail makes one final climbing push to reach the summit at 1.8 miles. Stop, stay, and enjoy the views. Don't hurry home—the longer you stay, the more you'll find to enjoy!

131 Colquhoun Peak

RATING/ DIFFICULTY	ROUNDTRIP	ELEV GAIN/ HIGH POINT	SEASON
***/2	1.1–2.6 miles	600 feet/ 5173 feet	July–Oct

Map: Green Trails Lester No. 239; **Contact:** Mount Baker–Snoqualmie National Forest, Snoqualmie Ranger District, Enumclaw office; **Notes:** NW Forest Pass required. Rough road for last mile to trailhead; **GPS:** N 47 07.930, W 121 27.588

The western Cascades south of Snoqualmie Pass have an incredible collection of old scenic fire lookouts, and this route provides a great experience at the former location of a summit watchtower in a rather secluded pocket of the land near Greenwater. Because the lookout has been abandoned so long, you'll find only filtered views from the actual summit. Trees have grown up since the heyday of fire suppression, but hikers will still enjoy grand views from the ridge just to the south of the summit. From this perch, about 100 feet below the old lookout station, the views sweep in Mount Rainier and the expanse of the Norse Peak Wilderness.

GETTING THERE
From Enumclaw drive east on State Route 410 (Chinook Pass Highway) to the small town of Greenwater. About 1 mile east of the Greenwater Fire Station (at the eastern

A buck stares at the photographer on a foggy morning while grazing in an open area of dry flowers and brush.

Views of Mount Rainier and much of the Norse Peak Wilderness from above the slide area on Colquhoun Peak

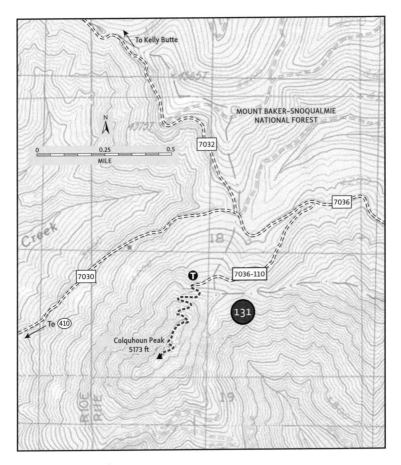

end of the community), turn left (north) onto Greenwater River Road (Forest Road 70). Drive 8.3 miles up FR 70 before turning left onto FR 7030. Continue 4 miles up FR 7030 to reach a T intersection. Turn right onto FR 7036, and after 0.4 mile find a somewhat brushy road angling uphill to the right. This is the road to the official trailhead. Hikers in low-clearance vehicles

or who don't like sliding their vehicles through rough branches at the start of the road should park here. Others can drive 0.6 mile up this road to the official trailhead at the road's end.

ON THE TRAIL

If you are starting from the lower "trail-head" on FR 7036, start walking the narrow, brushy road westward. At 0.6 mile you'll reach the end of the road and the start of the true trail.

After that rough section of road, the trail amazes—it's in great shape and provides easy walking all the way to the summit. At 0.1 mile from the true trailhead, the first of the views opens up, with nice looks off to the right toward Kelly Butte (Hike 130) and out toward the lower Greenwater Valley.

At 0.55 mile the trail pops out on the summit of Colquhoun. Though the ranger lookout station is gone, reminders of those old days of manned fire watchtowers remain: large, rusty steel cables serpentine around the rocks, and some old cabin essentials litter the area. On our last visit, an old rusted-out coffeepot and some broken furniture could be seen upon a close examination. Just remember: look but don't touch. Yesteryear's trash is today's historical relic. Leave the old items in place, please, after you snap a picture or two.

For the best views, continue south of the south face of the summit, and about 100 feet down a rough trail you'll find a grand snack spot above an old rock slide. The slide removed any view-blocking trees, so you get expansive views from Ravens Roost to the Norse Peak Wilderness to Mount Rainier!

132 Lake George–Noble Knob's Backdoor

RATING/ DIFFICULTY	ROUNDTRIP	ELEV GAIN/ HIGH POINT	SEASON
***/2	3.5 miles	1300 feet/ 6011 feet	July–Oct

Map: Green Trails Lester No. 239; **Contact:** Mount Baker–Snoqualmie National Forest, Snoqualmie Ranger District, Enumclaw

office; **Notes:** NW Forest Pass required; **GPS:** N 47 03.911, W 121 30.088

Hike through meadows nestled more than a mile above sea level, pass a crystal-clear trout-rich alpine lake, and explore a remote summit with stunning horizons capped by the snow-clad Mount Rainier. Add in a large resident herd of elk, some pretty doe-eyed mule deer, and a few hundred birds. Too much to ask? Maybe, but that's exactly what you get on this back-door route to the scenic summit of Noble Knob.

GETTING THERE

From Enumclaw drive east on State Route 410 (Chinook Pass Highway) to the small town of Greenwater. About 1 mile east of the Greenwater Fire Station (at the eastern end of the community), turn left (north) onto Greenwater River Road (Forest Road 70). Drive 5.8 miles up FR 70 before turning right onto Forest Road 72. Continue 0.7 mile on FR 72, then turn left onto FR 7220 and, in 1.3 miles, right onto FR 72-222. In 2.4 miles (4.4 from FR 72) stay left at a Y intersection to continue on FR 72-222 and, in another 1.2 miles, continue straight at the next junction. After another 1.2 miles (6.8 from FR 72) look for a parking space in a wide pullout to the right. The trail leaves from here.

ON THE TRAIL

The trail leaves the parking area and climbs the forested ridgeline to the south. At 0.6 mile, the first meadows are reached, with impressive views of Mount Rainier open to the west and sweeping views east into the Norse Peak Wilderness starting to open up—before you the rocky summits of Fifes

At as fine of a lunch spot as could ever be found, a hiker enjoys the views of Mount Rainier from the summit of Noble Knob.

Peak and Ravens Roost appear through the trees. As you climb, you'll look across the open expanse of Crow Lake basin and west into the heart of the Greenwater Valley.

A trail junction at 1.2 miles offers more views along with a choice. The trail to the left drops to Lake George, while the route to the right climbs steeply up the ridge to Noble

Knob. We suggest you go right for now to get the climb done so you can cool off in the lake later. So stay right, and at 1.7 miles, reach another junction, this time with the main Noble Knob Trail. Turn right and in less than 0.1 mile, crest the summit of this scenic peak. Enjoy the panoramic vistas before heading back down.

After leaving the summit and rejoining the main Noble Knob Trail, turn left and descend a faint way trail to the east from the ridge saddle. Take this boot-beaten way trail down to a shallow saddle and, from the saddle, down the open slope to the clearly seen Lake George shoreline at 2.15 miles.

Rinse off your trail sweat in the lake—or simply enjoy the cool lake basin's natural beauty if the day isn't hot enough for an alpine swim—then start up the trail back to that first junction you reached on the way

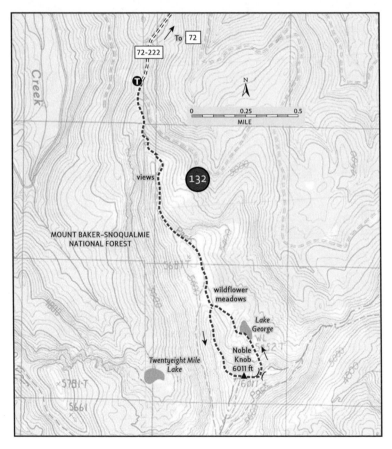

The PCT passing along the western shoulder of Blowout Mountain

up. Turn toward your car at the junction and complete your journey.

133 Blowout Mountain

RATING/ DIFFICULTY	ROUNDTRIP	ELEV GAIN/ HIGH POINT	SEASON
***/2	6.8 miles	1800 feet/ 5655 feet	July–Oct

Map: Green Trails Lester No. 239; **Contact:** Mount Baker–Snoqualmie National Forest, Snoqualmie Ranger District, Enumclaw office; **Notes:** NW Forest Pass required; **GPS:** N 47 08.270, W 121 20.848

 *Bring the kids and the dog. This gentle trail allows ample time to explore the local forest*

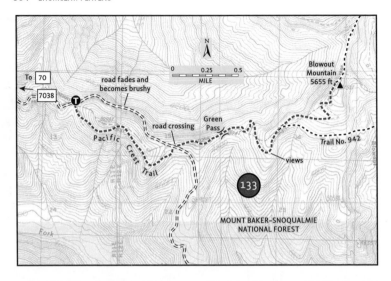

ecology and offers a fun way to enjoy a very-little-used portion of the Pacific Crest Trail (PCT)—one of the crown jewels of the National Trails System. Get the kids on this trail and tell them that if they hike south, they'll find themselves in Mexico in about 2400 miles, and if they turn north, it's just 200 miles to Canada! But the hike offers more than an immersion in the PCT. Visit in September and you'll find incredible fall colors lining the route. And any time of the year the traverse below the summit of Blowout Mountain provides wide-open views westward to the lonely deep forests of the central Cascades.

GETTING THERE

From Enumclaw drive east on State Route 410 (Chinook Pass Highway) to the small town of Greenwater. About 1 mile east of the Greenwater Fire Station (at the eastern end of the community), turn left (north) onto Greenwater River Road (Forest Road 70). Drive 8.3 miles up FR 70 before turning left onto FR 7030. Continue 4 miles up FR 7030 to reach a T intersection. Turn right onto FR 7036 and after 3.7 miles, pass a road on the right that takes you back to access the PCT and the hike to Pyramid Peak. Continue on FR 7036 and at 6.2 miles turn right at a junction onto FR 7038. Drive FR 7038 for 0.9 mile and pull off at a road to the right—the PCT crosses the road here. Park well clear of the road here to start your hike.

ON THE TRAIL

Leave the road and start uphill on the PCT heading south. The trail passes through forest until, at mile 1.2, it crosses a road to enter a forest glade full of trillium, vanilla leaf, and huckleberries.

At 1.5 miles the forest thins and views begin to open up, especially looking north-northwest into the Green River drainage. You'll be able to look out over Ravens Roost here.

ASAHEL CURTIS

Like the author of this book, Asahel Curtis and his family left the farmlands of southern Minnesota for Washington's more diverse landscape, and never looked back.

Curtis moved to Washington in 1888, along with his parents and siblings, and his brother Edward opened a photo studio in Seattle. Curtis went to work for him soon afterward. Curtis quickly developed skill in capturing the beauty and majesty of the native people of the Northwest, and the lands they occupied, with his camera. In the 1890s Curtis traveled north to document the Alaskan and Yukon gold rushes, and that led to the eventual bitter split with his brother and partner Edward when they disagreed over rights to the photos from that journey.

After that split, Curtis established his own photo studio and, until his death in 1941, continued to capture the beauty of the Northwest landscape and its people—both native and adopted—in stunning photographs. His catalogue of more than 60,000 photographic records resides largely within the Washington State Museum of History, and represents the best and most vivid documentation of Washington and Alaska during the end of the nineteenth century and start of the twentieth.

Curtis's love of mountains in general, and of Mount Rainier in particular, led him to promote wilderness recreation in the area. That in turn motivated him to help establish The Mountaineers in 1906. As a founding member, he led several climbs of Mount Rainier and its surrounding peaks, and worked to help promote Mount Rainier National Park as a place for all Americans to enjoy.

Another quarter mile of hiking puts you at Green Pass—a low saddle that doesn't represent much in the way of change in trail topography. No big elevation gain or loss on either side of the pass. But from here, the trail does present more views of Blowout Mountain as it looms before you.

At 2.4 miles, an open slope drops away to views south and east, with great fields of wildflowers and stunning fall colors come late September. Less than a half mile farther on, the PCT intercepts Trail 942 on the right. Continue straight ahead on the PCT, and at 3.4 miles the route reaches its high point on the northwest shoulder of Blowout Mountain. Enjoy the stellar views to the northwest here before turning for home. Or push on—to Canada?

134 Pyramid Peak

RATING/ DIFFICULTY	ROUNDTRIP	ELEV GAIN/ HIGH POINT	SEASON
***/2	6.5 miles	1000 feet/ 5715 feet	June–Oct

Map: Green Trails Lester No. 239; **Contact:** Mount Baker–Snoqualmie National Forest, Snoqualmie Ranger District, Enumclaw office; **Notes:** NW Forest Pass required; **GPS:** N 47 06.942, W 121 24.385

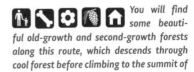 *You will find some beautiful old-growth and second-growth forests along this route, which descends through cool forest before climbing to the summit of*

Pyramid. This is one of the least-visited sections of the very popular and incredibly long (2600 miles) Pacific Crest Trail (PCT). Because few hikers venture out here, the local wildlife isn't as skittish as you'd find in more heavily traveled areas, so you'll have a decent chance to observe the resident deer and maybe even elk as you hike.

GETTING THERE

From Enumclaw drive east on State Route 410 (Chinook Pass Highway) to the small town of Greenwater. About 1 mile east of the Greenwater Fire Station (at the eastern end of the community), turn left (north) onto Greenwater River Road (Forest Road 70). Drive about 8.3 miles and turn left onto FR 7030. Continue 4 miles up 7030 to a T junction. Turn right onto FR 7036 and drive 3.7 miles before turning right again. In 0.7 mile you'll reach the trailhead where the PCT crosses the road.

ON THE TRAIL

Head south at the PCT parking area/trailhead and descend gradually into the fragrant cool pines and firs of the old second growth—and some true old growth—that surrounds this section of the PCT. In less than 0.1 mile you'll reach the official Windy Gap saddle. Continue south on the PCT as it follows the rolling ridgeline that separates the Green and Naches drainages.

A hiker takes a photography stop on the approach to the Pyramid Peak summit.

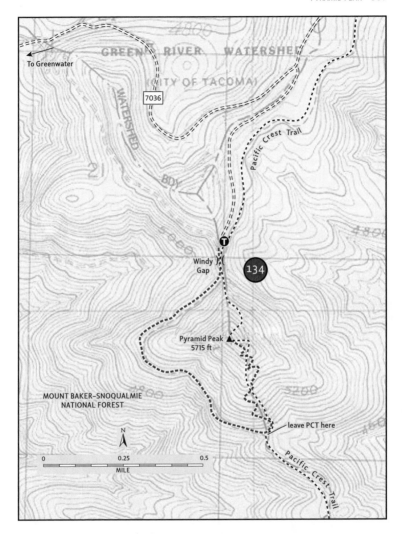

The trail loops west, then back east, reaching a trail junction on the left at 1 mile. Turn left here to leave the PCT and start the steep ascent of Pyramid Peak.

The summit trail climbs through several switchbacks, gaining nearly 750 feet in 0.6 mile to attain the 5715-foot summit. Take a well-deserved rest while enjoying the sweeping views from this former fire lookout site, then return the way you came.

135 Greenwater–Echo Lake

RATING/ DIFFICULTY	ROUNDTRIP	ELEV GAIN/ HIGH POINT	SEASON
***/3	14 miles	1600 feet/ 4100 feet	May–Nov

Map: Green Trails Lester No. 239; **Contact:** Mount Baker–Snoqualmie National Forest,

Snoqualmie Ranger District, Enumclaw office; **Notes:** NW Forest Pass required; **GPS:** N 47 6.335, W 121 28.475

Lush old-growth forest; dark, mysterious forest lakes; and a wonderful chance to meet and see wildlife await hikers here. The trail sticks to a deeply forested river valley, where it passes a wonderfully clear, cool lake—Greenwater—with good fishing. The route eventually reaches Echo Lake in a long 7 miles, but

The lush, mossy banks of the Greenwater River where it flows out below Echo Lake

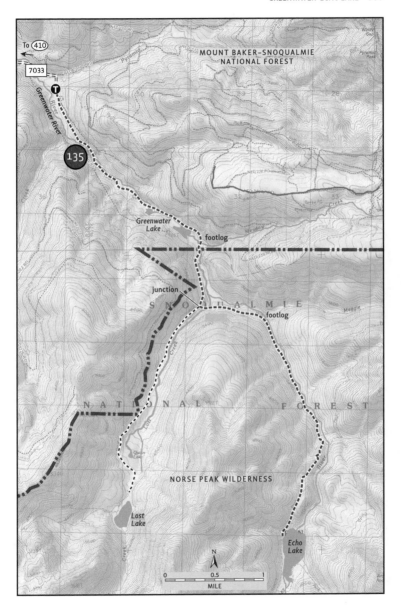

To (410)

7033

T

Greenwater River

Black River

135

MOUNT BAKER–SNOQUALMIE
NATIONAL FOREST

*Greenwater
Lake*

footlog

junction

footlog

S N O Q U A L M I E

N A T I O N A L   F O R E S T

NORSE PEAK WILDERNESS

*Lost
Lake*

*Echo
Lake*

N

0   0.5   1

MILE

these miles fly by as you stride through the cool forest. Footsore hikers will love the soft, duff-rich trail tread, and Echo itself is a wonderful place to rest and relax before hiking back down the pretty trail. But for all that, few people visit, perhaps because the trail doesn't offer sweeping panoramas. The distant views may be missing, but the route is remarkably scenic, and solitude is a high probability.

GETTING THERE

From Enumclaw drive east on State Route 410 (Chinook Pass Highway) to the small town of Greenwater. About 1 mile east of the Greenwater Fire Station (at the eastern end of the community), turn left (north) onto Greenwater River Road (Forest Road 70). Drive about 9 miles, crossing the Greenwater River, and turn right just past the bridge onto FR 7033. Drive up this narrow road about a half mile to the large trailhead parking lot.

ON THE TRAIL

Leave the trailhead and hike into the moss-laden forest, following the Greenwater River

A hiker's delight, a mountain huckleberry prime for the picking!

upstream. The trail is quiet and damp—even in summer—providing soft footing for those hiking in shoes rather than boots. As you hike up the trail watch for any sign of critters. Deer and elk browse through this valley, and where there are deer and elk there may be cougars, coyotes, and bobcats.

The trail crosses the Greenwater River three or four times before reaching the long, shallow Greenwater Lake at about 2 miles. Then for the next 3 miles the route maintains a slow, easy ascent of the valley, entering the Norse Peak Wilderness at about 2.3 miles. At about 3 miles, come to a junction; go left for this hike, but the righthand trail leads you 3 miles to Lost Lake.

At 5 miles the climb steepens substantially and another junction splits the trail—left is the little-known (and little-maintained) Maggie Creek Trail. Stay straight, and for 1.5 miles the path switchbacks up the valley wall before tapering off into a smooth, level glide into the Echo Lake basin at 7 miles. This pretty forest lake offers great swimming, sunning, and general wilderness R & R. Enjoy the relaxing atmosphere of the beautiful basin before heading back down the trail. If you so wish, camping here is wonderful, and you are then set for nearby day trips that can take you south of Echo Lake, up by Castle Peak, and to the Corral Pass regions above you on the ridge west of the lake.

Appendix A: Contact Information

Department of Natural Resources
South Puget Sound Region
(360) 825-1631
www.dnr.wa.gov

King County Parks and Recreation
(206) 296-8687
www.kingcounty.gov/recreation/parks.aspx

Mount Baker–Snoqualmie National Forest
Snoqualmie Ranger District
North Bend office
(425) 888-1421
Enumclaw office
(360) 825-6585
www.fs.fed.us/r6/mbs

Okanogan–Wenatchee National Forest
Cle Elum Ranger District
(509) 852-1100
www.fs.fed.us/r6/wenatchee

Puget Sound Energy
(509) 964-7815
http://pse.com/aboutpse/ToursandRecrea
tion/WildHorse/

US Bureau of Land Management (BLM)
Spokane Office
(509) 536-1200
www.blm.gov/or/districts/spokane/

Washington Department of Fish and Wildlife
(360) 902-2515
www.wdfw.wa.gov

Washington State Parks
(360) 902-8844
www.parks.wa.gov

Appendix B: Conservation and Trail Organizations

Conservation Northwest
1208 Bay Street #201
Bellingham, WA 98225
(360) 671-9950
www.conservationnw.org

Forterra (formerly Cascade Land Conservancy)
901 5th Avenue, Suite 2200
Seattle, WA 98164
(206) 292-5907
info@forterra.org
www.forterra.org

Issaquah Alps Trail Club
PO Box 351
Issaquah, WA 98027
http://issaquahalps.org

The Mountaineers
7700 Sand Point Way NE
Seattle, WA 98115
(206) 521-6000
info@mountaineers.org
www.mountaineers.org

Mountains to Sound Greenway
911 Western Avenue, Suite 203
Seattle, WA 98104
(206) 382-5565
info@mtsgreenway.org
http://mtsgreenway.org

Sierra Club, Washington State Chapter
180 Nickerson Street, Suite 202
Seattle, WA 98109
(206) 378-0114
cascade.chapter@sierraclub.org
http://cascade.sierraclub.org

Volunteers for Outdoor Washington
12345 30th Avenue NE, Suite I
Seattle, WA 98125
(206) 517-3019
info@trailvolunteers.org
www.trailvolunteers.org

Washington Trails Association
705 2nd Avenue, Suite 300
Seattle, WA 98104
(206) 625-1367
info@wta.org
www.wta.org

INDEX

ABOUT THE AUTHOR

Dan Nelson's personal and professional lives have always revolved around the outdoors. As a kid, he hunted, fished, and hiked the wild country around the Snake River canyons and the Blue Mountains of southeastern Washington.

After leaving college in 1989 with a BA in history, he put in a short stint as a general-news beat reporter for some daily newspapers before becoming executive editor of *Washington Trails* magazine. While there, he continued writing for the *Seattle Times* "Outdoors" section, providing features, and for a regular gear-review column. He also started working with several national outdoor magazines, including *Men's Journal*, *Backpacker*, and *Outside*. He has authored nearly a dozen guidebooks and has launched a number of popular series with Mountaineers Books, including the Snowshoe Routes and Best Hikes with Dogs series.

ABOUT THE PHOTOGRAPHER

Alan L. Bauer is a professional freelance photographer specializing in the natural and local history of the Pacific Northwest. Much of his love for the outdoors can be traced back to his growing up on a farm in Oregon's Willamette Valley—an experience he wouldn't trade for anything!

He has been published in *Backpacker*, *Odyssey*, *CityDog*, *Oregon Coast*, and *Northwest Travel* magazines, as well as numerous publications and books across sixteen countries. He was a featured master photographer for his macro work in *Smart Photography*, the top-selling photography magazine in India. Before the Day Hiking series, he coauthored *Best Desert Hikes* and *Best Hikes with Dogs: Inland Northwest* (Mountaineers Books). He frequently gives presentations around the Northwest on his photography and hiking guidebooks. He resides happily in the Cascade foothills east of Seattle with his caring family and dogs. Visit him online at www.alanbauer.com.

1% for Trails & Washington Trails Association

Your favorite Washington hikes, such as those in this book, are made possible by the efforts of thousands of volunteers keeping our trails in great shape, and by hikers like you advocating for the protection of trails and wild lands. As budget cuts reduce funding for trail maintenance, Washington Trails Association's volunteer trail maintenance program fills this void and is ever more important for the future of Washington's hiking. Our mountains and forests can provide us with a lifetime of adventure and exploration—but we need trails to get us there. One percent of the sales of this guidebook goes to support WTA's efforts.

Spend a day on the trail with Washington Trails Association, and give back to the trails you love. WTA hosts over 750 work parties throughout Washington's Cascades and Olympics each year. Volunteers remove downed logs after spring snowmelt, cut away brush, retread worn stretches of trail, and build bridges and turnpikes. Find the volunteer schedule, check current conditions of the trails in this guidebook, and become a member of WTA at www.wta.org or call (206) 625-1367.

OTHER TITLES YOU MIGHT ENJOY FROM MOUNTAINEERS BOOKS

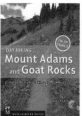

Day Hiking Mount Adams
Tami Asars
81 gorgeous hikes in the Goat Rocks, Indian Heaven,
and Mount Adams wildernesses—and more

Day Hiking the San Juans and Gulf Islands
Craig Romano
136 hikes on two dozen islands—plus Victoria,
Anacortes, Tsawwassen, and Point Roberts

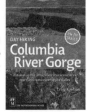

Day Hiking Eastern Washington
Craig Romano and Rich Landers
125 sunny hikes on the dry side of the
Cascades

Day Hiking Columbia River Gorge
Craig Romano
100 day hikes on both sides of the river

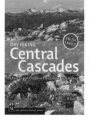

Day Hiking Central Cascades
Craig Romano and Alan Bauer
125 great hikes in the heart of Washington
State—including Lake Chelan

Backpacking Washington
Craig Romano
70 spectacular weekend routes,
from the lush Hoh River and Glacier Peak
Meadows to the open ridges of the
Columbia Highlands and beyond

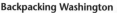

www.mountaineersbooks.org